MODERN HUMANITIES RESEARCH ASSOCIATION
TEXTS AND DISSERTATIONS
VOLUME 85

INSTITUTE OF GERMANIC AND ROMANCE STUDIES
(UNIVERSITY OF LONDON)
BITHELL SERIES OF DISSERTATIONS
VOLUME 40

BRIDAL-QUEST EPICS IN MEDIEVAL GERMANY
A REVISIONARY APPROACH

INSTITUTE OF GERMANIC AND ROMANCE STUDIES
BITHELL SERIES OF DISSERTATIONS

Launched in 1978, this series publishes outstanding recent doctoral theses, accepted by universities in the United Kingdom and Ireland, across all fields of Germanic studies. Since 1989 the series has been published in collaboration with the Modern Humanities Research Association.

Recommendations for theses which might be considered for possible inclusion in the series should be made by the supervisor and/or examiner(s), and sent to Professor Ritchie Robertson, Convenor of the Bithell Editorial Board, St John's College, Oxford OX1 3JP. Proposals must be accompanied by a copy of the Examiners' Report and Abstract.

Editorial Board
Dr Judith Beniston, University College London
Professor Sarah Colvin, University of Birmingham
Professor Pól O Dochartaigh, University of Ulster
Professor Ritchie Robertson (*Convenor*), St John's College, Oxford
Professor Bill Marshall,
Institute of Germanic and Romance Studies, University of London
Dr John Walker, Birkbeck College London
Dr Godela Weiss-Sussex,
Institute of Germanic and Romance Studies, University of London
Professor David Wells, Birkbeck College London

MODERN HUMANITIES RESEARCH ASSOCIATION
TEXTS AND DISSERTATIONS

Established in 1970, the series promotes important work by younger scholars by making the most accomplished doctoral research available to a wider readership. Titles are selected and edited by a Board of distinguished experts from across the modern Humanities.

Editorial Board
English: Professor Catherine Maxwell, Queen Mary, University of London
French: Professor William Brooks, University of Bath
Germanic: Professor Ritchie Robertson, University of Oxford
Hispanic: Professor Derek Flitter, University of Exeter
Italian: Professor Brian Richardson, University of Leeds
Portuguese: Professor Thomas Earle, University of Oxford
Slavonic: Professor David Gillespie, University of Bath

Managing Editor: Dr Graham Nelson

Bridal-Quest Epics in Medieval Germany

A Revisionary Approach

by
Sarah Bowden

Modern Humanities Research Association
2012

Published by

The Modern Humanities Research Association
1 Carlton House Terrace
London SW1Y 5AF
United Kingdom

© *Modern Humanities Research Association and the*
Institute of Germanic and Romance Studies, University of London, 2012

Sarah Bowden has asserted her right under the Copyright, Designs and Patents Act 1988 to be identified as the author of this work. Parts of this work may be reproduced as permitted under legal provisions for fair dealing (or fair use) for the purposes of research, private study, criticism, or review, or when a relevant collective licensing agreement is in place. All other reproduction requires the written permission of the copyright holder who may be contacted at rights@mhra.org.uk.

Copy-Editor: Nigel Hope

First published 2012

ISBN 978-1-907322-46-4 (hardback)
ISBN 978-1-907322-96-9 (paperback)
ISSN (Bithell Series of Dissertations) 0266–7932
ISSN (MHRA Texts and Dissertations) 0957–0322

CONTENTS

	Acknowledgements	vii
	Introduction: The Problems of *Spielmannsepik* and *Brautwerbungsepik*	1
	Genre and medieval literature	2
	The origins of the category *Spielmannsepik*	6
	Spielmannsepik without the Spielmann	12
	Brautwerbungsepik	19
	Solutions to the problem	25
1	*König Rother*: Rother and Dietrich	35
	Rother	39
	Dietrich	49
	Rother Again	55
	Conclusion	60
2	*Salman und Morolf*: Salme and Morolf	70
	Salme, the danger of love, and the drive of the narrative	75
	Morolf, practical knowledge, and normative behaviour	82
	Conclusion	94
3	The *Münchner Oswald*: Saint and King	102
	Lives of St Oswald	102
	Chastity and kingship	107
	Problems of interpretation in the *Münchner Oswald*	111
	Oswald's raven	122
	Conclusion	126
4	*Grauer Rock*: Orendel and the Grey Robe	137
	Grauer Rock and the *tunica inconsutilis*	137
	Robe and man: a relationship of indexicality?	142
	Orendel and the Holy Grave	149
	Conclusion: the reception of *Grauer Rock*	154
	Conclusion	163
	Bibliography	167
	Index	181

ACKNOWLEDGEMENTS

This book started life as a PhD thesis at Clare College, Cambridge, submitted in September 2010 and funded by an AHRC doctoral award. My first thanks must be to my PhD supervisor, Mark Chinca, whose help and enthusiasm have been tireless and criticism always insightful. Thanks too to my examiners, Chris Young and Henrike Lähnemann, from whose encouragement and critical eye I have benefited greatly, and to David Wells, who read and commented on the manuscript on behalf of the MHRA. The genesis of this book has been helped greatly by discussions with Esther Laufer, Victor Millet, Heike Sahm and Jürgen Wolf, as well as with all those who participated in the Cambridge Medieval German Research Seminar 2006–2010. I am grateful to Prof. Ursula Peters and Prof. Hans-Joachim Ziegeler for allowing me to spend a very fruitful semester at the University of Cologne. The process of editing the thesis has taken place in the first year of a research fellowship at St Hugh's College Oxford, and I am indebted to the principal and fellows for providing me with the ideal environment in which to work, as well as to the academic community of the Oxford Medieval German Research Seminar. I would also like to thank Graham Nelson, my editor, and Nigel Hope, my copy editor, for their help and for a remarkably efficient editing process.

This book is for Tom.

Part of Chapter 4 appeared in a different form in my 'Sehen, Sichtbarkeit und Reliquien im *Grauen Rock*', in *Sehen und Sichtbarkeit in der deutschen Literatur des Mittelalters*, ed. by Ricarda Bauschke, Sebastian Coxon and Martin Jones (Berlin: Akademie Verlag, 2011).

S. B., September 2011

ABBREVIATIONS

DVjs	*Deutsche Vierteljahrsschrift für Literaturwissenschaft und Geistesgeschichte*
MF	*Des Minnesangs Frühling*, ed. by Hugo Moser and Helmut Tervooren, 38th edn (Stuttgart: Hirzel, 1988)
MGH	*Monumenta Germaniae Historica*
PBB	*Beiträge zur Geschichte der deutschen Sprache und Literatur*
VL	*Die deutsche Literatur des Mittelalters: Verfasserlexikon*, 2nd edn, 10 vols (Berlin: de Gruyter, 1978–99)
ZfdA	*Zeitschrift für deutsches Altertum und deutsche Literatur*
ZfdPh	*Zeitschrift für deutsche Philologie*

INTRODUCTION

~

The Problems of *Spielmannsepik* and *Brautwerbungsepik*

The aim of this study is to do away with, once and for all, the genre labels of *Spielmannsepik* and *Brautwerbungsepik*, which have been regularly applied since the late nineteenth century to designate the following Middle High German narratives: *König Rother*, *Herzog Ernst*, the *Münchner Oswald*, *Orendel* (now more commonly known as *Grauer Rock*), and *Salman und Morolf*.[1] The intention is not to suggest another genre label for the texts, but rather to challenge the notion of their belonging together and to posit a more flexible framework for their interpretation.

The characteristics commonly attributed to *Spielmannsepik* were a rough, burlesque style (thought to indicate a lower-class author), an entertaining narrative, an interest in the Orient, the prevalence of bridal-quest motifs, and a closeness to orality, particularly as all the texts are traditionally dated to the twelfth century. The label itself, named after the *spilman* or minstrel, the class of person thought to be the author of the texts, is no longer held to be meaningful because the existence of an authorially productive 'Spielmann' is historically unfounded; yet it is still frequently used as a descriptive term. *Brautwerbungsepik* (alternatively *Brautwerbungsdichtung* or *Brautwerbungserzählung*), the genre label now often used instead of the outmoded *Spielmannsepik*, maintains some of these characteristics, focusing not on the problematic author-figure but rather on the bridal-quest schema (*Brautwerbungsschema*) said to form a common structural framework. The notion remains that the texts find their place in medieval German literary history between orality and fully literary courtly romance, both chronologically and typologically. *Herzog Ernst* is conventionally excluded from the genre of *Brautwerbungsepik*, as it is not shaped by a bridal quest and other works are brought into consideration, particularly *Ortnit*, *Kudrun*, and the *Dukus Horant* fragment.[2] For reasons of space, and because they are more frequently studied alone or in conjunction with other texts (that is, because their position as part of the genre is less traditionally ingrained), these texts shall not be studied in depth here. As the focus of the study will be on the problems of *Brautwerbungsepik* and the notion of the bridal-quest schema, there is also no individual chapter on *Herzog Ernst*, although its place in the history of *Spielmannsepik* will be taken into consideration.

The arguments of this study against the validity of *Brautwerbungsepik* as a genre are quite simple: the bridal-quest schema does not have the same thematic purpose or importance in any of the texts; 'schema' is moreover perhaps an inappropriate word for a motif that is used flexibly and with very different motivation in a wide range of medieval German texts. Indeed, there is very little evidence that all the texts in question were even composed in the twelfth century and there is no regional pattern in their transmission. Before dealing with *Brautwerbungsepik*, however, there are other matters that must be investigated: exactly what might be meant by genre (particularly in a medieval context) and why the texts were first grouped together as a genre, which will be explored in an analysis of scholarship from the early nineteenth century to the present day.

Genre and Medieval Literature

A theoretical discussion of the concept of literary genre could fill an entire study, but for the present purposes it is sufficient to distinguish three broad applications of the term.[3] The first is the notion of genre as a normative model to which authors are expected to conform. 'Prescriptive' genre definitions of this kind are a feature of some periods of literary history, such as the Baroque, which witnessed the serial production of 'arts of poetry' setting out rules and models for a whole range of literary genres. This model of genre is not relevant to the vernacular literature of the Middle Ages, so shall not be discussed here further.[4] The second and third applications of genre are more central to the problem discussed in this study, so will be examined in more depth: these are the permissive, rather than prescriptive, idea of genre as the set of implicit conventions and expectations that govern both the composition of literary texts and their reception, and the role of genre as a classification in literary history.

The second model of describing genre norms is termed permissive because these norms enable authors to locate their works in a particular tradition (from which they may nonetheless be trying to depart) and permit the audience to make sense of a new work by activating relevant norms for understanding. The particular problem with regard to medieval literature is that genre norms are always implicit, so can only be reconstructed with difficulty.

The classical definition of the three genres — drama, epic, and lyric — simply does not work for medieval literature written in the vernacular, seeing as '[E]s handelt sich hier um neu entstehende Literaturen, die weder durch ein humanistisches Prinzip strenger Nachahmung noch durch den Kanon einer verbindlichen Poetik von der vorangehenden lateinischen Literatur unmittelbar abhängig sind'.[5] We need scarcely mention the can of worms that is oral literature. Moreover, the triadic system of genre would exclude the majority of medieval texts, relegating them to 'Unter- oder Zwischenarten'.[6] In influential discussions of the problem of genres in medieval literature, Kuhn, Jauss, and — most recently — Grubmüller have offered alternative, often more flexible, suggestions of 'permissive' genre models.

Kuhn shows that there is no real conception of poetics in the vernacular literature of the German Middle Ages and that if generic terms, such as *minnesanc*, *aventiure*, or *liet*, are used, then they are flexible and undefined, requiring a prior understanding of the genre to be made comprehensible as genre labels.[7] Instead of suggesting a prescriptive system of genre, he highlights three 'problems' according to which a text may be described: type, level ('Schichtenproblem'), and entelechy. Type can describe purpose or point to a more vague orientation of function that crosses genre; the problem of level is a more sociological one, the level functioning according to the degree of literary consciousness. Entelechy then provides a kind of constancy, primarily through the three main genres (epic, romance, and lyric), the tendencies of which provide a kind of stability discernible in various types of text, 'eine Zielstrebigkeit bestimmter Gattungstendenzen, die sich quer durch begrenzte Typen durchsetzt und in der normativen Gestaltungs-Stunde des Hochmittelalters zu für lange gültigen "Naturformen" der mittelalterlichen Dichtung führt'.[8]

Despite the apparent openness of his three-pronged attack, Kuhn's method seems to advocate smoothing over the differentiating features of texts, rather than admitting to them and realizing their potential. His use of the Aristotelian term 'entelechy' ('the realization or complete expression of some function; the condition in which a potentiality has become an actuality')[9] suggests the desire to iron out difficulties and find the defining characteristic of a text in one of the 'classic' medieval genres. The same tendency is evident in the problem of type, which allows Kuhn a too generalized take on early Middle High German literature — all of the same type because it has as its aim the rather vague 'Weltbild- und Lebensorientierung'[10] — or, in another essay, on fourteenth-century texts.[11]

Jauss concentrates to a greater degree on the historical nature of classification, hoping to describe genres synchronically and investigate them diachronically. He stresses the active role of reader reception and the importance of historical horizons of expectation, suggesting a pragmatic model with the horizon of expectation of the reader taken into consideration, created 'aus einer Tradition oder Reihe der ihm zuvor bekannten Werke und aus einer spezifischen, vom neuen Werk ausgelösten und durch eine Gattung (oder auch mehrere) vermittelten Einstellung konstituiert'.[12] This model allows for diachronic change; as well as the synchronic perspective, which manifests itself in the 'inner form' of a genre and its unique blend of formal and thematic characteristics, genres exist diachronically in a 'zeitlichen Prozeß fortgesetzter Horizontstiftung und Horizontveränderung'.¹³ He argues that a medieval text can be described through various generic aspects, but that it always has a 'dominant' that can be recognized synchronically:

> Eine literarische Gattung im nicht-logischen, gruppenspezifischen Sinn ist demnach in Abhebung von dem weiteren Umkreis der unselbständigen Funktionen dadurch bestimmbar, daß sie Texte selbständig zu konstituieren vermag, wobei diese Konstitution sowohl synchronisch in einer Struktur nicht ersetzbarer Elemente als auch diachronisch in einer kontinuitätsbildenden Potenz faßbar sein muß.¹⁴

The idea of the 'dominant' is potentially a very useful one for medieval literature, in which — as we have seen — clear genres may be difficult to define, suggesting a flexible and varied understanding of generically related texts, which have a shared constant but can still differ considerably.¹⁵ Paradoxically, however, Jauss describes a very strict and detailed system of synchronic classification with the implication that other textual features could be considered unimportant.¹⁶

Grubmüller is heavily critical of this problem in Jauss's genre theory, offering a not dissimilar but more flexible theory of his own.¹⁷ As Kuhn has already done, he highlights the lack of conscious genre poetics in vernacular medieval literature and argues that the existence of genre poetics in Latin literature appears to have little influence on vernacular texts. The lack of a socially coherent literary life and the peculiarities of systems of communication in the Middle Ages also led to a rather disparate body of literature: 'Es gibt kein kohärentes literarisches Leben, keinen allgemeinen literarischen Austausch, kein stabiles historisches Kontinuum, kein zusammenhängendes literarisches System, sondern immer nur Teilsysteme und dementsprechend auch nur Partialität der literarischen Traditionen und Werkreihen'.¹⁸ As a result of this, texts appear that are 'punktuelle[n] Versuche[n], ohne konkretes Muster und ohne reihenbildenden Effekt, die als Einzelstücke aus ihren je konkreten Bedingungen erklärt werden müssen, für die Diskussion gattungshafter Zusammenhänge aber auszusondern sind'.¹⁹ Genres can, Grubmüller argues, only be described (or understood) historically, in the context of a process of change, hence his use of 'Werkreihen' or 'literarische Reihen' rather than systems:

> Sähen wir Gattungen hingegen nicht als klassifikatorische Systeme, sondern konsequent als literarische Reihen, von denen zu verlangen ist, daß die aufeinander folgenden Elemente oder Stufen sich — aber auf jeden Fall erkennbar und beschreibbar aufeinander beziehen [...], brauchten wir die Kriterien, die für den Anfang galten, am Ende nicht mehr unbedingt zu erwarten, könnten wir Spielformen, Erweiterungen und Umkehrungen eben als Beispiele für den Normalfall historischer Abläufe nehmen: für die Anverwandlung und Umwertung von Traditionen.²⁰

It is possible for a text to participate in more than one 'Werkreihe', and a genre can only be analysed and described when a 'Werkreihe' is clearly and historically discernible. Grubmüller's theory works very well for the genre to which he applies it — *Märe* — but what about texts (or groups of texts) that do not fit into to an obvious 'Werkreihe'? The examples of *Moriz von Craûn* and the *Prosa-Lanzelot* are mentioned as erratic works that do not fit in, but are explained away as entering German literature from another culture and exerting no literary influence.[21] How are we to describe these and other such 'Sonderlinge'?

It is noticeable that all three studies of medieval genre discussed attempt to solve the problem of a too fixed and rigid conception of genre without doing away with the idea altogether. They all insist on a kind of constant (entelechy; a dominant; a discernible 'Werkreihe'), more or less flexibly defined, that is maintained historically in a group of texts and (to a greater or lesser degree) altered or developed in time. The question to be considered in this study is whether the four texts under discussion — despite their differences — have a dominant, or can fit into a 'Werkreihe', in particular whether or not they obtain some kind of thematic or structural constant in the pursuit of the bridal quest.

The third model of genre, namely genre as a classification in literary history, almost always overlaps with one or both of the other models discussed above (prescriptive or permissive). This is understandable, because the literary historian will usually want to describe what concepts of genre (prescriptive and explicit or permissive and implicit) were operative in the relevant period, and to show how these concepts and norms contributed to an appreciation of the texts in their historical context. The classification of texts in literary history is vital both practically — it enables a manageable overview of a potentially unmanageably large body of work[22] — and reasonably, because a work of art can never exist in isolation from other works of art or cultural circumstances. Nonetheless, it is inevitably a difficult and controversial activity, an ordering device always applied to some extent retrospectively to facilitate historical understanding or to aid the literary historian's particular argument. Genre classification in literary history is always to some degree too narrow or something of a compromise; a description of a genre can never draw into consideration every element of every text it is said to contain and different texts will inevitably be included or excluded (for a variety of reasons) by different literary historians.

The role of genre as an organizing category of literary history is especially important for the study of the so-called *Spielmannsepen*, because the perception that they belong together in a group is the product of several generations of German literary historiography. It is therefore necessary to examine the history of their treatment in literary history in more depth.

The Origins of the Category *Spielmannsepik*

The majority of 'Forschungsberichte' on *Spielmannsepik* and *Brautwerbungsepik* begin with works written in the twentieth century, yet because they are both problematic genre labels — as we have seen and shall see in more detail — it is useful to step back further in an attempt to understand when and why the constituent texts were first grouped together.[23]

The eighteenth century saw the beginnings of a gradual awakening of interest in medieval German literature. Of central importance was the Swiss Johann Jakob Bodmer, who, convinced by the artistic merit of Minnesang, copied and published poems from the Manessische Liederhandschrift, his first attempts appearing in 1748, followed by a complete version in 1758–59.[24] The efforts of Bodmer and others had little success, however, largely because of the negative attitude of the Enlightenment movement to the Middle Ages and the corresponding enthusiasm for classical antiquity.[25] A few decades later, the awakening of nationalist feelings in Germany and the interests of the Romantics suited the rehabilitation of medieval literature much better, leading to the impulse to uncover particularly Germanic cultural origins and to search for the 'natural', a world in which everything — religion, politics, poetry — could be as one. Medieval literature seemed to offer a complete and natural expression of life.[26] According to Hunger, it is possible to distinguish four main motivational strands of scholarship on medieval literature in the early nineteenth century: the literary-romantic, represented primarily by Tieck, Uhland, and A. W. Schlegel; the national-political, found particularly in the work of Friedrich von der Hagen; the cultural-historical motivation of the brothers Grimm; and the philological, particularly the works of Karl Lachmann.[27] Hunger provides a useful overview, but it is important to emphasize (perhaps to a greater extent than Hunger himself) that these lines of scholarship were not clearly (or consciously) delineated and overlapped considerably; the notion of the importance of pure *German* poetry, for instance, was present in the works of all scholars. The present investigation will focus more on the efforts and ideas of specific individuals than schools of thought.

Central to Romantic thought at the start of the nineteenth century were Herder's writings on nature and poetry, particularly his relatively early *Auszug aus einem Briefwechsel über Ossian und die Lieder alter Völker* (1773), in which he took the German translation of Ossian as the starting point for an investigation into the possibility of translating early folk-literature and its essential characteristics.[28] According to Herder, Ossian's works were representative of 'Lieder des Volks, Lieder eines ungebildeten sinnlichen Volks',[29] a more natural form of poetry (and indeed feeling) to be contrasted positively with the 'artistic' (or even artificial) poetry ('Kunstpoesie') of the modern age.[30]

Herder's interpretation of 'Volk' as — for the first time — a non-derogatory, natural, national body and his legitimization of the study of medieval literature were of great importance for the beginnings of medieval literary scholarship;[31] the distinction he made between 'natural' and 'artistic' poetry ('Volkspoesie' and 'Kunstpoesie') was vital for the understanding of medieval epic and — as we shall see — for the development of the genre of *Spielmannsepik*.

At the start of the nineteenth century, however, all medieval German literature was in general thought of as 'Volkspoesie'. Tieck, whose work provided a vital foundation to much later study, understood the Middle Ages as a unified period, in which poetry, religion, and politics could coexist harmoniously. He wrote in the introduction to his Minnesang edition of 1803 that:

> Die Dichtkunst war kein Kampf gegen etwas, kein Beweis, kein Streit für etwas, sie setzte in schöner Unschuld den Glauben an etwas voraus, was sie besingen wollte, daher ihre ungesuchte, einfältige Sprache in dieser Zeit, dieses reizende Tändeln, diese ewige Lust am Frühling, seinen Blumen und seinem Glanz, das Lob der schönen Frauen und die Klagen über ihre Härte, oder die Freude über vergoltene Liebe. Kein Gedanke, kein Ausdruck ist gesucht, jedes Wort steht nur um seiner selbst willen da, aus eigener Lust, und die höchste Künstlichkeit und Zier zeigt sich am liebsten als Unbefangenheit oder kindlicher Scherz mit den Tönen und Reimen.[32]

Tieck is particularly important to *Spielmannsepik* because he rediscovered the most complete manuscript of *König Rother* (MS H) in the Vatican library during his stay in Rome in 1805–06. He copied it, and it was from this copy that Friedrich von der Hagen first published the text.[33] Believing it important to make medieval literature as accessible to as many lovers of poetry as possible,[34] Tieck also worked on an 'Erneuung' of *König Rother*, which he planned to publish as part of a 'Heldenbuch' project he never finished. The idea of an 'Erneuung' was the main impetus behind von der Hagen's editions of medieval literature, a 'renewing' of the original into modern language, as close to the original as possible, rather than a free retelling or new version.[35] Unlike von der Hagen, however, Tieck was not especially motivated by national-political concerns,[36] but his method of 'Erneuung' was much the same; he wanted to preserve the sound and metre of the original as much as possible.[37] His *König Rother* was not published in full until 1979 in an edition by Uwe Meves, and follows his conception of medieval literature as quoted above, consciously deleting all historical and political content from the text; neither Charlemagne nor the several noble Bavarian families, all of which play an important role in *König Rother*, are even mentioned. Religious emphasis is also considerably attenuated.[38] It is interesting to note that Tieck intended to publish *König Rother* as part of a 'Heldenbuch' with *Laurin*, *Rosengarten*, *Ortnit*, and *Wolfdietrich*, although he was not happy with the title of 'Heldenbuch' because *König Rother* was not to be found in any of the large late medieval collected 'Heldenbuch' manuscripts of heroic epics.[39] The fact that Tieck found the historical and religious dimensions of the text problematic also points towards the later categorization of *Spielmannsepik* as texts *different* to heroic epic, in that they are less 'natural', culminating in Gervinus's definition of them as 'Kunstpoesie innerhalb der Volkspoesie', as will be discussed in detail below.

Heroic epic was the preferred genre of medieval German literary scholars in this early period of scholarship, for it — in particular the *Nibelungenlied* — fulfilled the criteria of 'Volkspoesie' particularly well: it was German, without foreign influence (unlike romance), close to nature and immeasurably old. In his *Vorlesungen über die romantische Literatur*, given in 1803-04, A. W. Schlegel described the *Nibelungenlied* and the texts of the Heldenbuch manuscripts as 'Die zwey vornehmsten Denkmäler derselben, die auf uns gekommen'.[40] Textual investigation and historical interpretation were of great importance to Schlegel — he thought that history and theory should be as one[41] — and he considered medieval literature to be an expression of true romantic national poetry, comparable to Homeric epic.[42] He claimed that, as with the *Iliad*, it was impossible to attribute an author or redactor to the *Nibelungenlied*, because 'solch ein Werk ist zu groß für einen Menschen, es ist die Hervorbringung der gesamten Kraft eines Zeitalters'.[43] Importantly, however, the epic must still be thought of as a true work of art,[44] an opinion at odds with that of the brothers Grimm, who maintained a strong distinction between the 'Volkspoesie' (or 'Naturpoesie') and 'Kunstpoesie' within medieval literature, namely between the true German epic and the poetry written to suit the tastes of the nobility.[45] In his prologue to 'Über den altdeutschen Meistergesang' of 1811, Jakob Grimm wrote that:

> Man kann die Naturpoesie das Leben in der reinen Handlung selbst nennen, ein lebendiges Buch, wahrer Geschichte voll, das man auf jedem Blatt mag anfangen zu lesen und zu verstehen, nimmer aber ausliest noch durchversteht. Die Kunstpoesie ist eine Arbeit des Lebens und schon im ersten Keim philosophischer Art.[46]

Wilhelm Grimm was more negative, saying that given the existence of 'Volkspoesie', 'Kunstpoesie' was 'Manier' and 'überflüßig'.[47] Yet whether or not it was judged negatively, the fact that a distinction was being made between 'Volkspoesie' and 'Kunstpoesie' within medieval literature is of great importance.

The question of genre on a larger scale does not, however, really arise outside the writing of literary history. Prior to the nineteenth century, literary histories hardly existed; literature was included in large encyclopaedic works, but rarely discussed in detail, and individual attempts at more detailed descriptions were rarely taken seriously in intellectual circles.[48] Works resembling literary histories as we know them today began to be written from the end of the eighteenth century, but until Gervinus's famous work of 1835 — often thought of as the first 'true' history of German literature — they were generally written neither for nor by experts.[49] 'Germanistik' was, it is important to remember, at this time not an established subject taught at universities. Before Gervinus, there were not many comprehensive literary histories and they are often plagiaristic or very closely related to each other; individual texts are discussed very briefly and often only a synopsis is given.[50] Yet they still provide great insight into the reception and categorization of medieval literature.

Although many of these early literary histories were opposed to the ideas of the Romantics, they shared the same fundamental theory that a great flowering of literature can only come about in a period in which the whole 'Volk' is unified: so, in their opinion, in the High Middle Ages, at the Reformation, and in the latter half of the eighteenth century.[51] The High Middle Ages is usually thought to last from the twelfth century to the start of the fourteenth century and includes all the so-called *Spielmannsepen*, although they are never discussed together. *König Rother* is always classified as epic, usually in a subclass with *Ortnit* and *Wolfdietrich* and dated to the end of the twelfth century.[52] This type of epic is commonly thought to be different from the *Nibelungenlied* and the Dietrich epics, showing traces of a connection with the South.[53] *Salman und Morolf* and *Herzog Ernst* are described differently in almost every literary history; a relationship to heroic epic is usually mentioned, but they are always classed outside the circle of true German epic, more distant from it than *König Rother*. The historical side to *Herzog Ernst* is emphasized to a greater degree than the journey to the East, with the text sometimes classified as 'historical epic'.[54] *Salman und Morolf* is usually discussed in connection with the so-called 'Spruchgedicht' of Salomon and Markolf (which will be referred to as *Markolfs buch* in Chapter 2), but a thematic link to *König Rother* did not go unnoticed by Uhland.[55] Rosenkranz classified the text in the subclass 'die gemeine Wirklichkeit' of the class 'romantisches Epos' along with a series of short comic tales,[56] a comic side also emphasized by Pischon, who however classified it with a group of seemingly unrelated 'left-overs', including Ulrich von Liechtenstein's *Frauendienst*, Hartmann von Aue's *Der Arme Heinrich*, and Der Stricker's *Pfaffe Amis*, which he refers to as 'poetische Erzählungen';[57] similarly, Koberstein grouped it with *Der Arme Heinrich, Crescentia*, Konrad von Würzburg's *Gedicht von der Minne* and *Der Welt Lohn, Pfaffe Amis, Alexander und Aristoteles, von der Weiber List,* and *der Wiener Meerfahrt*.[58] There is no great interest in either *Orendel* or the *Münchner Oswald*, although a link between *Orendel* and heroic epic is occasionally mentioned.[59]

Next came Gervinus. In an article in the *Heidelberger Jahrbücher* from 1833 — ostensibly a review of literary histories by Bohtz and Herzog — he criticized the writing of literary history in general for a lack of historical perspective and a contradictory and biased nature.⁶⁰ His own literary history, the *Geschichte der poetischen National-Literatur der Deutschen*, appeared only two years later, and he laid out his theories in the introduction to the first edition. First, because of the political situation of the time, he thought it necessary to write a national literary history that emphasized the role of Germany as the real heir to the culture of ancient Greece.⁶¹ Then he stated that a literary history should not give an aesthetic judgement and that his own effort 'weicht besonders darin von allen literarischen Handbüchern und Geschichten ab, daß es nichts ist als Geschichte. Ich habe mit der ästhetischen Beurtheilung der Sachen nichts zu thun, ich bin kein Poet und kein belletristischer Kritiker'.⁶² The true literary historian:

> zeigt uns nicht Eines Gedichtes, sondern aller poetischen Producte Entstehung aus der Zeit, aus dem Kreise ihrer Ideen, Thaten und Schicksale, er weist darin nach was diesen entspricht oder widerspricht, er sucht die Ursachen ihres Werdens und ihre Wirkungen nach und beurtheilt ihren Werth hauptsächlich nach diesen, er vergleicht sie mit dem Größten der Kunstgattung gerade dieser Zeit und dieser Nation, in der sie entstanden, oder je nachdem er seinen Gesichtskreis ausdehnt, mit den weiteren analogen Erscheinungen in anderen Zeiten und Völkern.⁶³

Contrary to these claims, it is clear that Gervinus's work was shaped by strong opinions; it is for Germany and against France and Italy, for the classical period and against Romanticism, for the Reformation and against Catholicism.⁶⁴ It is also noticeable that he was not so favourably disposed to medieval literature as his predecessors.⁶⁵ Nonetheless, his work still resembles earlier readings of medieval literature in its nationalist tendencies and the distinction he makes between Volkspoesie and Kunstpoesie, the latter of which he viewed negatively, a symptom of his nationalist tendencies in the time of the founding of a unified German state. Art was, he argued, a struggle between national and foreign influences, won eventually in the eighteenth century in the works of Goethe and Schiller, which were truly German. The Kunstpoesie of the Middle Ages, however, was tinged with foreign influence, so Gervinus disapproved of it as literature that detracted from the national Volkspoesie.⁶⁶ Nonetheless, Gervinus was the first to sketch a process of development in the literature of the Middle Ages (even if this development is not an entirely positive one), towards the texts of what is today known as the *Blütezeit*, a chronological progression not dissimilar to that most commonly found in literary histories today.

When it comes to the so-called *Spielmannsepen*, one of the most important moves Gervinus made was to take *König Rother* out of the epic context in which it had previously been considered and to describe it as a forerunner of works from what we now call the *Blütezeit*. The text is discussed in the chapter 'Übergang zur ritterlichen Poesie der hohenstaufischen Zeit' in the subcategory 'Ausartung der Volkspoesie', a section in which, importantly, *Herzog Ernst* and

Salman und Morolf are also discussed; *Salman und Morolf* is connected to *König Rother* thematically — they both have a Byzantine influence — whereas *Herzog Ernst* is, he argued, stylistically similar. This section also briefly discusses *Graf Rudolf* and *Biterolf und Dietleib*. According to Gervinus, Volkspoesie came to an end when it was no longer received by Everyman; the change from orality to written texts was also of great importance:

> Denn Volkspoesie kann nur heißen, was den Weg zu seiner Vollendung unter der Theilnahme Aller gemacht hat; was später von Geistlichen oder solchen Dichtern, die schon standes- und kastenmäßig eine Kunst oder ein Gewerbe aus der Dichtung machen, gleichviel, ob Erfundenes oder Gefundenes bearbeiten in Schriften und Büchern, hört man auf Volksdichtung zu sein, und sollte es sich auch noch so tief im Volke verbreitet haben.[67]

From the expression 'Ausartung der Volkspoesie' it is possible to infer that Gervinus did not have a particularly high opinion of the texts, which was indeed the case. He asserted that they were no longer real German Volkspoesie, but were also not yet true Kunstpoesie; instead, they were 'eine Kunstpoesie gleichsam innerhalb der Volkspoesie'.[68] He described them as follows:

> Das Geschichtliche ist [...] in stetem Sinken, die Erdichtung und das Wunderbare in stetem Wachsen; die objective Treue, Scheu vor der Tradition, Wahrheit und Lebendigkeit halt Schritt mit jenem und die subjective Zudringlichkeit mit diesem; der würdevolle Ernst fällt mit jenem und das Komische steigt mit diesem; die Wirkung des Ganzen wechselt mit der Wirkung der Theile; die alten Verhältnisse werden von neuen verdrängt, größere von kleineren.[69]

In the second edition of his literary history, Gervinus changed his interpretation slightly. The texts keep their place in the course of the history of German medieval literature, but are considered in a slightly more positive light. The section in which they are discussed is now called 'Veränderungen in der deutschen Volksdichtung' and the style of the texts — which this time include the *Münchner Oswald* — is argued to point to a period of transition. They have 'keinen inneren Mittelpunkt' and are a mix of courtly themes and folk poetry, an interpretation that has endured until the present.[70] Gervinus was also the first person to link this group of texts explicitly to a Spielmann-figure, suggesting 'eine Klasse von fahrenden Sängern und Spielleuten' as redactors.[71] His theories were soon very influential, and a firmer definition of the group was given by Wackernagel in his literary history of 1848. The category he termed 'Byzantinisch-palaestinische Dichtung' — thanks to the influence of oriental sagas and Byzantine stories — was made up of *König Rother*, *Herzog Ernst*, *Salman und Morolf*, and *Orendel*.[72] The *Münchner Oswald* is classed as a saint's life, although he does see similarities to *Orendel*.[73]

To summarize, the texts that became known as *Spielmannsepik* were first put together by Gervinus in his literary history because they were neither Volkspoesie nor Kunstpoesie but helped to demonstrate a historical progression between the two. The similarities he highlighted between the texts are not particularly well defined and his argument resonates with his own political stance; yet the notion of *Spielmannsepik* as a mid-point between orality and serious written literature, or between heroic epic and courtly romance, has persisted, as has an insistence on their belonging together as a group, even if the reasons adduced for such a grouping are often vague and frequently change.

Spielmannsepik without the Spielmann

Unsurprisingly, the status of the texts between Volkspoesie and Kunstpoesie led to the assumption of an author-figure placed halfway between 'the people' and a serious, self-consciously artistic poet. The 'Spielmann' or 'singer' had already been the subject of discussion — without direct relevance to our texts — and was first mentioned by Wilhelm Grimm as a transmitter, rather than productive author, of Volkspoesie.[74] Uhland, on the other hand, argued in his lectures held at Tübingen in 1830–31 that the 'Spielmann' could also have a productive role, changing stories as he sang them.[75] The role of the Spielmann with respect to our texts was first examined in detail by Wackernagel, who thought that the Spielmann of the twelfth century was a productive poet, whereas earlier Spielmänner were not, and that the works later known as *Spielmannsepen* were composed by a travelling poet.[76]

A firm definition of the singer or minstrel was given in 1875 by Friedrich Vogt, who argued that all such people belonged to the class of *gernde liute* (he classed many kinds of people under this term), travelling people considered very important in the pre-Christian period as well as at the time of the crusades, on which they travelled as musicians and from which they brought back Eastern tales to influence their songs. The defining characteristic of these people, who travelled with old songs, developed new ones, added contemporary political arguments and entertained courts, was that they performed for money, something for which they were reproached by other scholars, although Vogt defended them by saying they paradoxically gained honour for themselves by giving others honour through their songs. Our texts, particularly *Salman und Morolf*, were said by Vogt to be the most typical examples of the work of these people.[77]

The problem with Vogt's argument is there is no evidence that the *gernde liute*, described in the *Sachsenspiegel* as being without rights, were in fact minstrel-poets. Indeed, there is no evidence that the *spilman*, a figure who is mentioned in many medieval texts (including *König Rother* and *Salman und Morolf*) is a poet at all, let alone one who produces new works. Indeed, discussion of the productive (or not) presence of the Spielmann appears to be the result of the Romantic interpretation of medieval literature, particularly that of the brothers Grimm, influenced by Herder's concepts of Volkspoesie and Kunstpoesie. As argued by Bahr:

> Die These, daß Spielleute die Verfasser der um den Rother gruppierten Epen seien, wurde daher auch niemals bewiesen: sie ist aber auch nicht die willkürliche Behauptung eines einzelnen Gelehrten, sondern das notwendige Nebenergebnis einer Jahrzehnte dauernden Folge literaturgeschichtlicher Darstellungen auf der Grundlage des Grimmschen Literaturbildes. Die These vom dichtenden Spielmann verdankt ihre Existenz nur dem Versuch, die Sonderstellung jener Epengruppe zu erklären.[78]

Bahr was not the first to doubt the Spielmann; Naumann's essay of 1924 argued that there was no evidence for the creative abilities of this class of person and suggested a new type of author for the *Spielmannsepen*. The appearance of a Spielmann in several of the texts was, he said, no reason to suppose that he was also the author since — following this line of reasoning — he could just as easily have been a king or a giant; moreover, the stylistic arguments concerning the 'rough style' bear little weight. Naumann stressed instead the religious dimension of the texts and posited religious men as the poets, 'Propagandageistliche', who spread the word of God through secular literary forms:

> jene bestimme Art von Klerikern, deren Aufgabe es war, Heiligenleben und Legenden in epischer und liedmäßiger Form vorzutragen, voller weltlicher Zugeständnisse an ritterlichen Kämpfen und Brautfahrten, Abenteuern im Heiligen Land, Moniagen, heimatlichen und gelehrten fremden Motiven — kurzum an ein Institut der inneren Mission sozusagen.[79]

Even though Bahr criticized Naumann's argument, suggesting that it placed too much emphasis on the religious dimension of the texts, it is notable that neither believed the texts did not belong together as a group, which might seem to be the natural conclusion of an examination of the history of their classification.[80] Bahr argued that, despite their misleading name, the *Spielmannsepen* were similarly neither religious nor courtly and had a shared style; he suggested that they were works of town and marketplaces, a theory surely as unprovable as Naumann's 'Propagandageistliche'.[81]

Despite the authorial problem, the name *Spielmannsepik* has persisted as an empty term and the existence of the group has been hardly challenged. The 1960s and 1970s saw a resurgence of interest with an introductory handbook and edited collection of older scholarship by Walter Johannes Schröder and a monograph and 'Forschungsbericht' by Michael Curschmann, all of which attempted to clarify the status of the genre.[82] Schröder defines *Spielmannsepik* as a group of twelfth-century texts that belong neither to heroic nor to courtly epic, although they are thematically linked to both. The main characteristic feature is the style of the works:

> Man versteht darunter einen Komplex bevorzugter Motive, typischer Vorgänge und formelhafter Wendungen in der sprachlichen Darstellung, Mischung von Ernst und Scherz, bunte Fülle der Ereignisse, geringe Sorgfalt in Metrik und Reim, alles in allem eine gewisse Unbekümmertheit der Erzählweise, die mehr auf Unterhaltung und Belustigung des Publikums aus ist als künstlerische Form.[83]

Also important is the structural schema of wooing, the background of the crusades, and a relationship to historical events.[84] Curschmann's monograph is more complex and has exerted a greater influence, making a case for the 'spielmännische Epik' (as he calls it) as a developmental stage towards courtly romance. He claims that the texts are early examples of the exploration of the theme of reconciling worldly life and love with God, a theme central to the courtly romances of the *Blütezeit* that culminates in the works of Wolfram von Eschenbach, and understands them as a mid-point between earlier religious poetry — with which they share many stylistic features[85] — and these romances, which take *minne* and transform it into something with a higher, spiritual possibility.[86] Following Naumann's line of argument, he argues that the poets were probably religious men who reshaped 'trivial' secular literature for their own purposes, reforming the material into a style between that of epic and that of romance, and exploring contemporary religious needs.[87]

There are a few simple problems with Curschmann's argument. First, his alternative genre label, 'die spielmännische Epik', does not solve any of the problems of *Spielmannsepik*. Second, to understand the texts as the successors to twelfth-century religious 'Buchepik' and precursors to Wolfram is to ignore the possibility of a later dating for *Oswald*, *Orendel*, and *Salman und Morolf* (this is one of the fundamental problems of situating all the *Spielmannsepen* chronologically before the *Blütezeit*). Third, the focus on the *Münchner Oswald* at the expense of the other texts leads to a more heavily religious interpretation than might be merited.

Despite all the problems that have been outlined above, the *Spielmannsepen* have however been almost invariably grouped together in twentieth-century literary histories, and a number of supposedly defining characteristics are often adduced: the 'spielmännisch' style; the status of the works on the threshold between orality and written texts; the bridal-quest structure; the depiction of the Orient. A short overview of some of the most important literary histories should help to demonstrate just how arbitrary and often ill-defined the links between the texts appear to be.

In his influential history of medieval German literature, first published in 1922 (so before the appearance of Naumann's essay), Ehrismann grouped *König*

Rother, Salman und Morolf, Oswald, and *Orendel* together under the heading 'Das Spielmannsepos'.[88] All of these narratives are said by him to have been written by a Spielmann, an essential member of courtly society who entertained others to make a living, but who lost his privileged status after the clericalization of society in the eleventh century. These epics treated a wide variety of material in an entertaining style, particularly favouring the bridal quest;[89] *König Rother* represents the greatest achievement of the genre and *Salman und Morolf* the purest expression of its style.[90] All the epics are dated to the twelfth century.

De Boor took an important step forward in grouping all five texts as 'die sogenannten Spielmannsepen'; the qualifier 'sogenannt' reflects his dissatisfaction with the notion of a Spielmann as author. He argued that the Spielmann was probably only a musician and transmitter of oral literature, whereas the authors of these works were probably members of the rural nobility and perhaps even religious men.[91] The genre is founded on stylistic similarities: '[F]reude am Stofflichen, Sinn für das Bunte und Grelle, im Humor für die Burleske, Sorglosigkeit des Aufbaus, geringe Ansprüche an die Form, überwuchernde Formelhaftigkeit gelten also die bestimmenden "spielmännischen" Merkmale'.[92] His description concentrated, however, primarily on the individual characteristics of each text and he created a subclass — which would influence many later literary historians — of 'Legendenromane' for *Salman und Morolf, Orendel*, and *Oswald*, texts that fall outside the supposedly Bavarian audience of *König Rother* and *Herzog Ernst*, although he admitted that *Salman und Morolf* had no real religious motifs. Importantly, he doubted the early dating of these 'Legendenromane', stressing the fifteenth-century characteristics of each text and questioning how closely related any twelfth-century versions might be to the extant texts.[93]

Schwietering also appeared to move away from *Spielmannsepik*, discussing the five texts together, with *Brandan* and *Tundalus*, in his chapter 'Weltliche Erzählungen, volkstümliche Legende und Jenseitsvision'. Stylistic similarities are drawn between *König Rother* and *Herzog Ernst* on the one hand and *Oswald, Orendel*, and *Salman und Morolf* on the other, although within the latter grouping *Salman und Morolf* is described as more worldly. On the whole, however, each text is treated individually; whether Schwietering intended to challenge the generic label *Spielmannsepik*, or even assign the works to a different grouping, is not entirely clear, since he avoided all explicit discussion of either the term 'Spielmann' or the bridal-quest schema.[94]

Erb's literary history, in contrast, offers a positive and expansive definition of the Spielmann, heavily influenced by the political conditions of writing in the former GDR. In his chapter 'Der spielmännische Versroman im 12. Jahrhundert', he devotes more space to 'Der "Stolze Spielmann"' than to any of the five texts (*König Rother, Herzog Ernst, Oswald, Orendel, Salman und*

Morolf), emphasizing the cultural potential of the people (rather than simply the nobility) and the social importance of the Spielmann himself, a central and vital figure at court.[95] For Erb, *Spielmannsdichtung* is entertaining, combines a wide variety of material, is interested in the Orient, and often centres on the bridal quest, 'das älteste unter den unverwüstlichen Motiven mittelalterlicher Erzählkunst'.[96] There are also overlaps with religious poetry, so that it is difficult to tell exactly what class of author a text might have.[97] Erb discusses the Spielmann so widely, drawing in sources from a wide number of texts to stress his importance — including Tristan's disguise as Tantris to give evidence of his authority and potential courtliness[98] — that it is surprising he does not attempt to widen the genre, only giving details about the five texts in which it traditionally consists, as well as the so-called 'Spruchgedicht' of *Salomon und Markolf*. *Orendel* and *Oswald* are assigned to the subcategory of 'spielmännische Legendenepen' and all texts are dated to the twelfth century, although he admits that it is impossible to know how those with an exclusively fifteenth-century transmission may have changed in the intervening period.[99]

In his chapter 'Höfisches im Orient-Bild der Spielmannsepen und im *Graf Rudolf*', Ruh retains the word *Spielmannsepik* without quotation marks, because 'es scheint mir heute möglich, sie nach Struktur und Erzähltechnik so präzis zu fassen, daß sich das romantische Bild des Spielmanns nicht mehr vorzuschieben braucht'.[100] Much like Curschmann, Ruh wants to show how the genre is in some way courtly, stressing its place between orality and written texts, with the Spielmann successfully translating his material into the new medium. Courtly features discussed include the use of rhyming couplets, new ideological influences (such as the 'Reichsgeschichte' in *König Rother*), the 'Problemstruktur' of the bridal quest, which becomes an expression of virtue and honour, and the depiction of the Orient, eventually integrated into courtly romance in *Parzival*.[101]

Wehrli describes all five texts in his chapter 'Vom Zeitlied zum historischen und legendarischen Roman', with three subsections for *Herzog Ernst* and *König Rother*, 'Legendenromane', and *Graf Rudolf*.[102] He does not use the term *Spielmannsepik*, arguing that de Boor's term 'Legendenroman' is more fitting and clearly defined for the latter three texts, but he does describe *Salman und Morolf*, *Orendel*, and *Oswald* as 'spielmännisch' and argues for their early dating.[103] Even if the validity of the traditional genre label is questioned and the five texts split into two categories, these categories are still related and adjacent, and no attempt is made to suggest that they do not belong together. A similar solution is offered by Bumke, who, in his chapter 'Die Anfänge der höfischen Literatur', discusses *König Rother* and *Herzog Ernst* as 'Epen aus mündlicher Stofftradition' and *Oswald*, *Orendel*, and *Salman und Morolf* as 'Die spielmännischen Legendenepen'.[104] He is doubtful about the term

Spielmannsepik, arguing that the former texts are similar because of their political themes and probable audience of Bavarian nobility, and expressing general uncertainty about the latter three: 'so bleibt ein großes Fragezeichen hinter dieser Epengruppe'.[105] Bräuer also uses de Boor's term 'Legendenroman' for *Salman und Morolf*, *Orendel*, and *Oswald*, keeping the five texts together as a group in his chapter 'Orientabenteuerepik'.[106] He asserts that all the texts are motivated by either religious or (pseudo-) historical concerns, are entertaining, and show signs of the influence of orality. He claims that they were written most likely by intellectuals who were neither noble nor religious men, but most probably lived by their writing.[107]

Röcke, in Mertens's guide to medieval epic material, discusses *Spielmannsepik* (a name with which he is dissatisfied) together with other verse narratives (*Apollonius*, *Wilhelm von Wenden*, *Die Gute Frau*, *Friedrich von Schwaben*, *Flore und Blanscheflur*, *Wilhelm von Österreich*) as examples of loosely defined genres which nonetheless have a dominant (he follows Jauss closely), and groups these loose genres together under the heading of 'Minne- und Abenteuerromane'. The dominants of this new genre are the theme of questing for a lover or bride, an emphasis on love and adventure, separation of lovers, and the testing of the hero. *König Rother* and *Herzog Ernst* are discussed under the subcategory 'Heroisch-politische Romane', *Oswald*, *Orendel*, and *Salman und Morolf* as 'Legendenromane'.[108] A similar division is offered by Ebenbauer in Glaser's collective literary history. He discusses the texts in a chapter called 'Andere Großepen', under the subheading 'Brautgewinnung in der *Spielmannsepik*', stressing the thematic link of the bridal quest and excluding *Herzog Ernst*, which is discussed elsewhere in the same chapter. His main title, however, barely disguises the fact that his chapter contains the leftover texts that cannot be fitted in elsewhere, including *Flore und Blanscheflur*, *Wilhelm von Orlens*, Konrad von Würzburg's *Engelhard* and *Partonopier und Meliur*, *Friedrich von Schwaben*, and *Apollonius*. The general themes argued to be characteristic of this group are remarkably broad: love and marriage, travel, historicization, enjoyment, a mix of intentions, didacticism, legitimation of rulers, and so on.[109]

Vollmann-Profe retains the name *Spielmannsepik* despite the fact that she is unconvinced by both the Spielmann as author and the so-called 'spielmännisch' style; for her, the essential feature of all five texts is their early dating in the second half of the twelfth century and their position on the cusp between orality and written literature that is conscious of its status:

> Die entscheidende Gemeinsamkeit der Epen sehen wir darin, daß sie den Moment der Transformation von der Mündlichkeit in die Schriftlichkeit noch festhalten — oder besser: jenen Moment, in dem die Begegnung der beiden literarischen Existenzformen noch offen und im Stadium des Experiments war.[110]

The texts may differ considerably, but they all offer similar literary answers to similar experiences and share themes of 'bridal quest', 'journey to the East', and 'how the hero should live in the world'. The twelfth-century dating of each text is emphasized — understandably, given her main thesis. The major problem is that it is unclear what 'de[r] Moment der Transformation' consists in; how can we see it, test it?[111] The idea of progression is, paradoxically, a rather backward one — how can texts know (it seems) what they are aiming at? What is the point in reading them for what they are not yet, instead of for what they are?

Such a problem is only one of many when it comes to describing *Spielmannsepik*. Without the Spielmann as author, the name itself is meaningless, yet alternative suggestions have rarely been made (or, in the case of 'Legendenroman' for *Salman und Morolf*, are inappropriate). The different thematic emphases of the texts are either discussed in some depth without justifying to any considerable degree the texts' generic classification, or — more frequently — glossed over in favour of generalizing statements. The late transmission of *Oswald*, *Orendel*, and *Salman und Morolf* is scarcely mentioned and even less frequently granted any importance — a fact stressed by Brandt, who shows convincingly that literary histories take little account of the transmission or editorial history of the texts. Some older editions attempt to recreate earlier versions of the *Münchner Oswald*, *Salman und Morolf*, and *Orendel*, but more recent editions of the former two texts have maintained the fifteenth-century language, treating the text as it would have been received at that time.[112] As Brandt says:

> Fur die Gesamtgruppe der 'Spielmannsepen' bedeutet das, dass sie editorisch heute praktisch nicht mehr existiert — man muss schon die älteren Editionen von Bartsch (*HE*), Frings/Kuhnt und De Vries (*Roth*), Baesecke und Fuchs (*Münchener Osw*, *Wiener Osw*), Steinger (*Or*), Vogt (*S&M*) zusammenfassen, um dieses Bild noch beibehalten zu können. Parallel dazu ergibt sich auch kein einheitliches Bild der Editionen mehr: In den alten Editionen kann die Fiktion einer relativ festen Gruppe von 'Spielmannsepen' weiterexistieren, in den neuen bietet sich dafür kaum noch ein Anhaltspunkt.[113]

The problem of dating the texts is, however, insufficient to dismiss their belonging together as a genre; indeed, the theories of genre discussed above are diachronic, based on a central idea that may change with time, such as Jauss's dominant or formative of Grubmüller's 'Werkreihe'. Nonetheless, the impression remains from the above review of literary histories that the so-called *Spielmannsepen* are in some sense 'problem' texts, however they are categorized in each specific case, and despite the fact that the notion of *Spielmannsepik* is never explicitly dismissed and the texts are rarely discussed in contexts away from one another.

INTRODUCTION

Brautwerbungsepik

The answer to the problem of *Spielmannsepik* could be to think of the texts as *Brautwerbungsepik* (or *Brautwerbungsdichtung* or *Brautwerbungserzählung*), a term that highlights a clear thematic link between them. There is, after all, some kind of bridal quest in each one of the texts: Rother woos the daughter of Constantin, King of Constantinople; Salman has wooed Salme, who is in turn wooed by various heathen kings and must be won back; Oswald woos Paug, the daughter of King Aron; Orendel woos Bride, Queen of Jerusalem. As mentioned above, *Herzog Ernst* is not considered within this definition of the group, because it is not shaped by a bridal quest; Ernst's mother is wooed by Kaiser Otto, but this is very brief, and Ernst never seeks a wife himself (an implicitly possible wife, the Indian princess, is killed by monstrous crane-men before he can rescue her).

The idea of *Brautwerbungsepik* as a genre is relatively new, but discussion of the bridal-quest schema ('Brautwerbungsschema'), the structural feature supposedly common to all the so-called *Spielmannsepen*, has been a feature of criticism for many years. *Brautwerbungsepik* as a genre designation has not yet appeared in any literary histories, but is used increasingly in monographs and articles, and studies that discuss the bridal-quest schema usually understand it as a clear structural matrix in which the texts subsist. Although its nuances are always identified differently, a rough idea of the schema can be given as follows:

— The hero (usually a king) decides, or is told, that he needs a wife, usually to secure his lineage.
— There is a council scene, in which his most trusted advisers suggest a suitable bride. She lives across the sea.
— The hero or a messenger sets out to woo her.
— There is some kind of obstacle to the marriage.
— The hero returns home with his wife.[114]

The first scholar to address the matter of the bridal quest was Frings. Although he still referred to the texts as *Spielmannsepik* and believed in the Spielmann as author (even if the latter was in his view a partially romanticized figure), his approach represented a departure from hitherto dominant concerns because it discussed the texts primarily with respect to the structural feature of the bridal quest.[115] He did not seem to view the bridal quest as constitutive of genre, but rather as a widespread story-motif, the particular medieval German shaping of which is found in *Spielmannsepik*. According to Frings, there were two types of bridal quest, the Northern Germanic violent wooing expedition and the Mediterranean wooing expedition achieved by cunning, which are combined for the first time in the *Spielmannsepen*.[116] He set out the developmental theory of Urlied — Erblied — Neulied, which argued that the versions of the texts we have today did not come directly from oral songs (Urlied) but rather through an intermediary early written stage (Erblied), a notion embodied in the archetypal Erblied 'Ur-Rother', the original combination of violent and cunning bridal-quest types.[117] The 'Ur-Rother', similar to the first part of *König Rother* as we know it, led to the development of the first epics about Siegfried and Brünhild and the double structure of the new *König Rother* enabled epics such as the *Nibelungenlied* and *Kudrun*.[118]

Frings's concept of the 'Ur-Rother' seems outdated to the modern scholar. Archetypal ur-texts are now largely dismissed — common sense dictates that it is foolish to hypothesize in any detail about something that may well have never existed — and the attribution of the development of much Germanic epic to the influence of only one early text seems highly unlikely. Equally, Frings's two types of bridal quest are problematic, not least because his concept of the Mediterranean seems vague and to stretch into Southern Germany.[119] Nonetheless, Frings's study has been highly influential, particularly with regard to the commonly expressed idea that the *Spielmannsepen* (especially *König Rother*) should be considered as an early stage in the development of German literature, a necessary step on the path to the works of the *Blütezeit* and a midpoint between oral and written poetry.

Haug's essay 'Struktur, Gewalt und Begierde' can be seen as a next step on from Frings, for, although it certainly does not discuss archetypes, it maintains and complicates the idea of the bridal-quest schema as an oral form. Haug treats the 'Brautwerbungserzählungen', as he calls them, as examples of early written forms: 'Brautwerbungserzählungen vom Typus *König Rother* sind die ersten deutschsprachigen narrativen Großformen, die heimisch-profane Stoffe verschriftlichen'.[120] Characteristic of each text (and its written state) is the way it 'breaks' from the 'Grundthematik' of the bridal quest.[121] Variation between different oral presentations of an orally composed song cannot, he argues, indicate intentional reinterpretations of that song; these can only occur when something is written down. Oral presentations can vary in aesthetic ability, can shorten or expand, but

> all dies berührt die Identität der Erzählung nicht, und das impliziert: es berührt auch nicht ihren Sinn, denn der Sinn stellt sich nicht im Akt des Improvisierens her, sondern er liegt jenseits der Variation in der Struktur der Handlung selbst: der Sinn und die Identität der Erzählung sind eins.[122]

Written texts, on the other hand, present opportunities to bring the laws of the framework into discussion and are fixed, so:

> Dabei kann jedes Wort wichtig sein; eine Kleinigkeit kann den Sinn signalisieren. Oder anders gesagt: das, was hier fest bleibt, der Text, ist nicht mehr identisch mit dem Sinn. Der Sinn konstituiert sich vielmehr erst in

der Lektüre, und wenn ich die Lektüre wiederhole, dann tritt er nicht etwa deutlicher heraus, sondern es öffnet sich ein Spielraum für die Sinngebung: jede Lektüre kann eine neue Deutung bringen.[123]

Written texts can facilitate reflection upon the framework — which, in the case of the bridal quest, is no longer simply an expression of violence and desire — particularly by repeating the quest and therefore doubling the structure. In *König Rother*, for example, the repetition of the quest is able to demonstrate the way in which power and Eros are sanctioned by God, and the *Münchner Oswald* uses comedy (particularly in the figure of the raven) to 'break' the bridal-quest structure so as to relativize the action and hence paradoxically to make it more serious.[124] The double structure of the bridal-quest narratives marks out a literary turn, a development towards courtly romance with its characteristic double cycle form.

There are several problems with Haug's analysis, not least the fact that it is impossible to claim convincingly that all so-called bridal-quest narratives are characterized by a double structure. The most obvious difficulties, however, are with his treatment of oral poetry. It is both unjustifiable and unprovable to state that orally transmitted narratives cannot promote reflection (for example in the case of *König Rother* on the strategic use of power) or change meaning between retellings; perhaps the opposite is necessarily true.[125] Moreover, his interpretation relies on the possibility of reading a written text repeatedly and does not bear in mind medieval conditions of reception, which in the majority of cases would have scarcely been different than for an orally composed work: the audience would have heard it read out loud.[126]

The — not dissimilar — alternative to such an approach is to concentrate to a greater degree on the structural realizations of the schema itself, the emphasis thus being primarily morphological. The 'classic' structural study of the bridal-quest schema is Schmid-Cadalbert's work of 1985, in which he attempts to establish a genre of 'Brautwerbungsdichtung' consisting of texts whose actions are dependent on a consciously delineated schema. These texts are *Dukus Horant*, *König Rother*, *Kudrun*, *Orendel*, *Ortnit*, the *Münchner Oswald*, and *Salman und Morolf*; the *Nibelungenlied*, *Tristan*, *Dietrichs Flucht*, and *Wolfdietrich* B conform partially to the schema, but for this reason cannot be counted within the genre.[127] Schmid-Cadalbert argues that medieval literature is always schematic; he understands medieval literary reality as a fixed system and medieval literary behaviour as a series of fixed norms:

> Mittelalterliches Erzählen unterscheidet sich grundsätzlich von modernem Erzählen, da es auf einer Erkenntnisweise beruht, welche die objektive Realität als Ausprägung eines festgefügten Systems betrachtet. Menschliches Handeln wird nicht als kausaler Prozeß verstanden, sondern als Ringen um eine Norm, die es in einem eng verzahnten, hierarchisch gegliederten Wertsystem immer wieder zu erfüllen gibt.[128]

Bridal-quest narratives therefore provide a matrix for modelling the appropriate behaviour of a member of society. They should not be thought of as pure entertainment, but — as is also argued by Curschmann, albeit in a different context — as teaching their readers how to live in the world: '[S]ie lassen sich verstehen und interpretieren als Verhaltensentwürfe, d. h. als Dichtungen welche auf der Basis eines tradierten Handlungsschemas mittels relevanter Schemavariationen und -individuationen mögliche Existenzmuster und Verhaltensweisen beispielhaft vorführen'.[129] Such an instructive purpose is achieved by variation on the schema, variation that can fulfil, set, or challenge norms: '[E]rst in der Abweichung vom Schema, im Schemabruch, vermittelt der sich des Schemas bedienende Autor thematische Relevanz. Schemabrüche signalisieren, welche Normen und Werte zur Diskussion gestellt werden, und geben dem erzählten Text als Schemaindividuation die Funktion eines Verhaltensentwurfs'.[130] In order for this thesis to hold water, it is necessary to bear all (or at least several) bridal-quest narratives in mind at once and for the audience to have a good knowledge of the schema. Schmid-Cadalbert argues that 'Brautwerbungsdichtungen [...] können als isolierte Texte nur lückenhaft verstanden werden. Eine isolierte Betrachung widerspricht der Existenzweise dieser Texte und muß deshalb scheitern', because 'Autorität und kritische Instanz der Brautwerbungsdichtungen ist die Erzählgemeinschaft [...] selbst, denn sie ist aufgrund ihres Vorwissens in der Lage, eine gebotene Erzählung zu beurteilen und aufgrund relevanter Variationen Autorintentionen zu erkennen'.[131] He attempts to show how the variation from the schema functions in a reading of *Ortnit AW*, which he argues creates meaning by deliberate departure from the schema, a departure that is indicative of Ortnit's failure. Ortnit is inextricably linked to the wilderness, or wild-ness (*wilde*) through his father, Alberich, and the scenes that depart most obviously from the bridal-quest schema — particularly Ortnit's first meeting with his father and his eventual death at the hands of the dragon — are those most particularly shaped by and located in the *wilde*. In this sense, Ortnit's failure takes place in a world outside what Schmid-Cadalbert considers to be the conventional world of the bridal-quest narrative and the very departure from this world signals the fact that he will fail.[132]

Such an interpretation of *Ortnit* is highly restrictive. There is little space to go into detail here, but suffice to say that Schmid-Cadalbert ignores all links to the *Wolfdietrich* narratives, which form a continuation to *Ortnit*-stories, Wolfdietrich eventually killing the dragon and marrying Ortnit's widow. The interdependency of the two texts is a much-discussed problem, as is the question whether or not *Ortnit* can ever be thought of as an entirely independent text; there is no written evidence of an Ortnit-narrative before the twelfth century and no theories about the sources and origins of such a narrative are entirely convincing.¹³³ More important is the fact that *Ortnit* is always transmitted with *Wolfdietrich*, the only exception being the fragmented *Ortnit* W. In the case of *Wolfdietrich* B and D, part of the Ortnit story is, to use a phrase of Miklautsch, 'einmontiert' in the main Wolfdietrich narrative.¹³⁴ The relationship with *Wolfdietrich* — rather than deviation from the bridal-quest schema — is also perhaps the best way to explain the curious and highly unusual death of the protagonist. In the words of Millet, '[I]n der Ortnitgeschichte lässt sich der Tod des Helden nur dadurch erklären, dass man einen Rächer einbauen wollte. Der Ortnit lässt seinen Helden versagen, damit ein anderer die Aufgabe lösen kann, die er nicht zu vollenden vermochte'.¹³⁵

The problem of interpreting *Ortnit* solely in relation to the bridal-quest schema signals the problems that plague this kind of interpretation in general. First, it does not take into account transmission (*Ortnit* is mainly transmitted in collected manuscripts of heroic epic); in the case of the so-called *Spielmannsepen*, none of the texts are transmitted together and are transmitted in different regions at different times. This leads to the second problem: if there is no evidence that so-called bridal-quest narratives were ever read together, is it possible to accept Schmid-Cadalbert's argument that the audience would have a clear understanding of the schema (through other bridal-quest narratives) and be able to recognize conscious deviation from it? There is, of course, no ideal prototypical realization of the bridal-quest schema. From this point, we can also move to a third problem, perhaps the most simple and the most important, namely the fact that the bridal-quest schema can in no way be thought to constitute a 'dominant' in all the texts described as 'bridal-quest narratives'. Where it is present, it is simply not important enough to create the entire system of meaning of each of the texts.

I do not want to challenge the fact that there is some kind of story motif about a bridal quest or that it appears particularly prevalent in medieval German texts. It is true that when it does appear, it often has the same constant features, for example the council scene, in which the protagonist asks his court for advice, that occurs in all four texts to be discussed here. Yet the bridal-quest motif always appears in a different context and has a different function within the narrative, not attributable to conscious variation on a fixed and meaningful matrix. A sentence of Hugo Kuhn is illuminating here; discussing the bridal-quest structure in passing, he says that 'die Motivationen und Stationen — die Höhe, Ferne und Gefährlichkeit der Braut, die Fähigkeiten, Listen und Wunder bei ihrer Gewinnung und Wiedergewinnung — variieren so stark, daß der Typ eher wie eine Handlungshülse wirkt, denn als Handlungsstruktur'.¹³⁶ Moreover, the bridal-quest motif is very rarely the dominant structural or thematic feature of a text and reading a text solely through the use of this motif can be highly restrictive, as is demonstrated by Schmid-Cadalbert's analysis of *Ortnit*.

I therefore reject the term 'bridal-quest schema', because the word 'schema' is too all-encompassing and suggests something much more fixed and all-determining than the bridal-quest motif we find in the texts. 'Schema' also implies something fully realizable and clearly defined, which is not the case. Siefken, who does not reject the term 'schema' in his study of *Kudrun*, nonetheless is careful about its application, and understands it as an 'überindividuelle Form' that influences individual conceptions of it and is only attainable within them; it is 'weder typische Darstellung eines typischen Verlaufs noch auch eine feste Motivverbindung [...], sondern überindividuelle Form, die die Einzelgestaltung beeinflußt und nur in ihr greifbar wird'.[137] In this sense, '[Ü]berspitzt gesagt: es gibt das Schema nicht. Es begegnet uns immer nur verborgen in dichterischer Gestaltung'.[138] This is certainly a more productive understanding of the schema, similar to the one advocated by Deutsch: 'Es [das Schema] wäre dann zu sehen als ein motivlicher Ermöglichungsrahmen für die Narration, und nicht als ein mündlich möglichst einfaches Erzählmuster, das man vergleichend rekonstruieren kann, um dann in den schriftlichen Realisationen Abweichungen und Brüche zu konstatieren'.[139] The bridal-quest motif is a basic motif for the exploration of possibility and the creation of narrative; perhaps this is why it often only appears at the beginning of a story, a narrative possibility to start an action that can develop in different directions, such as in the *Nibelungenlied*, *Tristan*, *Grauer Rock*, even the *Münchner Oswald*. For this reason, I find 'schema' a misleading word and prefer not to use it.

I also reject the term *Brautwerbungsepik* because the bridal-quest motif does not constitute a 'dominant' (Jauss) or allow the texts to form a clearly delineated 'Werkreihe' (Grubmüller). When the texts are read separately, and closely, it becomes clear that they do not have the same 'Sitz im Leben'; they cannot be thought to have been written in the same period or for the same reasons. It is striking that other texts contain a bridal-quest motif but are very rarely read solely according to it — notably the *Nibelungenlied*, *Tristan*, *Kudrun*, and (other than by Schmid-Cadalbert) *Ortnit* — because they are thought to belong to another genre (heroic epic or romance) and, in the first two cases at least, because they are thought to be more skilfully crafted and valuable as individual works of art. There is no doubting this judgement, admittedly, but it does not necessarily mean that the lesser works are more 'schematic', or that they should be read as such. Jan-Dirk Müller argues that the concept of schematic literature is simply inappropriate for medieval literature, in which there does not exist the modern impulse for originality:

> Schema ist das Automatisierte, Stereotype, Veräußerlichte im Gegensatz zum Neuen, Individuellen, Authentischen. In diesem Sinne ist der Begriff 'Schemaliteratur' sinnvoll nur für Epochen, in denen sich die Forderung durchgesetzt hat, jedes literarische Werk müsse möglichst einmalig und besonders sein. Dies widerspricht der Traditionsgebundenheit mittel-

alterlicher Literatur; Erzählen ist wesentlich 'Wiedererzählen', literarische Produktion 'Arbeit am Muster' und Weiterbilden und Variation von Konventionalität.[140]

Perhaps a better way of understanding the matter, therefore, would be to suggest that some texts simply use and combine different motifs (or 'Muster') more intelligently and in a more sophisticated fashion than others. The bridal-quest motif furnishes us with a concrete example. The presence of such a motif in a text does not make it automatically part of a bridal-quest genre against the ideal criteria of which every text containing the motif is to be judged. Different motifs are infinitely combinable and different combinations can be used in a variety of contexts. The combinatorial multiplicity of such motivic elements is not taken into account sufficiently in essays on genre theory and helps to explain why the notion of genre in medieval texts is so problematic; the same motif can appear in a variety of seemingly unrelated works. It is not the appearance of the motif that defines a work, but rather its particular mode of combination and the function for which it is employed in a particular situation.

Solutions to the Problem

The remainder of this study consists in individual chapters on *König Rother*, *Salman und Morolf*, the *Münchner Oswald*, and *Grauer Rock* (*Orendel*). It is not my intention to suggest an alternative genre classification for each text, but rather to read each one away from the hitherto dominating context of *Spielmannsepik* or *Brautwerbungsepik*. Each chapter also focuses on a particular problem of interpretation.

More than any of the other so-called *Brautwerbungsepen*, *König Rother* has been read as a transitional work between orality and courtly romance, with many interpretations focusing entirely on the repetition of the bridal quest (the 'double-structure') as a source of narrative meaning. I offer a reading that looks neither forward nor back, but focuses on the text in its contemporary context and the problems of names and disguise, concentrating on the difference between the undisguised Rother and his disguised self, Dietrich.

Salman und Morolf is often thought to be the least harmonious of the texts in question here, with conflicting themes and characters. The second chapter concentrates on its two major protagonists, Salme (not Salman) and Morolf, and the way in which they play out the two most common lines of interpretation of the work, either as a moralistic fable about the dangers of love and women or as a topsy-turvy narrative, breaking conventions of behaviour and genre. I challenge both of these ways of reading, but show their productivity in that the problems of both can aid a greater understanding of the two central characters and the text as a whole.

The chapters on the *Münchner Oswald* and *Grauer Rock* both examine their text in its particular context: the development of the cult of St Oswald and the *translatio* of the seamless robe of Christ to Trier cathedral respectively. In each case there is a specific interpretative difficulty to consider: in the *Münchner Oswald*, the reconciliation of the roles of saint and king and the functions of comedy and devotion, and in *Grauer Rock* the comparative importance of relic and man and the relationship between the text and the cult of the relic at Trier.

Notes to the Introduction

1. The title of the text that has until recently been referred to in scholarship as *Orendel* is now increasingly being referred to as *Grauer Rock*, for reasons that will become clear in Chapter 4. I will also use the title *Grauer Rock* in my study on the text. In much of the earlier scholarship discussed in this introduction, however, it is called *Orendel*, so I will mainly use this title here to avoid confusion.
2. See in particular Christian Schmid-Cadalbert, *Ortnit AW als Brautwerbungsdichtung* (Bern: Francke, 1985).
3. A comprehensive overview of genre is given by Alastair Fowler, *Kinds of Literature: An Introduction to the Theory of Genres and Modes* (Oxford: Clarendon Press, 1982). See also Claudio Guillén, *Literature as System: Essays toward the Theory of Literary History* (Princeton: Princeton University Press, 1971).
4. A possible exception to this are treatises on the composition of troubadour poetry, most famously the *Leys d'amors* ('Laws of Love'); on these see Suzanne Fleischmann, 'The Non-lyric Texts', in *A Handbook of the Troubadours*, ed. by F. R. P. Akehurst and Judith M. Davis (Berkeley: University of California Press, 1995), pp. 167-84 (pp. 178-80).
5. Hans-Robert Jauss, 'Theorie der Gattungen und Literatur des Mittelalters', *Grundriss der romanischen Literaturen des Mittelalters*, 6 (1972), 93-138 (p. 108).
6. Hugo Kuhn, 'Gattungsprobleme der mittelhochdeutschen Literatur', in Kuhn, *Dichtung und Welt im Mittelalter* (Stuttgart: Metzler, 1959), pp. 41-61 (p. 44). Jauss, 'Theorie der Gattungen', p. 108, finds a similar difficulty: '[W]o Grundunterscheidungen wie: zweckbestimmt oder zweckfrei, lehrhaft oder fiktiv, nachahmend oder schöpferisch, traditionell oder individuell, die seit der Emanzipation der Schönen Künste das Literaturverständnis regeln, noch nicht empfunden und reflektiert wurden, hat es auch keinen Sinn, mit einer diesem Emanzipationsprozeß verdankten Dreiteilung der Dichtung zu arbeiten und den darin nicht aufgehenden, im Mittelalter gewiß größeren Rest einer problematischen vierten "Dichtart", dem Didaktischen zuzuschlagen.' See also Klaus Grubmüller, 'Gattungskonstitution im Mittelalter', in *Mittelalterliche Literatur und Kunst im Spannungsfeld von Hof und Kloster: Ergebnisse der Berliner Tagung, 9.-11. Oktober 1997*, ed. by Nigel F. Palmer and Hans-Jochen Schiewer (Tübingen: Niemeyer, 1999), pp. 192-210 (pp. 194-95), who discusses the problem of the 'dramatische' in a medieval context, drawing into consideration the works of Hrotsvita of Gandersheim, Easter, Passiontide, and Carnival plays, all of which function with a very different kind of performativity in mind (or not, in the case of Hrotsvita) and certainly do not comply with Aristotelian ideals.
7. Kuhn, 'Gattungsprobleme', p. 46.
8. Ibid., p. 59.
9. <www.oed.com, 'entelechy', *philos.*, 1> [accessed 10 September 2010].

10. Kuhn, 'Gattungsprobleme', p. 49.
11. Hugo Kuhn, 'Versuch einer Literaturtypologie des 14. Jahrhunderts', in *Kleine Schriften*, III: *Liebe und Gesellschaft*, ed. by Hugo Kuhn and Wolfgang Walliczek (Stuttgart: Metzler, 1980), pp. 121–34. See Grubmüller, p. 199, on the lack of explicitness and the avoidance of complicated examples in Kuhn's essay.
12. Jauss, p. 110.
13. Ibid., p. 124.
14. Ibid., p. 112.
15. On the Formalist notion of the 'dominant', influential to Jauss, see Roman Jakobson, 'The Dominant', in *Readings in Russian Poetics: Formalist and Structuralist Views*, ed. by Ladislav Matejka and Krystyna Pomorska (Ann Arbor: University of Michigan, 1978), pp. 82–87.
16. Jauss, pp. 114–18, for a precise description of the synchronic model of medieval epic, romance, and novella.
17. Grubmüller, p. 199, says of Jauss that: '[S]ein auf Merkmalbündeln aufgebautes Gattungssystem, besonders das der 'kleinen Gattungen der exemplarischen Rede' ordnet die mittelalterlichen Werktypen so vollständig und explizit wie möglich — und macht gerade damit die Unzulänglichkeit diese Versuches offenbar: Überschneidungen, verfließende Ränder, willkürliche Zuordnungsentscheidungen und immer wieder ad hoc einzuführende Zusatzbedingungen führen von Augen, wie ein in sich kaum verbesserungsfähiger systematischer Zugang scheitert.'
18. Grubmüller, p. 205.
19. Ibid., p. 210.
20. Ibid., pp. 200–01.
21. Ibid., pp. 203–04.
22. David Perkins, *Is Literary History Possible?* (Baltimore: Johns Hopkins University Press, 1992), p. 61: 'Classification is fundamental to the discipline of literary history. A literary history cannot have only one text for its subject, and it cannot describe a great many texts individually. The multiplicity of objects must be converted into fewer, more manageable units, which can then be categorized, compared, interrelated and ordered.'
23. The most thorough 'Forschungsbericht' for *Spielmannsepik* — even though it is now out of date — is Michael Curschmann, '*Spielmannsepik*: Wege und Ergebnisse der Forschung von 1907-1965', *DVjs*, 40 (1966), 434–78; 597–647. See also Walter Johannes Schröder, *Spielmannsepik* (Stuttgart: Metzler, 1962), pp. 2–9, and most recently (and in English) Thomas Kerth, *King Rother and his Bride: Quests and Counter-Quests* (Rochester, NY: Camden House, 2010), pp. 1–20. A more critical overview is given by Rüdiger Brandt, 'Spielmannsepik: Literaturwissenschaft zwischen Edition, Überlieferung und Literaturgeschichte. Ein nicht immer unproblematisches Verhältnis', *Jahrbuch für internationale Germanistik*, 37 (2005), 9–49 (pp. 13–34). One essay that takes into account earlier scholarship — but does not question the belonging together of the five texts — is Joachim Bahr, 'Der "Spielmann" in der Literaturwissenschaft des 19. Jahrhunderts', *ZfdPh*, 73 (1954), 174–96, repr. in *Spielmannsepik*, ed. by Walter Johannes Schröder (Darmstadt: Wissenschaftliche Buchgesellschaft, 1977), pp. 289–322.
24. Gerard Kozielek, *Mittelalterrezeption: Texte zur Aufnahme altdeutscher Literatur in der Romantik* (Tübingen: Niemeyer, 1977), pp. 1–2
25. Ibid., p. 4.
26. Ibid., pp. 7–10; he also mentions the rise of capitalism in Germany as a reason for turning to something more 'natural'.
27. Ulrich Hunger, 'Romantische Germanistik und Textphilologie: Konzepte zur Erforschung mittelalterlicher Literatur zu Beginn des 19. Jahrhunderts', *Sonderheft*

zur DVjs, 61 (1987), 42–68. See also Christopher Young, 'Ulrich von Liechtenstein in German Literary History: The Don Quixote of the Steiermark', in *Ulrich von Liechtenstein: Leben, Zeit, Werk, Forschung*, ed. by Sandra Linden and Christopher Young (Berlin: de Gruyter, 2010), pp. 1–44 (p. 4).
28. Johann Gottfried Herder, *Auszug aus einem Briefwechsel über Ossian und die Lieder alter Völke*, in *Werke*, ed. by Martin Bollacher, II: *Schriften zur Ästhetik und Literatur 1767–1781*, ed. by Gunter E. Grimm (Frankfurt a. M.: Deutscher Klassiker Verlag, 1993), pp. 447–97.
29. Ibid., p. 448.
30. Ibid., pp. 473–74: 'In der alten Zeit aber waren es Dichter, Skalden, Gelehrte, die eben diese Sicherheit und Festigkeit des Ausdrucks am meisten mit Würde, mit Wohlklang, mit Schönheit zu paaren wußten; und da sie also Seele und Mund in den festen Bund gebracht hatten, sich einander nicht zu verwirren, sondern zu unterstützen, beizuhelfen [...] bis endlich die Kunst kam und die Natur auslöschte. In fremden Sprachen quälte man sich von Jugend auf Quantitäten von Sylben kennen zu lernen, die uns nicht mehr Ohr und Natur zu fühlen gibt: nach Regeln zu arbeiten, deren wenigste, ein Genie, als Naturregeln anerkennet; über Gegenstände zu dichten, über die sich nichts denken, noch weniger *sinnen*, noch weniger imaginieren läßt; Leidenschaften zu erkünsteln, die wir nicht haben, Seelenkräfte nachzuahmen, die wir nicht besitzen — und endlich wurde Alles Falschheit, Schwäche und Künstelei.'
31. Kozielek, pp. 7–10. See also Bahr, pp. 290–91.
32. Ludwig Tieck, 'Die altdeutschen Minnelieder', in *Kritische Schriften: Zum erstenmale gesammelt und mit einer Vorrede herausgegeben von Ludwig Tieck*, I (Leipzig: Brockhaus, 1848), pp. 185–214; repr. in Kozielek, pp. 44–62 (p. 50). See also Uwe Meves, *Alt-deutsche epische Gedichte: Großentheils zum erstenmahl aus Handschriften bekannt gemacht und bearbeitet von Ludwig Tieck. 1. König Rother* (Göppingen: Kümmerle, 1979), pp. xx–xxi.
33. Meves, *Alt-deutsche epische Gedichte*, pp. v–vi.
34. Ibid., p. xxiv.
35. Hunger, pp. 50–52.
36. Ibid., p. 47.
37. Meves, *Alt-deutsche epische Gedichte*, pp. xxvi–xxviii. See also Kozielek, pp. 13–14, on Tieck's *Minnesängern aus dem schwäbischen Zeitalter* (1803), a well-received 'Erneuung' of Minnesang that worked on the same principles.
38. Meves, *Alt-deutsche epische Gedichte*, p. xxxiii.
39. Ibid., p. xlv.
40. A. W. Schlegel, *Kritische Ausgabe der Vorlesungen*, ed. by Ernst Behler, II/I: *Vorlesungen über Ästhetik*, ed. by Georg Braungart (Paderborn: Schöningh, 2007), p. 85.
41. Perkins, p. 9.
42. Young, pp. 11–12, Kozielek, pp. 22–26.
43. Schlegel, p. 91.
44. Ibid., p. 92: 'Allein nicht bloß ein Wunderwerk der Natur ist dieses Heldengedicht: nach allen meinen Ansichten muß ich es auch für ein erhabenes Werk der Kunst erklären, dergleichen seitdem noch nie wieder in Deutscher Poesie aufgestellt worden'.
45. Bahr, pp. 291–95.
46. Jakob Grimm, 'Vorrede zu: Über den altdeutschen Meistergesang', repr. in *Spielmannsepik*, ed. by Schröder, pp. 1–7 (p. 3).
47. Wilhelm Grimm, 'Ueber die Entstehung der altdeutschen Poesie und ihr Verhältniß zu der nordischen', in *Studien*, ed. by Carl Daub and Friedrich Creuzer, 6 vols (Frankfurt and Heidelberg: Mohr, 1805–11), IV (1808), 75–121, repr. in Kozielek, pp. 124–50 (p. 144).

48. Michael S. Batts, *A History of Histories of German Literature: Prolegomena* (New York: Lang, 1987), pp. 133–34: 'The literary historical works published up to the 1830s can be categorized relatively easily. At the one end of the scale are the chronological tables that provide nothing beyond facts and figures, the names of authors, their dates, works, etc. At the other end of the scale are those works that consist entirely of selections from literary works over the whole period of literary history; these are usually ordered chronologically and/or by genre. In between the two poles are the literary historical works that may tend more to the pragmatic and annalistic side, may offer in addition to an historical overview also some selections from literature, or may even attempt to combine chronology, historical outline, and appropriate selections.' See also Young, p. 6, on the reception of early literary histories.
49. Batts, p. 133.
50. Young, pp. 6–9.
51. Batts, p. 136.
52. August Koberstein, *Grundriß der Geschichte der deutschen National-Litteratur* (Leipzig: Vogel, 1827), p. 43, sets it in his third period, which starts with the beginning of the Hohehstaufen dynasty, grouping it with *Ortnit, Wolfdietrich, Hugdietrich, Dietrichs Flucht, Rabenschlacht, Alpharts Tod, Hildebrandslied, Rosengarten, Sigenot*, and *Eckelied* as 'gothisch-langobardische Sagen'. Friedrich August Pischon, *Leitfaden zur Geschichte der deutschen Literatur*, 4th edn (Berlin: Duncker und Humblot, 1838; 1st edn 1830), p. 15, classifies *König Rother* in the epic subclass 'Heiterer Kreis' and, within that, in a 'Lombardischer Kreis und Kämpfe mit dem Morgenlande'. It has unfortunately proved impossible to consult the first edition of Pischon's work, published in 1830. Karl Rosenkranz, *Geschichte der Deutschen Poesie im Mittelalter* (Halle: Anton und Gelbcke, 1830), pp. 153–56, classes it with the same texts, but adds *Kudrun* to the group, calling it 'Die Deutsche Odyssee' within the larger category of 'Das reine Epos'. Ludwig Uhland, *Werke*, ed. by Helmut Fröschle and Walter Scheffler, III: *Geschichte der deutschen Poesie im Mittelalter* ed. by Helmut Fröschle (Munich: Winkler, 1981), pp. 35–37, classifies it with *Ortnit, Wolfdietrich, Hugdietrich*, and various of the Dietrich epics in the subclass 'Die Amelung' within 'Deutsche Gestaltung der Sage', in turn within 'Die Heldensage'. Uhland's literary history was first published in 1865–66, but was begun in 1823 and given as lectures in 1830–32. See Young, p. 16.
53. See also W. Grimm, p. 128: 'Wie jede Nation eine ihr mehr eigenthümliche Sage gehabt hat, so scheint der hörnerne Siegfried, Wittlich Wielands Sohn etc., nordisch, Wolfdietrich und Ottnit (sic) und die constantinopolitanischen Geschichte südlich, wahrscheinlich später etwas entstanden zur Zeit, wo die Longobarden in Italien blühten, das Nibelungen-Lied, Attila, Hagen, Günther, Chriemhilde, eigentlich deutsch zu seyn. Denn so zeigt sich in den ersten die nordische Tiefe, das Ungeheuere und Riesenhafte, in den andern schon ein viel farbigeres und wärmeres Colorit, manche Erinnerung an den Orient und seine Ueppigkeit [...]'
54. Rosenkranz, pp. 373–76, classifies *Herzog Ernst* within 'Das historische Epos' as 'Die deutsche Geschichte', comparing its depiction of the East unfavourably with that in Byron's *Childe Harold*, and Pischon, p. 21, sets it in the subclass 'Historische Gedichte'. Koberstein, pp. 52–53, mentions it in a section on 'Gedichte, welche Thaten und Begebenheiten einzelner historischer Personen zum Inhalt haben'.
55. Uhland, p. 313; p. 372.
56. Rosenkranz, pp. 350–58. He compares the text negatively with *König Rother*, contrasting the Semitic with the Germanic (p. 352): 'Die Liebe selbst erscheint ziemlich schwunglos, wie man von einem Juden, auch wenn er König ist, nicht anders erwarten kann. Man vergleiche hier den in so vielen Puncten verwandten Rother, um den Unterschied dieser Liebe von einer Germanischen und ritterlichen zu sehen.'

57. Pischon, pp. 23–24.
58. Koberstein, p. 54. He describes the text as follows: 'In dem größern, selbst seiner Form nach ganz volksmäßigen Gedichte von Salomon und Morolf wechseln komische Abenteuer mit ernsthaften ab; das Ganze nähert sich der größern epischen Gedichten. Durchaus komisch, oft satirisch und nicht selten sehr muthwillig und leichtfertig sind die einzelnen Schwänke, welche theils aus fremden Quellen geschöpft, theils aus Ereignissen und Gewohnheiten des wirklichen Leben damaliger Zeit unmittelbar genommen sind.'
59. The relationship between *Orendel* and heroic epic is mentioned by Uhland, p. 315; p. 506. Uhland's discussion of *Orendel* is in fact remarkably modern, as he emphasizes the connection of the text to the seamless robe in Trier (pp. 509–10), which does not become a main feature of its interpretation until Tonnelat's essay of 1924. He considers it to be a curious mix of *translatio* and heroic lay: '[D]er Umstand, daß die Legende von der Erwerbung des Heiltums, wie sich sich zu Trier erhalten, mit der Erzählung unsres Gedichtes nichts gemein hat, bestätigt die Ansicht, daß in letzterem die legendenhafte Überlieferung sich eines alten Heldenliedes bemächtigt habe' (p. 510).
60. Georg Gottfried Gervinus, review, 'Geschichte der neuern deutschen Poesie. Vorlesungen von August Wilhelm Bohtz. Göttingen 1832; Geschichte der deutschen National-Literatur mit Proben der deutschen Dichtkunst und Beredsamkeit. Von Dr Karl Herzog. Jena 1831', *Heideberger Jahrbücher der Literatur*, 26 (1833), 1194–1239. See also Batts, pp. 145–50.
61. Georg Gottfried Gervinus, *Geschichte der poetischen National-Literatur der Deutschen*, I: *Von den ersten Spuren der deutschen Dichtung bis gegen das Ende des 13ten Jahrhunderts* (Leipzig: Wilhelm Engelmann 1835), p. 9: 'es erforderte eine so mäßige und weise Nation, wie die deutsche, um von der unmäßigen Vergeudung aller Gefühle, wie von der einseitigsten Pflege des Verstandes, von den unseeligsten Verirrungen in Religion, in Kunst, in Wissenschaft und Staat zu der alten Besonnenheit, Gesundheit und ruhigen Thätigkeit zurückzuführen.'
62. Ibid., pp. 10–11.
63. Ibid., p. 11.
64. Batts, p. 148.
65. Gervinus (1835), pp. 12–17.
66. Uwe Meves, 'Zur historischen Bedingtheit literarischer Wertung: Das Beispiel "Spielmannsepik" in der Literaturgeschichtsschreibung', in *Textsorten und literarische Gattungen: Dokumentation des Germanistentages in Hamburg vom 1. bis 4. April 1979*, ed. by Vorstand der Vereinigung der deutschen Hochschulgermanisten (Berlin: E. Schmidt, 1983), pp. 317–34 (pp. 319–20).
67. Gervinus (1835), p. 159.
68. Ibid., p. 184.
69. Ibid., pp. 185–86.
70. Gervinus, *Geschichte der poetischen National-Literatur der Deutschen, Zweite Auflage*, I: *Von den ersten Spuren der deutschen Dichtung bis gegen das Ende des 13. Jahrhunderts* (Leipzig: Wilhelm Engelmann 1840), p. 239.
71. Ibid., p. 223. See also p. 224: 'In jedem einzelnen sehen wir auf einen sagenhaften, volksthümlichen Grund zurück, einfach genug, um in dem öffentlichen Gesange eines Spielmanns Raum zu haben; in jedem sehen wir diesen einfachen Sagenstoff so unendlich breit getreten, oder so verbunden mit fremdartigen Elementen aus Büchern und andern fremden Dichtungen, daß wir die willkührlichen Ausstattungen dürftiger Erfinder und Erzähler gleichsam verfolgen können.'
72. Wilhelm Wackernagel, *Geschichte der deutschen Litteratur* (Basel: Schweighauserische Buchhandlung, 1848), pp. 180–83.

73. Ibid., pp. 163–64.
74. W. Grimm, pp. 126–27. See Schröder (1962), p. 2: 'So erscheint der Spielmann als der typische Mann aus dem "Volke", wie es die Romantik sieht, gleichsam als eine Inkarnation der Volksseele, naturhaft wie diese und daher der Träger der "Naturpoesie"'.
75. Bahr, p. 303, Schröder (1962), pp. 2–3.
76. Wackernagel, p. 180. See Bahr, pp. 311–14.
77. Friedrich Vogt, 'Leben und Dichten der deutschen Spielleute im Mittelalter', in *Vortrag gehalten im wissenschaftlichen Verein zu Greifswald am 29. November 1875* (Halle: Niemeyer, 1876), pp. 3–32, repr. in *Spielmannsepik*, ed. by Schröder, pp. 18–48.
78. Bahr, p. 314.
79. Hans Naumann, 'Versuch einer Einschränkung des romantischen Begriffs Spielmannsdichtung', *DVjs*, 2 (1924), 777–94, repr. in *Spielmannsepik*, ed. by Schröder, pp. 126–44 (p. 138).
80. For a critique of Naumann, see Bahr, pp. 320–21.
81. Ibid., pp. 321–22. See also Piet Wareman, *Spielmannsdichtung: Versuch einer Begriffsbestimmung* (Amsterdam: van Campen, 1951), who challenges the concept of the 'Spielmann' but does not offer a comprehensive solution to the problem.
82. Schröder (1962 and 1977), Michael Curschmann, *Der Münchener Oswald und die deutsche spielmännische Epik* (Munich: Beck, 1964) and '*Spielmannsepik*'.
83. Schröder (1962), p. 1.
84. Ibid., pp. 13–15.
85. Curschmann, *Der Münchener Oswald und die deutsche spielmännische Epik*, pp. 141–44.
86. Ibid., pp. 127–28.
87. Ibid., pp. 153.
88. Gustav Ehrismann, *Geschichte der deutschen Literatur bis zum Ausgang des Mittelalters*, II: *Die Mittelhochdeutsche Literatur. I. Frühmittelhochdeutsche Zeit* (Munich: Beck, 1922), pp. 284–345.
89. Ibid., pp. 284–90.
90. Ibid., p. 319: 'Das Spielmannsgedicht von Salman und Morolf stellt unter den verwandten Dichtungen die spielmännische Art am reinsten dar. Hier ist der niedere, volksmäßigere Geschmack am besten getroffen. Ergötzt und belustigt will diese Publikum werden, es hat seine Freude an derberer Kost.'
91. Helmut de Boor, *Die deutsche Literatur von Karl dem Grossen bis zum Beginn der höfischen Dichtung 770–1170: Geschichte der deutschen Literatur von den Anfängen bis zur Gegenwart*, ed. by Helmut de Boor and Richard Newald, I (Munich: Beck 1949), pp. 239–40.
92. Ibid., p. 238.
93. Ibid., pp. 250–58.
94. Julius Schwietering, *Die deutsche Dichtung des Mittelalters* (Darmstadt: Gentner, 1957), pp. 107–19.
95. Ewald Erb, *Geschichte der deutschen Literatur von den Anfängen bis 1160*, 2 vols: *Geschichte der deutschen Literatur von den Anfängen bis zur Gegenwart*, I, I–II, ed. by Klaus Gysi and others (Berlin: Volk und Wissen Volkseigener Verlag, 1965), pp. 753–66. Earlier in his history he criticizes other Germanists for underemphasizing the importance of the Spielmann, which he argues is for political rather than scholarly reasons, comparing the 'bürgerlich' attitude favourably to the 'nazistisch' stance of Naumann, whose dismissal of the Spielmann still affects contemporary scholarship (p. 370). On Erb's political motivation, see Meves, 'Zur historischen Bedingtheit', pp. 331–33.
96. Erb, p. 766.

97. Ibid., p. 760: 'In manchem Epos liegt eine solche Verquickung von Spielmännischem und Geistlichem, bzw. bildungsmäßig erhöhtem Niveau vor, daß man schwerlich entscheiden kann, ob man selbständige Spielmannsdichtung vor sich hat oder ein spielmännisch umgearbeitetes Werk eines Geistlichen oder ob schließlich hier ein Geistlicher aus kluger Kenntnis des Publikumsgeschmackes selbst sich spielmännischer Thematik, Motive und Kunstmittel bedient hat, also Spielmannsdichtung schuf.'
98. Ibid., p. 755.
99. Ibid., p. 780 on *Oswald*, p. 784 on *Orendel*, p. 787 on *Salman und Morolf*.
100. Kurt Ruh, *Höfische Epik des deutschen Mittelalters*, I: *Von den Anfängen bis zu Hartmann von Aue* (Berlin: Schmidt, 1967), p. 58.
101. Ruh, pp. 58–61.
102. Max Wehrli, *Geschichte der deutschen Literatur vom frühen Mittelalter bis zum Ende des 16. Jahrhunderts* (Stuttgart: Reclam, 1980), pp. 221–33.
103. Ibid., pp. 228–29.
104. Joachim Bumke, *Geschichte der deutschen Literatur im hohen Mittelalter* (Munich: dtv, 5th edn, 2004, 1st edn, 1990), pp. 74–82.
105. Ibid., p. 79.
106. *Dichtung des europäischen Mittelalters: Ein Führer durch die erzählende Literatur*, ed. by Rolf Bräuer (Munich: Beck, 1990), pp. 286–304.
107. Ibid., pp. 20–21.
108. Werner Röcke, 'Höfische und unhöfische Minne- und Abenteuerromane', in *Epische Stoffe des Mittelalters*, ed. by Volker Mertens and Ulrich Müller (Stuttgart: Kröner, 1984), pp. 395–423.
109. Alfred Ebenbauer, 'Andere Großepen', in *Deutsche Literatur: Eine Sozialgeschichte*, ed. by Horst Albert Glaser, I: *Aus der Mündlichkeit in die Schriftlichkeit 750–1320*, ed. by Ursula Liebertz-Grün (Hamburg: Rowohlt 1988), pp. 279–89.
110. Gisela Vollmann-Profe, *Wiederbeginn volkssprachlicher Schriftlichkeit im hohen Mittelalter (1050/60–1160/70): Geschichte der deutschen Literatur von den Anfängen bis zum Beginn der Neuzeit*, ed. by Joachim Heinzle, I/II (Königstein/Ts: Athenäum, 1986), p. 215.
111. Vollmann-Profe's interpretation of the texts fits well as a culmination of the general argument of her history, that early Middle High German literature acts as a gradual progression towards the *Blütezeit*.
112. *Salman und Morolf*, ed. by Alfred Karnein (Tübingen: Niemeyer, 1979); *Der Münchner Oswald*, ed. by Michael Curschmann (Tübingen: Niemeyer, 1974). A new edition of *Orendel* would be of great use to the field.
113. Brandt, p. 40.
114. For more detailed realizations of the schema see Schmid-Cadalbert, pp. 87–95; Hinrich Siefken, *Überindividuelle Formen und der Aufbau des Kudrunepos* (Munich: Fink, 1967), pp. 21–35.
115. Theodor Frings, 'Die Enstehung der deutschen Spielmannsepen', *Zeitschrift für deutsche Geisteswissenschaft*, 2 (1939/40), 306–31, repr. in *Spielmannsepik*, ed. by Schröder, pp. 191–212 (p. 192).
116. Ibid., p. 204.
117. Ibid., p. 208: 'In der Mitte des 12. Jahrhunderts baute ein begnadeter Dichter in Verschmelzung vorhandener liedhafter Dichtung des Themas "Werbung durch Gewalt" und des mittelmeerisches Schemas "Werbung durch List" ein spielmännisches Kurzepos, den [...] Ur-Rother'.
118. Ibid., pp. 209–10. See also Frings and Max Braun, *Brautwerbung*, I (Leipzig: Hirzel, 1947) (volume II was never published), the beginnings of an exploration of the use of

the bridal-quest schema in the oral composition of songs throughout Europe. On this work, see Schmid-Cadalbert, pp. 28–30.

119. See Claudia Bornholdt, *Engaging Moments: The Origins of Medieval Bridal-Quest Narrative* (Berlin: de Gruyter, 2005), pp. 7–11; p. 215. One of the main theses of Bornholdt's study is to show that there is evidence of the 'cunning' bridal quest in earlier Germanic literary traditions. Through a reading of the Hilde legends, she also shows that there is no substantial difference between the earliest heroic lays of bridal abductions and the later tales, in which the bride is won through disguise.

120. Walter Haug, 'Struktur, Gewalt und Begierde: Zum Verhältnis von Erzählmuster und Sinnkonstitution in mündlicher und schriftlicher Überlieferung', in *Idee — Gestalt — Geschichte: Festschrift für Klaus von See*, ed. by Gerd Wolfgang Weber (Odense: Odense University Press, 1988), pp. 143–57, repr. in Haug, *Brechungen auf dem Weg zur Individualität: Kleine Schriften zur Literatur des Mittelalters* (Tübingen: Niemeyer, 1997), pp. 3–16 (p. 4).

121. Ibid., p. 5.
122. Ibid., p. 8.
123. Ibid.
124. Ibid., pp. 11–12. On the *Münchner Oswald*, see Walter Haug, 'Das Komische und das Heilige: Zur Komik in der religiösen Literatur des Mittelalters', *Wolfram-Studien*, 7 (1982), 8–31. *Salman und Morolf* is interpreted in a similar fashion in Haug, 'Brautwerbung im Zerrspiegel', in *Sammlung, Deutung, Wertung: Ergebnisse, Probleme, Tendenzen und Perspektiven philologischer Arbeit. Melanges de littérature médiévale et de linguistique allemande offerts à Wolfgang Spiewok à l'occasion de son soixantième anniversaire par ses collègues et amis*, ed. by Danielle Buschinger (Amiens: Université de Picardie, Centre des études médiévales, 1988), pp. 179–88.

125. A comprehensive critique of Haug's theories is given by Lorenz Deutsch, 'Die Einführung der Schrift als Literarisierungsschwelle: Kritik eines mediävistischen Forschungsfaszinosums am Beispiel des *König Rother*', *Poetica*, 35 (2003), 69–90. On this particular problem, he argues that '[M]ündliche Texte sind aufgrund ihrer fehlenden Speicherung grundsätzlich nicht wiederholbar. Vielmehr ist jeder vorgetragene Text prinzipiell als ein eigener Text aufzufassen' (pp. 80–81).

126. Ibid., p. 80. On the practices of reception and performance in the Middle Ages, see D. H. Green, *Medieval Listening and Reading: The Primary Reception of German Literature 800–1300* (Cambridge: Cambridge University Press, 1994).

127. Schmid-Cadalbert, pp. 79–80.
128. Ibid., p. 20.
129. Ibid., p. 204.
130. Ibid., p. 20.
131. Ibid., p. 205.
132. Ibid., pp. 110–229.
133. Wolfgang Dinkelacker, *Ortnit-Studien* (Berlin: E. Schmidt, 1972), pp. 23–56.
134. Lydia Miklautsch, *Montierte Texte, hybride Helden: Zur Poetik der Wolfdietrich-Dichtungen* (Berlin: de Gruyter, 2005), p. 19.
135. Victor Millet, *Germanische Heldendichtung im Mittelalter* (Berlin: de Gruyter, 2008), p. 385. Contrary to this, Schmid-Cadalbert, p. 201, argues that *Wolfdietrich* could not exist without *Ortnit*, but that *Ortnit* could exist without *Wolfdietrich*.
136. Hugo Kuhn, 'Allegorie und Erzählstruktur', in *Formen und Funktionen der Allegorie*, ed. by Walter Haug (Stuttgart: Metzler, 1979), pp. 206–18 (p. 209).
137. Siefken, p. 40.
138. Ibid., p. 38.

139. Deutsch, p. 85.
140. Jan-Dirk Müller, *Höfische Kompromisse: Acht Kapitel zur höfischen Epik* (Tübingen: Niemeyer, 2007), p. 30.

CHAPTER 1

~

König Rother
Rother and Dietrich

König Rother is the work that has suffered least from its consideration within the genres of *Spielmannsepik* and *Brautwerbungsepik*. First, because it can certainly be dated to the twelfth century, thanks to its transmission;[1] second, because the narrative quite clearly consists in the story of a king, Rother, setting out on a wooing expedition; third, because it is thought to have literary value (or at least an important place in literary history), which means it is read for itself more frequently than *Salman und Morolf*, the *Münchner Oswald*, or *Grauer Rock*. Nonetheless, there is a trend in scholarship on *König Rother* that concentrates on what it is not any more or what it is not yet, either looking back to an older, oral original or forwards to courtly romance. The intention of this chapter is to move away from this trend.

In the case of *König Rother*, the structure of the text — the so-called bridal-quest schema and its doubling — is generally thought to be constitutive of meaning, by which I mean that meaning of some kind is believed to be produced by the way in which the structure is repeated, varied, and played with. The reason for this structural emphasis is located primarily in the understanding of *König Rother* as an early text on the threshold between the oral and the written, a stage of literary development at which, it has been argued, meaning is not created by the conscious fictionality of poetical reflection but mainly by the use of form, schemata, and structural frameworks.[2] This interpretative tendency has had, historically, two important — and problematic — variations, both of which are temporally determined. The first looks forward; this type of reading often concentrates on the 'earliness' of *König Rother* and its status as a text preparing the way for the courtly romances of the *Blütezeit*. The second looks back; it is often shaped by the notion of something concrete, ancestral to the *König Rother* we have, an oral something (an original, an 'Ur-Rother', a framework), to which our narrative reacts. These two types of reading often combine to create a 'noch nicht' and 'schon nicht mehr' interpretation of the text.[3] A brief overview of scholarship will help to clarify this.

Although Frings's concept of the 'Ur-Rother', a short epic similar to the first half of *König Rother*, written down in the middle of the twelfth century, is no longer accepted, the idea persists that the first half of *König Rother* reflects some kind of original version and that its division into two parts is of vital importance to its symbolic meaning.[4] The fact that Rother undertakes two quests — that he successfully woos the princess but must woo her again after she has been recaptured — has formed the crux of the majority of interpretations. The theory that the two halves of the work were composed separately and should not be read as a homogeneous whole, owing to the closeness of the first half only to the Osantrix story in the Vilcinasaga, is now largely out of fashion, given the current interest in reading texts with an eye to how the versions we have would have been received, rather than investigating sources.[5] Understanding *König Rother* as a homogeneous work also demands investigation of the purpose of having two quests, however, and the significance of this structure is often thought to be in some way developmental.[6] 'Developmental' in two interlinked senses: the development of the text from a simple oral form to a double structure and the developmental process within the narrative itself, which is usually considered to become more religious and historical in its second half.

Curschmann's interpretation is largely thematic rather than structural; he believes that the first half of *König Rother* is mainly concerned with worldly power and law, with an interest in *minne* predominating in the second half. He asserts that the text had one redactor who, for the first time, explored in a literary text the theme of how to live in the world and the question of *minne*, which had growing importance at the time.[7] Curschmann's general thesis is that the 'spielmännische Epen' (as he calls them) are precursors of the works of the *Blütezeit* and represent the first attempts at dealing with the themes that will come to shape the great courtly romances — worldly life and love, and their reconciliation with God. *König Rother* fits, for him, into an early stage in the emergence of this thematic complex.

Haug, as we have already seen, persists in the notion that *König Rother* is a reaction to something older — not something as clearly defined as the archetypal 'Ur-Rother', but rather the oral form of the bridal-quest structure, which is reflected upon in the written text, where the oral themes of violence and desire are qualified with an exploration of the religious sanctioning of worldly power and love. Of great importance is the doubling of the bridal quest in *König Rother*, again interpreted as a developmental step towards the structure of courtly romance.[8] In this sense, Haug's interpretation is typical of both kinds of development found in studies of *König Rother*; the double structure of the text is both a sign of genetic growth away from orality and a structure that enables the 'moral' development of the text, a characteristic central to studies of courtly romance.

The 'doppelter Kursus' of courtly romance has been given much attention since its elaboration in relation to *Erec* by Hugo Kuhn, the basic premise being the 'Wiederholung und Steigerung' of the first half of the text in the second.[9] These principles reflect the development of the hero, not in the modern psychological sense, but in the sense of making amends after a crisis suffered at the mid-point of the story and taking responsibility for his social role and place in God's world. Such a line of interpretation can be applied to both of Hartmann's romances as well as to *Parzival*, even if the 'doppelter Kursus' is never so clear as in *Erec*.[10] The link with courtly romance pushes the reader into reading *König Rother* as a developmental narrative and encourages the notions (seen in the interpretations of both Curschmann and Haug above) that the second quest must reflect and improve on the first, and that Rother himself must grow in some way in the course of the story.[11] A developmental view of Rother's character is, however, problematic and inappropriate.

Haug's interpretation of *König Rother* is made doubly problematic because of the explicit link to orality and the assumptions made about the nature of oral storytelling, as has been discussed at length in the introduction.[12] Yet even if later scholars have moved away from speaking explicitly about the different natures of oral and written storytelling, Haug's interpretation of *König Rother* has been hugely influential, particularly with regard to the transitional status he assigns to the text. Focus has moved away from the double-structure and towards individual episodes or textual trends in order to demonstrate the way in which the text stands on a 'Literarisierungsschwelle' between archaic, oral storytelling and more courtly written literature. Kiening argues that the emphasis on the double structure depends on the premise of an older, perhaps oral epic, which is a 'problematische Große' and restricts interpretation of the text, yet nonetheless bases his analysis on the notion of increasing distance from oral forms and the resulting sense of 'Literarisierung'.[13] He concentrates on individual episodes to demonstrate the way in which the text distances itself from the 'Muster' of 'gefährliche Brautwerbung' by making this story-model obvious and more complex.[14] Unlike Haug, Kiening does not argue that the written form has 'overcome' the oral themes of violence and desire, but instead attempts to clarify the process of the change of medium, seeking out traces or reflexes of orality.

Schmitz also makes a case for the status of the text as an early literary product, although from a more narratological perspective. The narrator, she argues, is a withheld figure in the text, who comments on the action only very rarely; yet the episode towards the end of the text in which a *recke* narrates to Rother what has happened in Constantinople in his absence demonstrates an awareness of a very different style of narration, one in which the narrator is very present, and provides a reason for saying what he does and an interpretation of events described. In this sense, she argues, the Rother-poet makes it clear that events narrated can be interpreted in different ways and that such interpretation is to be desired: a sign of the first steps into the world of literature.[15]

Fuchs-Jolie admits the problem, discussed with respect to Haug in the introduction, of a reliance on an empirically undefinable 'before', stating that: '[D]ie Zirkularität indes, die solcher Argumentation mit Gestalten und Erfordnissen eines uns empirisch nicht fassbaren archaisch-mündlichen Erzählens bei aller Subtilität und bei allem Erkenntnisgewinn droht, ist kaum zu entkommen'.[16] His interpretation of *König Rother* nonetheless maintains the idea that the text plays a developmental role in the medieval literary history of Germany, but is culturally rather than medially determined: he focuses on the cultural boundary on which *König Rother* sits, namely the onset of the courtly programme of narrative and culture. This cultural transition is expressed in moments of eruption of spontaneous violence, particularly within ritual court scenes such as feasts or greetings. Later courtly literature depicts courtly rituals as separate from narrative action, so is able to distance them from the problems of the narrative, but here violence marks out and forms the basis for every performance productive of courtly culture.[17]

Even though he distances himself from the orality-based discussion, the result of Fuchs-Jolie's argument is much the same: an interpretation of *König Rother* as a transitional text, based on the 'evidence' of individual passages. Markus Stock's criticism of Haug and Kiening is thus equally pertinent here:

> Es ist fraglich, ob man die zuletzt vorgestellten Positionen 'am Text belegen' kann. Aber darum geht es nicht. Wichtig ist vielmehr, daß diese Arbeiten unabdingbare methodisch-theoretische Vorentscheidungen repräsentieren, die den Blick auf den Text entscheidend determinieren: Was 'am Text' überhaupt sichtbar werden kann, wird durch diese theoretischen Entscheidungen stark mitbestimmt.[18]

Stock's own argument is more promising; he argues that the identity of the hero is stable throughout the text and that there is no problematization or process of development. Instead, the bridal-quest schema is used to work through questions of legitimation, that is, how to maintain stability and longevity of rule: '[E]s gibt hier keine fundamentale innere Krise des Herrschaftsverbands [...], sondern lediglich eine Herausforderung der Handlungsfähigkeit und des Handlungsvermögen des Verbands'.[19] The second quest, therefore, is not an improvement on the first but acts as affirmation, and '[H]errscherliche Idealität wird nicht einmal bestätigt, sondern muß immer wieder bestätigt werden'.[20]

Such a synchronic form of interpretation is desirable, but Stock's reading, as is also the case with the others mentioned above, is reliant on the notion of the bridal-quest schema as a fixed framework that structures the whole narrative. The narrative of *König Rother* resembles the ideal schema most closely and is often considered the first written bridal-quest narrative; indeed, deviations in other texts sometimes seem to be more deviations from *König Rother* than from a schematic model. I do not want to deny that there was probably some kind of oral story-model of a bridal quest, but — as discussed in the introduction — I reject the notion of the bridal-quest schema as a structure that can create meaning in deviation or breaks from the schematic form. Instead, it seems rather to be a motif of narrative possibility; that is, a basic and loose motif that is often employed at the start of a narrative and develops in different directions. In the case of *König Rother*, more than in the other texts that are to be discussed in this study, gaining a bride forms the central drive to the narrative action. Yet there is no justifiable reason to argue that textual meaning is created by the relationship of the narrative to a schema.

The interpretation of the text offered here will concentrate on the use of disguise: Rother travels to Constantinople for the first time in disguise as the exile Dietrich. The fact that Rother and his men are in disguise for a large proportion of the text is rarely taken into much consideration, other than as the motif of 'cunning' common to the so-called 'Brautwerbung durch List'. Although I agree with Stock that there is no development of the protagonist, there are differences in behaviour between Rother and Dietrich that have not yet been noted sufficiently. It is likely that there exists in medieval literature a topos of 'Brautwerbung durch List', that is, winning a bride through some sort of cunning (such cunning is applied, for example, in *Ortnit* and the *Nibelungenlied*, as well as the *Münchner Oswald*), but there is no reason to suggest that the action of wooing a bride demands such cunning and that the fact cunning is applied is a necessary part of the bridal-quest schema. In the case of *König Rother*, the way in which the cunning is employed is interesting, particularly the all-determining nature of the disguise adopted. This disguise helps to illuminate what kingly behaviour is and how it works; it does this by exposing the machinations of kingly behaviour outside the context of kingship and, simultaneously, by exposing the weaknesses in Constantin's own system.

My reading of *König Rother* is perhaps culpably simple. I do not hope to make any overarching statements about the text, but rather show plainly the effects of the disguise and change of name adopted by the main protagonist, without implying any kind of character development. Consequently, my analysis will be set out in three parts, according to the name of the protagonist (Rother — Dietrich — Rother).

Rother

At the start of *König Rother*, the reader is introduced to Rother the king, who sends messengers to Constantinople to woo the daughter of Constantin. After his messengers fail to return, Rother disguises himself as Dietrich to travel to

Constantinople, rescue them, and win the hand of the princess. She is then kidnapped back by her father, and her husband returns to Constantinople — this time as Rother — to retrieve her. The way in which the names of Rother and Dietrich are used is striking — from the point that Rother decides to disguise himself he is referred to as Dietrich not only by all his men but also by the narrator — as is the different way in which Rother and Dietrich are able to behave. I intend to show how the change of name provides the author with a means for exploring different norms of social conduct, without however implying that the protagonist who exhibits different behaviours according to his name undergoes any sort of character development. The difference between Rother and Dietrich illuminates what it means to be a king and how kings behave.

The most complete manuscript of *König Rother*, MS H, is linguistically curious, a mixture of different dialects. Thomas Klein has shown that it was most probably written down by a Mid-Franconian scribe from an older manuscript, written by a Low German scribe in a mix of Low German and Middle German.[21] MS M and the manuscript of fragments E, L, and N are Bavarian in origin. Nonetheless, the transmission of *König Rother* follows the general trend of the transmission of other secular texts written in the second half of the twelfth century (*Rolandslied*, *Eneasroman*, *Herzog Ernst*, Eilhart's *Tristrant*), centring on the south-east of Germany, with manuscripts in North German dialects (particularly Eastphalian) and West Middle German as well. The dispersion of manuscripts follows the location of ruling houses at the time, particularly the duchy of Bavaria and the Welfs in East Swabia, Bavaria, and Saxony.[22] It is well known that the composition of the *Eneasroman* was connected to the relationship between the houses of Cleves and Thuringia,[23] and relatively likely that the patronage of the *Rolandslied*, *Tristrant*, and the *Kaiserchronik* (which has a similar pattern of transmission) was Welfish.[24] A variety of suggestions has been offered for the patron of *König Rother*, the only consensus being that he was probably a member of the Bavarian nobility, given the transmission and the frequency of naming Bavarian noble families in the latter part of the text. Suggestions include the circle of Welf VI (1115–91), who had friendly relations with Roger II of Sicily, one of the possible models for Rother; a descendant of the Tengeling dynasty, mentioned in such glowing terms in the text; or a member of the Hohenstaufen dynasty, which saw itself as the heir to Charlemagne and held — roughly — the lands that Rother shares out among his men at the end of the text at the probable time of its composition.[25]

It is not my intention to align myself with one of these points of view, nor to argue for a particular source for *König Rother*.[26] It seems more likely that *König Rother* resonates more with contemporary literary trends — the *Rolandslied*, *Kaiserchronik*, Lamprecht's *Alexander*, *Herzog Ernst*, and the *Eneasroman* all display, to varying degrees, an interest in kingship, the foundation of empire, and (in the case of the first two works) Charlemagne — than with the other so-called bridal-quest epics. There is insufficient space here to investigate links with such texts in depth, but such comparative work seems a good direction for future scholarship; indeed, some fruitful inroads have already been made.[27]

The following reading of *König Rother* will split the text into three parts, according to the name of the protagonist: thus the first part lasts until l. 801, the second until l. 2932.[28] This is primarily a thematic rather than a structural move; although I intend to move away from reliance on the double-structure for an interpretation of the text, there is no doubting that there are two journeys to Constantinople, which parallel one another (indeed, the split between my second and third sections roughly corresponds to the traditional division of the plot in a bipartite reading). The present tripartite reading foregrounds thematic differences in the portrayal of the protagonist according to which of his two names he is called.[29]

Jan-Dirk Müller discusses names and naming as a particular point of interest in medieval literary texts, arguing that from the end of the twelfth century there was a growing interest in the individual, although the predominant concern for the collective did not diminish.[30] Names provide a suitable compromise between these poles as they suggest individuality but also point to family, provenance or status — the kind of collective of which the individual is a part:

> Der Name faßt Identität in der Sicht der anderen zusammen. Name bedeutet Status. Neben dem Eigennamen trägt man den des Standes, der die Verpflichtung zu bestimmten Taten einschließt [...]. Der Name bezeichnet nicht nur die kontingente Person, sondern immer auch, was sie gilt. [...] Mit dem Eigennamen verknüpft sich nie nur eine individuelle Biographie. Im Namen treffen individuelle und ständisch-gesellschaftliche Komponenten zusammen.[31]

The combination of personal and collective implications, as well as the variety of parts that can constitute the whole of the name, provide, according to Müller's analysis, a frequently used *Erzählkern*, a component of the social imaginary that can give impetus to literary production and constitutes a 'problem' for literary examination.[32] Names — their discovery, provenance, etymology, concealment — thus form central loci of narrative crystallization in a number of texts.

In *König Rother*, the loss and regaining of a name does not signify a process of growth or change in the protagonist, and in this sense the text is considerably less complex than *Iwein* or *Parzival*.[33] 'Rother' marks out a fixed entity, recognized by an established feudal status, set of character traits, and reputation. Despite the double-structure of the plot, the depiction and narrative of the protagonist are not what we have come to expect from a conventional reading of Arthurian romance and the structure does not enable change, but rather affirmation of what was already there.[34] The use of the name 'Rother' is perhaps more easily recognized in Müller's description of names in heroic epic: '[I]n der Heldenepik stimmen Eigen- und Gruppenname, Einzelperson und Fama zusammen. [...] Im Heldenepos ist der Eigenname metonymisch, schließt unermeßlichen Ruhm, unermeßliche Kraft und hohen Rang ein'.[35] Yet it is doubtful whether 'Rother' signifies a collusion of 'Sagenruhm' and 'kontingente Person', for if this were the case, it would suggest that there were a sense of innate person, distinguishable from reputation (or rather how the person is perceived by others), which would then combine to form the complete character. It is important that Rother is a king rather than a hero, and accordingly seems unable to act alone and without the group of his men about him. Such a mode of behaviour is at odds with that of the hero of epic, whose alone-ness, separate from his collective allegiance, is of great importance, as '[D]er Held verkörpert zwar weiterhin eine überindividuelle Norm, zu der bestimme ständische und ethische Qualitäten gehören, doch tut er es in radikaler Vereinzelung'.[36] Quite what happens when Rother becomes Dietrich remains to be seen, but when he is Rother the emphasis is on communal rather than individual action, which is embodied by Rother as the head of the group. Kingship is fully institutionalized and the king has become a symbol of his order, and therefore his name has very little to do with his contingent personal identity.

König Rother begins with a description of the king, who lives *mit vil grozen erin* (l. 5), is lord over seventy-two kings (l. 7), and is a model ruler: *er was der aller heriste man, | der da zu Rome | ie intfinc die cronen* (ll. 10–12).[37] The narrative continues with an exposition of the system of government he embodies, in which there is no distinction between private and collective affairs. Although the way in which Rother is introduced is not unusual for a medieval narrative, it is usually the case that the hero is presented as part of an established lineage,[38] yet despite occasional mentions of a nameless father, Rother has no family. As will be discussed later, however, he becomes a founding myth in himself, affirmed not by the history of his own past, but the history of the 'real' past that comes after him in his son Pippin and grandson Charlemagne. The silence about a family at the beginning of the text also serves to emphasize that Rother has no wife. Without a wife, there can be no descendants, and without descendants, the ruling order cannot be maintained. Marriage is a profoundly public concern, affecting the security of all the men at court:

> unde virsciede er [Rother] an erben,
> so waneden se irsterben,
> weme sie dan die cronen
> solden gebin zo Rome (ll. 29–32)

Accordingly, the choice of wife must be approved by everyone (l. 44) and although Lupold, Rother's most loyal adviser, names an appropriate princess (ll. 55–56), the decision is discussed by everyone present and is expressed communally: *si nanten ein megetin* (l. 62). The marriage in *König Rother* is primarily a feudal affair, enabling political alliance — a link between the great powers of Western and Eastern Christianity, Rome and Constantinople — as well as political stability, and its most important product is an heir, emphasized by the fact that Rother's future wife becomes pregnant on the way back to Italy from Constantinople (ll. 2943–46) and gives birth on the day they finally return to Bari (ll. 4764–66).[39] It is also noticeable that the princess is never given a name and that Rother does not claim to love his prospective bride; only later, when she is pregnant, does Rother declare that his wife is his 'lip' (l. 4652), but until then, there is no demonstration of attraction on his part, and in this instance his declaration that she is his 'life' may be taken more literally, as she ensures his continuation. The lack of explicit declaration of love is perhaps surprising, as 'distant' unions such as this are often qualified with a claim of love from afar ('Fernliebe').

The notion of 'Fernliebe' is connected to the maxim of the suitability of the 'best' man for the 'most beautiful' woman, and vice versa, often said to be a core feature of the bridal-quest schema, although it is prevalent throughout medieval literature, and found widely in both epic and romance. The features of the potential partner that are heard of and consequently desired centre on social ideals: both partners are of equal (high) status, the man exceptionally strong and powerful, the woman exceptionally beautiful. In this sense, 'Fernliebe' can seem political rather than personal: '[D]er Herrscher erklärt, eine Frau zu lieben, die er noch nie gesehen, von deren Schönheit, Adel, Machtstellung er aber gehört hat; es sind allesamt überindividuelle Vorzüge, so daß seine persönliche Entscheidung immer schon mit den Motiven feudaler Heiratspraxis übereinstimmt'.[40] In *König Rother*, the absolute suitability of the princess is stressed, and she fulfils Rother's desire for a wife powerful enough to be queen over his men (ll. 38–41) in that her nobility and beauty are both unmatchable:

> siu luchtit vor anderen wiben
> so daz golt vor der siden.
> siu ist in miden also smal,
> sie gezeme eime herren wol
> unde mochte von ir adele
> gezeme eime koninge (ll. 73–78)

The bridal quest in *König Rother* is not about one man, but is emphatically the concern of the whole realm. Moreover, the use of the bridal-quest motif is used to explore the nature of king and kingship and, as such, the actual 'quest' may be sidelined; it has already been mentioned that a bridal quest is a good way to start a narrative, which may then explore other concerns. Here, Rother sets out to Constantinople not to woo the princess, but to rescue his messengers, two activities that become inextricably linked; moreover, the decision to quest for a bride provides an impetus for the establishment of the primary characteristics of Rother's system of government, one of the most important of which is the centrality of advice.

It has already been mentioned that the choice of wife was expressed communally, and this sets a pattern for what is to come. A messenger must be chosen to send to Constantin, the father of the chosen bride, to ask for her hand, and the choice of messenger — Lupold — is voiced by another noble, Herman, although it is implied that he is the spokesman for a communal decision (l. 85). Yet Lupold is not present at this council scene, so messengers must be sent to him; he must be 'wooed' in order to go wooing himself. The manner in which this scene is extended clarifies the process of government and Lupold's absence allows emphasis on the way in which 'things are done', creating what Müller refers to as 'Inszenierung von Rat'.[41]

Such scene-setting also occurs in the second extended advice scene after the messengers have failed to return. When Berchter — another of Rother's most loyal vassals — has given his own opinion, Rother declares *nu wil ich uffe den hof gan!* (l. 505), and it becomes apparent that private advice, even from the most trusted adviser, is not sufficient:

> wir suln iz den herren allen sagen
> unde kunden iz goten knehtin
> — dar an to wir rechte —,
> wie iz in gevalle,
> unde bedenken unsich alle. (ll. 506–10)

Rother's speech, quoted above, explains why Berchter, usually the best of advisers, suggests a plan that is not accepted. Two of his sons, Lupold and Erwin, are among the messengers, and he proposes taking Greece by storm (ll. 492–95), a plan that Rother considers too much of a risk (ll. 514–24). Berchter's status as leading adviser makes his intemperate proposal seem rather odd, and it is possible to suggest that his judgement is clouded by grief at the loss of his sons, or that the purpose of the scene is to demonstrate Rother's superior tactical skills.[42] Yet Rother does not propose an alternative plan himself and it seems that the primary reason for Berchter's 'failure' is to establish the importance of communal advice — which would have been unnecessary had Berchter's plan been infallible — and enable the necessary 'Inszenierung von Rat'.

The final decision, for Rother and his men to cross the sea in disguise as a band of exiles, is voiced by the common voice in the impersonalized plural *sie sprachen* (l. 584). The one objector to this, who believes nothing should be done, is quite literally silenced with a blow to the head by Berchter. This man does not care about the disappearance of the messengers, a sign of his lacking loyalty to the group, so must be distanced from the decision-making process; such distance is achieved successfully by Berchter, as the dissenter cannot hear nor speak, both vital for an advisory role, for three days (ll. 570–71). Before Berchter hits him, there is a rare narratorial comment to make it clear that this violent act is — unlike the other violent act Berchter suggested, of attacking Constantin with force — appropriate behaviour: *do half der vatir sinin kindin!* (l. 565).[43]

The result is an emphasis on the importance of the collective. The ruling system may have a figurehead, but it is not a dictatorship and its success shows how reciprocity and 'parliamentary' government can be the most sensible option for the medieval king. In a time of constant upheaval, stability is needed in the ruling order and can be attained by maintaining union with lords and vassals as well as by producing the longed-for heir. Hence the importance of *milte*, the generosity of the king, which Rother has in abundance. Wealth is given out gladly and men are rewarded for their actions; the messengers, for example, are given silver and gold (ll. 146–48). In comparison to Constantin, who sits on his nest-egg (see, for example, ll. 1120–27), Rother is not scared to share out his wealth, and the effects of *milte* are clear: generosity brings about greater loyalty, and loyalty brings about stability and strength. *Milte* is not to be thought of as bribery; its manipulative side comes into play at Constantin's court, but under Rother's kingship it is a natural part of the established system.

The gold and silver worn by the messengers sent to Constantinople not only ensures their status as the epitome of loyalty (*sie waren deme kuninge alle holt*, l. 146), but also acts as a reflection of the strength of their king, for they are described as the most splendid messengers ever seen: *iz quam in nie in chein lant | so manic bate wol getan* (ll. 159–60). When they arrive at their destination, Lupold asks a merchant to guard the ships and promises to reward him well for it (ll. 206–07), a scene that is unnecessary to the progression of the narrative. What it establishes, however, is that the attributes of 'Rother' are not simply those of a single figure, but permeate the whole order he represents, for Lupold behaves here in the manner of 'Rother' and justly rewards a man through his *milte*. Even in the absence of Rother himself, the ethos of his system remains constantly present.

The presence of Rother's kingship continues when the messengers enter Constantin's court. Their splendid appearance is described at length (ll. 218–33) and attracts the attention of all present, who gaze at their brilliant clothing (ll. 247–49; l. 279) and consequently think positively of their king. Constantin's queen declares that a *statehafter man* (l. 258) must have sent them and the speech of an old woman, Herlint, provides a culminating summary of the effect they have had:

> swannen dise herren kumen sint,
> daz ist ein wunderlichiz lant:
> sie tragen so manigen iachant

> gezirot mit deme golde.
> daz daz goth wolde,
> daz wer den kuninc gesehen
> des dise boten weren! (ll. 281-87)

It is striking that the manner in which the messengers can intimate the power of their land and ruler is stressed to such a degree. Furthermore, despite their failure to win the hand of the princess, they are not rejected in the same way as other wooers and their honour and superiority are upheld even in refusal. Constantin says that if he were to give his daughter to anyone, Rother would be an honourable choice (ll. 328-31), and he does not behead the messengers, as is his usual custom (ll. 82-83), but imprisons them instead because Lupold asked to speak before speaking (ll. 333-34). Although this decision may seem tenuous and motivated merely by the demands of the subsequent narrative (the messengers must stay alive so that they can be rescued), it stresses nonetheless the superior behaviour of Rother's men.

The main emphasis in the opening section of the text seems not to be on the superiority of Rother as a person, but rather on how this superiority is structured politically and how it is demonstrated by others. The group reflects back to Rother, but Rother is equally inconceivable without the group. 'Rother' consists in the system constituted by the king and his men and the manner in which they function politically, a notion clarified by the way in which each of Rother's vassals can be seen to embody a particular attribute of kingship, through which he is often described: thus Berchter is 'advice', Lupold 'loyalty', and Asprian 'strength'. Although each of these characters chiefly fulfils this main function, he does not act exclusively according to it; thus Lupold may be praised for his prowess in battle and Asprian sometimes displays more intelligence and subtlety than expected. The result is that there is a heightened feeling of 'group' action and all the men may act together in a battle scene or moment of cunning, stressing the importance of communality, while still principally fulfilling one role in the 'Rother' system. Berchter, Lupold, Asprian, and the others may have traits that distinguish them from each other and allow them to be recognizable as characters, but these traits come together to form the attributes of the greater whole, effectively extinguishing any independence from function.

The way in which characters are named by the narrator contributes to their association with an attribute, a technique that can be called 'delayed naming', in which the narrator only names the character after he has been described otherwise, or performed some kind of action. A particularly dramatic and visual example of this is the first entrance of the giant Asprian:

> do san sie in deme melme gan
> einin wunderlichen man,

> den ne mochte niehein ros getragen:
> der duchte sie ein seltsene knape.
> der troch eine staline stangin
> vier und zwienzich ellene lange,
> des wart sie ein michel kaffen angetan.
> sie brachte ein riese der hiez Asprian. (ll. 652-59)[44]

The effect of this delayed naming is to build up a good knowledge of the attributes of a character before the application of a name, making these attributes seem all the more important. When this technique is used for a character who has already appeared in the narrative, he can then be recognized by his attributes alone.

The fact that Rother wishes to undertake a bridal quest and rescue his messengers provides an opportunity for all the attributes of his kingship to be gathered together in one place; advice can be given, loyalty demonstrated, physical strength displayed. Rother sends envoys to all his men, calling them to court, and sheer numbers mirror the extent of the power of his kingship; there are so many knights that he can even choose which ones to take with him (ll. 748-52). Importantly, this summons brings the giants, whose symbolic function has been much discussed and is surely multifaceted. As exotic creatures, they are a sign of the extent of Rother's dominion, and they bring with them exotic attributes, such as the ivory-legged chairs Asprian takes to Constantin's feast (ll. 1608-09) and the *blatvuze* he gives 'Dietrich' (ll. 1871-73). Stock interprets them as elements of the 'fabulous', usually obtained by rulers (such as Herzog Ernst and Alexander) as part of a process of growth; Rother's kingly status is already affirmed, however, so the giants are already under his control.[45] They are also not quite civilized, at times a little uncourtly, a source of comic relief and a sign that Rother has, at least to some extent, conquered the untameable.[46] The giants' narrative functionality (or rather their potential for strategic cunning and enabling plans) comes into play in the second part of my analysis of the text, particularly in the manipulation of physical strength and fear. This, in turn, is made possible by what I believe to be the primary significance of the giants, their presence as a symbol of physical strength.[47] Physical strength is a vital attribute of Rother's system of government, and in the giants he has this in abundance.[48] The exoticism and difference of the giants makes this physical strength stable and unbeatable, for as soon as they enter the text, it becomes clear that there is absolutely no possibility of Rother being outdone in terms of physical strength. The most loyal man and best adviser have already been introduced, but now the very fact that Asprian, Witold, and the others are giants is sufficient. Witold is even chained, emphasizing further the extreme supremacy of his physical strength, but also that this violence is potential, not actual, for, importantly, 'Rother' is characterized by the constant, stable possibility of physical power, not a wild, uncontrollable violence. Stability and constancy is vital, not just of strength but of every attribute in which the system consists. The first section of the text (according to this interpretation) exists to establish this, and it is the impetus of the bridal-quest motif that makes its exposition possible.

To summarize, the bridal-quest motif is employed at the start of *König Rother* to allow an exposition of what constitutes Rother's ruling system and how it functions. It provides an opportunity to demonstrate how the system is founded on the principles of communality, advice, loyalty, and the presence of physical strength, and that an implication of all of this is contained within the name of 'Rother'. It is vital that the system is introduced in such detail because of what happens next: the system is removed from its ruling context and disguised as Dietrich, an exile banished by Rother, and his men. Loyalty is an intrinsic part of the system, so there is no question but that the messengers must be searched for and rescued or avenged — indeed, wooing the princess is no longer mentioned — but why accomplish this by disguise rather than by violent attack? A violent attack on Constantinople has also been explicitly thematized and rejected and is avoided until the introduction of the heathen king Ymelot, at which point it gains the justification of crusading and protecting Christianity from heathen attack.[49] It has been noted relatively frequently that in *König Rother* the option of violence is often made explicit and denied, but that its latent threat always remains and occasionally rises to the surface, particularly in scenes that involve the giants.[50] Instead of acting as a sign of the 'archaic' or pre-courtly, not yet overcome, the possibility and avoidance of violence seems rather pragmatic; it demonstrates that physical strength (and with it, the possibility of violence) is a vital part of the ideal ruling system, but that it is to be used in moderation and only when entirely necessary. Unless it happens to be religiously motivated, large-scale violence is clearly not the ideal path for a ruling system such as that of Rother, although the possibility of it must necessarily always be present under the surface, epitomized here in the characters of the giants. The very presence of the giants and the establishment of the 'Rother'-system as ideal, stable, and unbeatable also means that a violent attack would be of little narrative interest, let alone morally acceptable. Furthermore, *list* (cunning) is not depicted here — or indeed elsewhere in medieval literature — as a negative characteristic.[51] The decision to employ cunning and travel to Constantinople in disguise also means that the characteristics of 'Rother' (so carefully established) can remain unthreatened and unharmed because they stay, as far as the world is concerned, distant and at home. The disguise necessarily 'expatriates' the 'Rother' system, because it is removed from its usual context; the primary characteristic of Rother and everything the name refers to is that it rules, that it is a system of governance. Yet it cannot be a ruling system in someone else's space of rule.

Dietrich

Surprisingly, the implications of the 'Dietrich'-disguise have been little discussed in criticism, the emphasis being largely on the difference between the two halves of the text without consideration of the disguise motif, other than as a necessary feature of the 'Brautwerbung durch List'. The assumption of the name 'Dietrich' is, strikingly, the first decision Rother makes without advice. It has been decided collectively to travel to Constantinople *in reckewis* (l. 560), but the renaming is an individual act:

> der kuninc gedachte eine wisheit.
> er sprach zo [den] herren allen samint:
> [...]
> ich bit uch alle geliche
> armen unde riche,
> heizit mich Thiderich. (ll. 811–20)

According to the model of the 'Rother' system discussed above, the expression of such a decision without advice is unusual and surprising.[52] Yet this action sets an example for what is to come: Rother, a symbol of institutionalized kingship, has become Dietrich, who, as an exile, is tied to no political system and thus has greater possibilities for acting alone.

The disguise adopted is not a change of appearance — Rother and his men do not don recognizable clothes of another class of person, such as a pilgrim or beggar — but a change solely of name. Noticeably, as soon as Rother assumes the name 'Dietrich', he is always called by this name by the narrator and by his men, even when it is implied he is acting as Rother, and the narrative never explicitly points to the fact that Dietrich is not who he says he is.[53] The loss of the name 'Rother' is not synonymous with crisis or loss of place in the world as is the case in Hartmann's *Iwein*, for example.[54] Here, no damage to personal honour has occurred — on the contrary, it has been made very clear that sending messengers to Constantinople was an appropriate course of action and that these messengers behaved very well.[55] The status implied by the name 'Rother' is untouched and any feeling of victory that Constantin may harbour (l. 992) is laughable in the eyes of the audience, who know about the disguise. Indeed, one of the main effects of Dietrich is to reflect back on the splendour of Rother's order. Dietrich may appear in Constantinople as a rich and powerful man, but he has supposedly been banished by Rother, who must therefore be even more powerful.[56] The latent presence of Rother is part of the tactical plan, for if Dietrich can put on a show of extreme strength, then Rother must be quite remarkable: '[D]ie 'übermäßige Präsenz der (angeblich) Vertriebenen macht also nicht nur die latente Präsenz Rothers — in den eingekerkerten Boten — immer wieder deutlich, sondern auch die tatsächliche Präsenz Rothers zur beständigen Drohung'.[57] The latent presence of Rother finds particular expression in the voice of Constantin's queen, who is persistently critical of her husband, telling him for example that he was foolish not to give his daughter to Rother when she sees Witold in chains (ll. 1065–68).[58] Yet, when it comes to Dietrich, the attributes that were established to constitute Rother remain, but the name does not. The change of name means that the connotations of Rother, of kingship and its contingent attributes — wealth, power, generosity, and so on — become estranged from their systemic context. In the first part of the text, these attributes were part of a system and formed the stable and functioning core of Rother's order, but now they have been transplanted from their context and are applied so obviously and consciously by Dietrich and his men that they are evidently being strategically manipulated.

The strength of 'Rother', represented by the giants, becomes strategically staged terror. As soon as they reach Constantinople, the giants begin to show-fight on the beach (ll. 832–33) and they are sent to guard Dietrich's treasure in as terrifying a way as possible, so that their presence may be felt more strongly. One giant, Witold, is so aggressive he must be chained up, and thus maintains a constantly present threat of latent violence, as discussed above. There are two important scenes in which violence erupts: the death of Constantin's pet lion (ll. 1146–71) and the argument over the chairs (ll. 1593–1773).

It is striking that many of the moments discussed by Kiening, Fuchs-Jolie, and others as examples of the avoidance of violence or the manipulation of courtly rituals occur when Rother is disguised as Dietrich. It is true that when *König Rother* was written the romances of Chrétien had not yet exerted a great influence in Germany and that the ethical code of courtliness was not yet fully developed, but it does not necessarily follow that this code should be unconsciously half-thematized, half interrupted by some kind of pre-courtly or 'archaic' spontaneous that erupts periodically in the narrative; or indeed why these moments should be 'Irritationen'. Surely more important is that such moments occur when Rother is disguised as Dietrich. This is not to suggest that Dietrich represents some kind of heroic 'epic' past (although the name surely must resonate);[59] instead, the adoption of a disguise enables an exposure of kingly behaviour, and how this is changed when the protagonist and his men are *not* a king and his men.

While entertaining Dietrich at court, Constantin brings in his pet lion, which steals some of Asprian's food. As a result of this, Asprian flings it against a wall *daz her al zerbrach* (l. 1152), an action that provokes fear and so prevents reaction (ll. 1153–54). It is questionable whether Asprian's behaviour is an expression of his uncontrollable nature or is tactically motivated, for unlike the giant Witold, who must be kept in chains, Asprian seems more reasoned and 'human', and is a lord in his own right. Whatever the motivation behind his action, however, the event is manipulated to make it tactically beneficial. Berchter recognizes its positive effect (*iz kumit uns wole, daz Asprian | deme lewen so we hat getan*, ll. 1225–26) and as a result Dietrich and his men are given the freedom to establish their own court to rival that of Constantin.

Importantly, Asprian's action is not unprovoked or unnecessarily aggressive, because the very presence of the lion appears to be a provocation on the part of Constantin:

> Do zohc man vor Constantinis disch einen lewen vreissam,
> der ne wolde niemanne vor nicht han.
> her nam den knechten daz brot,
> her tet en over deme dische groze not. (ll. 1146–49)

The lion is not only a symbol of Constantin's kingship, which is exposed by Asprian to be easily toppled, but also an aggressive demonstration of it.[60] If the lion is meant to be a sign of Constantin's own latent physical strength, then it is overcome by that of Dietrich without any difficulty; the difference, however, is that the giants do not behave inappropriately or aggressively without provocation, whereas the lion actively disrupts the feast, stealing food from the plates of others. Constantin's attempted show of power thus fails on two accounts: it is overcome by a superior power, and also exposes his understanding of kingly behaviour as flawed, because it is unnecessarily and actively aggressive.

The tactical potential of the giants comes into play similarly in the argument over the chairs. Constantin holds a feast for Whitsun and all the chamberlains set out chairs for their lords; for Dietrich, this duty falls to Asprian. The chamberlain of a certain Duke Friedrich tries to muscle in on Dietrich's allotted space, the space of honour opposite the king.[61] Asprian reacts peaceably at first, asking the other chamberlain to go to his allotted place and not argue (ll. 1627–37), but this man reacts by throwing a bench at him, so Asprian kills him. Witold wants to attack further, breaking his chains and coming to the aid of his lord Asprian, but Asprian tries to stop him, claiming that Friedrich's men behaved towards him in a kindly manner. A fight breaks out nonetheless and news of it reaches Constantin, who says that Dietrich must judge what to do. Dietrich says that if Witold has done wrong, he must be put to death publicly (ll. 1748–50), a decision that terrifies Friedrich so much that he takes back his accusation. The excuse is given that it would be shameful to treat an exile in this manner (ll. 1758–65), a rather transparent cover for the real reason that Friedrich and his men are scared of the public presence of Witold:

> ettelicher forte sere,
> her wurde des roufens geclagit
> mit vil grozen bulslagen,
> ob der helit kone
> uf den hof queme. (ll. 1767–71)[62]

Dietrich is wronged on two counts: his honour is damaged when an attempt is made to unseat him from his place next to the king, and then his man, Asprian, is attacked without provocation. Yet the result is that he emerges with both his honour intact and his potential physical strength confirmed. He suggests, honourably, that Witold (who responded violently to the attack on Asprian) should be killed, but even this act, selfless and noble as it appears, has the paradoxical result of confirming Witold's strength further; even Witold's public presence at the place of execution is seen as too threatening. Much like the lion scene, an unprovoked moment of aggression towards Dietrich and his men is manipulated to assert their own superiority without any damage to their honour.[63] Stable in their own physical superiority, the giants have the potential to stage terror (or to be staged as terror) and manipulate their power (or have it manipulated) into a 'show' both entertaining and alarming. In l. 2170, Asprian is described as a *riesen spileman*, perhaps a rather apt epithet.[64]

The strategic manipulation of *milte* is perhaps even more strongly delineated. After the lion episode, Berchter suggests Dietrich make use of his new freedom and retire to his own quarters in order to help other exiles (ll. 1237–43). He and his men share out their wealth, helping the poor at court, something that would not otherwise be done by Constantin; this seeming altruism soon becomes an explicit way of gaining men:

> Do ne stund iz borlange,
> er Dietherich der manne
> ses dusint gewan,
> die ime waren underdan
> mit dieniste aller tagelich:
> sin ingesinde was herlich. (ll. 1387–92)[65]

Even Constantin's men are lured by this generosity, changing sides explicitly because of material gains:

> her [Dietrich] gab en tageliche
> mit golde deme rotin
> de pellele ungescrotin,
> dar zo mantele snevare:
> dar nach hoven sie sic dare. (ll. 1508–12)

It is clear now why Berchter advised withdrawing to their own quarters, as from there Dietrich and his men could establish a rival court, separate from the royal court, which they could then undermine from within. The result is that *milte*, a fixed policy in the 'Rother'-system, is recontextualized, which makes it seem more manipulative and similar to bribery. The attributes that shaped Rother's ideal order are used to expose the weaknesses of Constantin's system, but removed from the context of kingship, another, more blunt functionality becomes clear. Rother and his men, as Dietrich, are manipulating what it is that constitutes themselves for their own gains.

It must therefore be considered whether or not Dietrich makes the attributes of good kingship ambivalent by manipulating them. He returns to Italy with only those men he brought with him, sending those who joined him in Constantinople back to Constantin (ll. 2843–44); it is thus implied that their allegiance to him was only functional, martial power to be gained where necessary and then cast off again, and they are not irreplaceable. Dietrich also swears by God that Constantin and his men are all dead in order to escape successfully with the princess (l. 2861), another morally dubious act. Yet most of his cunning has an altruistic side, for in gaining martial strength, he does still help exiles out of poverty, an action that guarantees the allegiance of Arnolt, so vital for the third section of the text. His escape with the princess and his rescue of the messengers are also particularly impressive, a deception achieved remarkably unselfishly, by winning a battle, killing heathens, capturing an evil king, and saving Constantin's empire.[66] Dietrich's schemes can also be compared with the schemes of Constantin's minstrel, who is sent to recapture the princess. The minstrel makes a poor mockery of Dietrich's *milte*, selling his potions for money and promising false cures to the sick, whom he then throws unceremoniously from the side of his ship (ll. 3231–32).[67] There is no negative tendency such as this to Dietrich, rather a tactical cunning that is not part of the stability of 'Rother'.

It has been suggested above that Dietrich can act autonomously, unlike Rother, who must remain the symbol of institutionalized kingship. A good example of this is the famous 'Schuhprobe' scene, in which the princess and Dietrich meet and he reveals his true identity. 'Fernliebe' comes again into play, since the princess has become attracted to Dietrich because of his reported prowess at court, despite the fact she has never seen him.[68] Herlint, the princess's lady-in-waiting, is sent to Dietrich to invite him to the princess's chamber; he refuses, but sends her back with bracelets, a cloak, and two shoes to fit the same foot (Dietrich has two pairs of shoes made, one silver and one gold, but sends one shoe from each pair, ll. 2014–31). On discovering that the shoes fit only one foot, the princess sends Herlint back to Dietrich and this time arranges a visit in person, where he fits the shoe himself. The 'Schuhprobe' scene has been the subject of much critical discussion, and Schulz's argument that it is a judicial, ritual act of betrothal, symbolic of the mutual agreement of both parties, is convincing.[69] Yet it is surely important that the process is carried out not by Rother, but by Dietrich.

Near the end of the scene, Dietrich asks the princess whom she would ideally marry (ll. 2202–08) and she replies that he, Dietrich, is the best man she has ever seen (ll. 2213–23), but that if she had the choice she would have to marry Rother (ll. 2224–32). According to Stock, her response is tied up with the maxim of 'die Schönste' and 'der Beste', for logic (and narrative schemata) require that she marry the 'Besten', who is Rother, not Dietrich.[70] Indeed, from the perspective of the audience, her speech may be amusing, for we know very well the paradox that the superlatives characteristics of Dietrich assert the superiority in all respects of the man who supposedly banished him. Paradoxically, she should love both Dietrich and Rother: Dietrich, because of his superlative presence at court; Rother, for the sake of the success of the narrative. The narrative demands that Dietrich cannot be preferred, so the problem is solved by the separation of the men into two different sorts of attraction, with Rother coming out on top. For not only do Dietrich's qualities reflect positively on Rother, but his status as exile enables the establishment of a personal relationship, free from political ties or official wooing. Dietrich is the man the princess is attracted to, Rother the official wooer represented by messengers, a name implying great kingship and status.[71] The 'Kemenatenszene' — the scene that constitutes a private moment between wooer and bride, a moment for the expression of mutual consent — is often discussed and thought to be of central importance in a bridal quest (indeed, such a scene appears in the majority of medieval texts that contain any form of betrothal). Importantly, it is Dietrich who carries out this private moment, keeping Rother entirely separate from 'private' affairs, or those in which he must act individually. In this sense, the princess's speech provides a point of crystallization for the function of the disguise, clarifying the separation between Dietrich and Rother and the different implications of these names.

The princess believes that Dietrich is Rother's messenger (ll. 2247–57) — which, in a sense, he is — and he answers that he really is Rother: *ia stent dine voze | in Rotheris schoze!* (ll. 2261–62). She demands that he prove this, and he suggests she take the captured messengers into her care so that they can be used as witnesses, thus making explicit the mutual dependence of his two aims in Constantinople, wooing and rescuing. Despite the fact that Dietrich has revealed himself to the princess as Rother, he is still referred to by the narrator as Dietrich and the freed messengers do not recognize him or his men immediately. Lupold and Erwin do not even recognize their father, Berchter, something made more curious when they admit a potential similarity: *'daz is war, brodir min, | her mach wole unser vatir sin!'* (ll. 2481–82). The lack of recognition on the part of the messengers can be thought of as an 'isolation' episode, in Lugowski's terminology, an episode that does not seem to 'make sense' but is motivated retroactively within the narrative.[72] Here, Dietrich must prove to the princess that he is Rother, so he must be recognized officially; much as there was a 'staging' of advice earlier, here there is a 'staging' of recognition. The possibility of such a scene is signalled earlier in the text when the messengers depart from Bari and Rother plays lays on the harp by which they may recognize him: 'kummit ir imer in decheine not, | swa ir virnimet die leiche dri, | da suld er min gewis sin.' (ll. 175–77).[73] This is indeed the case: Dietrich hides behind a curtain to play the lays and is immediately recognized as Rother (ll. 2509–29).

Yet the lack of recognition points to more than the necessity of a public coup de théatre. Personal identity is much like naming as discussed by Müller; it consists in separate parts, brought together and unified by the name. In this sense, physical appearance is not enough to allow recognition, for the person is equally made up from skills and status, indeed everything that may be implied by a name. The messengers are freed by Dietrich, who can only be identified as Rother by performing an act that only Rother would be able to, and the messengers can only recognize him in the way in which they have been instructed.[74] This is not to suggest that physical appearance is not at all important. In fact, *ansehen* is often stressed in the text, along with the desire of onlookers to 'see' beautiful clothing or appearance. Yet *ansehen* signals status, not personal identity, such as when Arnolt is recognized as a noble, despite his poverty (ll. 1405–06).[75] It is rather the case that specific physical traits, such as a large nose or blond hair, that mark out one person and are not symbolic of his status seem irrelevant.

This dependence of personal identity in some way on name is why Dietrich continues to be so called without exception after he has revealed himself to be Rother. Dietrich must remain Dietrich until all the intentions of this name have been fulfilled. It seems impossible to have a partial identity, that is, to have two names at once, so while the Dietrich disguise is still functioning, 'Dietrich' is how he must remain. This name can only be shed after the battle against Ymelot, when the messengers and the princess are safely on board ship and the anchor has been weighed. Only then can Rother say *ione heiz ich niwit Dietherich* (l. 2918) and the queen can express her happiness *nu du Rother bist* (l. 2932). Rother can only return when Dietrich's plan is completed and his full function is at an end.

Rother Again

As soon as Rother and his men return to Bari, the realities of kingship become apparent, for the kingdom has been thrown into disarray in their absence; Amelger, the chosen regent, has died and Hademar von Dießen has attempted to seize power.[76] Rother and his men manage to resolve the situation fairly swiftly (ll. 2967–86), but this short episode indicates that we are now firmly back in the domain of kingship; Rother is even fulfilling his kingly duties, preaching to widows and orphans, when his wife is kidnapped (ll. 3106–07).

Dietrich is gone and the attributes established in the first part of the story are now restored to their original context.

The restoration expands on that which was established in the first part of the story: the system is challenged and put into action in battle; stability and continuity are demonstrated in the birth and accession of an heir and withdrawal of the old king, which nonetheless keeps the system intact; there is the added dimension of historical 'reality', or rather references to the world outside that of the text. This expansion is not a negative reflection upon the Dietrich-episode, nor does it suggest the growth or development of the king and his system. The Dietrich-episode does not exist for the purposes of value judgement or development; it is merely a transposition of attributes established in the first section into a different context. As we have seen, the change of name to Dietrich signalled a change in behaviour, even in personal identity, and there was the possibility to act more freely without the constant necessity to uphold an ideal system. The return to Rother leads to a return to behaviour as a system of kingship and, with this, a more idealized state, hence, for example, the increased number of moral aphorisms.[77]

After his wife has been kidnapped, Rother decides to travel to Constantinople in disguise as before, but this time as a pilgrim. As with the Dietrich-disguise, he speaks this decision himself, *harde wisliche* (l. 3665), but, importantly, it is qualified immediately by his men. Wolfrat says that *du ne salt nicht eine dare gan!* (l. 3673) and insists he take Berchter and Lupold with him, as well as a horn to summon the rest of his men, a suggestion supported by Asprian. Rother, Berchter, and Lupold disguise themselves as pilgrims and discover that Constantin's kingdom has been overtaken by the since-escaped Ymelot, whose son is now betrothed to Rother's kidnapped wife. They enter Constantin's court and manage to hide under a table during the feast, whence Rother passes his wife a ring. She smiles, which gives away his presence, and, after a swift under-table advisory session — necessary even in the most uncomfortable situation — Rother reveals himself and is condemned to death by hanging.[78]

Rother's discovery and capture has been interpreted as both a mistake and as a cunning ploy. According to Schröder, 'die eigentliche List ist nicht die Verkleidung, sondern die Sich-Gefangennehmen-Lassen', because it enables the battle against the heathens and the final rescue of the princess;[79] Stock, on the other hand, argues that it is a mistake, symptomatic of the more difficult world of the second half of the text, in which Rother and his men are not entirely in control and aware of all that is happening.[80] This scene can be clarified by closer consideration of several moments.

It is first important to note the difference between the Dietrich-disguise and the pilgrim-disguise, the former of which was a complete assumption of a different personal identity, the latter more simply a covering, a large cloak under which to hide one's person: *do sluffen die helede guode | in pilegrimis gewete* (ll. 3694–95). In contrast to the 'Dietrich' section of the text, the narrator still refers to Rother by his 'real' name, and the disguise as a whole is therefore considerably more transparent. In this episode unexpected events are also encountered for the first time; with the invasion of Ymelot, something has happened without Rother's (or Dietrich's) knowledge or influence.[81] Yet this is not the first time that something bad has happened in his absence: without him present the messengers are captured, the land falls into disarray, the queen is kidnapped, and Ymelot invades Constantinople. The association of negative events with the king's absence means that his restored presence can assert and affirm superiority[82] — but in this case, however, Rother's presence only seems to make the situation worse. On the other hand, Rother chooses the manner of his death, which could be interpreted as a tactical move, because hanging is a public event from which he can easily be saved;[83] his getting caught also legitimizes the attack of his men and gives them the opportunity to prove their superiority in a final and concrete manner.

It seems irrelevant whether Rother 'fails' here or not, because what this episode shows is that Rother *is* the group, that he needs his men in order really to be Rother, and that success can happen through the group working together and the system functioning in the way that it should. This fact is demonstrated by Rother 'failing' alone and by, paradoxically, this 'failure' enabling a demonstration of the success of the group and the way in which it functions. Thus the ensuing battle is won by *triuwe*, *milte* (epitomized by Arnolt, the exile helped by Dietrich) and advice (Wolfrat advises Rother to take the horn with which he summons the army), as well as military strength.

Rother takes no active part in the battle, even after he has been let down from the gallows, and the description of the battle centres on the brave deeds of his men. His individual deeds are of no importance, for he is emphatically not a hero and individual heroics are not a constituent part of his kingship; instead, he is the symbolic figurehead of an institutionalized ruling order.[84] This is made particularly apparent by Arnolt's use of crusading language in encouraging his men to fight. Arnolt, who as an exile was rescued by Dietrich's *milte*, now repays the favour by rescuing Rother from the gallows and his hortatory speeches are reminiscent of crusading sermons: *ia vore wir godis recht! | swer hie hute wirt irsclagin, | des sele sal genade haven* (ll. 4072–74). Yet God is not the only motivation, for they must fight for Rother, *der aller turiste man | de ie koninriche gewan* (ll. 4079–80). Such duality is clarified in Arnolt's second speech: *nu horet, gote knechte, | warumbe wir hute vechtin: | uns sind gebotin zwei lon* (ll. 4125–27). The first of these rewards is the promise of eternal salvation, the second is more practical:

> daz ander ist also getan:
> generder den getruwin man,
> er vorit uch in sin lant
> unde behalt unsich alle samt! (ll. 4135–38)

Rother will provide them with a home. When qualified in this manner, the religious vocabulary seems rather more a matter of style than an indication of a primarily religious motivation; crusading jargon is adopted perhaps more emphatically than its ideals.[85] The battle is nonetheless fought against heathens, the Babylonian King Ymelot and his men, but as mentioned above, they function as a kind of *deus ex machina*, a legitimation for the conclusive demonstration of Rother's superiority over Constantin without recourse to violence against him. Crusading should still be considered a serious and positive action, however, for religion, and the defence of it, are as intrinsic a part of Rother's kingship as any other of its attributes. Kingship in the model of Charlemagne and the Hohenstaufen emperors, on the throne at the time in which *König Rother* was probably written, was based ideally on a combination of secular and spiritual values (the *sacrum imperium*); without going so far as to argue that *König Rother* is Hohenstaufen propaganda, it seems likely that such a combination of worldly and spiritual is at the root of Rother's system of kingship as well.[86] The end of the text, when Rother withdraws from worldly life, is therefore not incongruous.[87]

The battle is the final challenge to confront Rother's system, the last time that loyalty, generosity, strength, and so on must be put to use as responses to a problem. Despite it being made clear that the system is stable and constant, the narrative has centred so far on such problems and their associated responses, but at the end of the story it becomes equally clear that, even without a problem to tackle, the system remains unchanged. When Rother and his men return to Bari, Rother divides up his kingdom. In a simple political sense, sharing out lands between the most devoted men is the most effective way to ensure stability, peace, and a lasting hold over the empire. Yet this is a peace-time representation of what has been happening in war, with Rother as a figurehead emperor and his vassals responsible for a part of his kingship. These attributes (loyalty, strength, and so on) are now translated, in the most extreme act of *milte*, into physical parts of the kingship: lands.[88]

The division of lands also makes the extent of Rother's kingship apparent. In this part of the text it has become clear that he is emperor over the whole known western world; he is referred to as *keyser* in l. 3106, a title handed down to his son Pippin (l. 5064). The language used to describe Rother's kingdom changes as well, with more emphasis on the Roman Empire; Rother is the *koninc von Rome* (l. 3653; 3789–90; 3912), his men the *romiske diet* (l. 4060), and the kingdom the *romesche riche* (l. 4760).[89] The effect of this emphasis on

Roman inheritance is to make the text seem more historically 'real'; Rother is not just a king, but recognizably a ruler of the Holy Roman Empire. He is given a concrete historical identity when we discover that his unborn son is Pippin, father of Charlemagne (ll. 3479–91), a circumstance from which the truth of the text can be asserted: *von du nis daz liet | von lugenen gedihtet niet!* (ll. 3490–91). Much the same is said after Pippin's birth:

> von du ne sulit ir dit lit
> den andren gelichin nit,
> wandit so manich recht hat,
> danne ime die warheit in stat. (ll. 4791–94)[90]

The character of Wolfrat is also introduced as an ancestral representative of the Tengeling family, and, along with Berchter (von Meran) and Hademar of Dießen, who tries to seize power in Rother's absence, a dimension of 'true' dynastic relevance is added.[91] The text now wants to make statements about reality external to the narrative.

This section of the text may have more connection to the time of composition, but there is also a stronger feeling of the past and Rother's men are praised as old-fashioned heroes: *an den lach die alde zucht | unde die wereltliche vorcht* (ll. 3654–55; see also ll. 4263–68). Despite being depicted as *helede*, these men still uphold Rother's system, introduced in the first section and employed here, and they are not challenged in the traditional manner of the hero. Broadly, the hero is set upon by enemies, beasts, and the elements, the sort of tests which assess the properties of the innate person, his strength and daring. These men are fighting for the social order and are representative of the unquestionable superiority of Rother's system of kingship — there is no possibility that they might lose the battle. On the one hand, therefore, the text refers to contemporary social ideals — the notion of the *sacrum imperium* — and to contemporary families, although the familial references are loose and the ideals are not specifically realized around one historical figure. On the other hand, the ideals are made 'historical', that is, they are located in an idealized past, which is in turn given historical truth through the link to Pippin and Charlemagne.[92]

In the first part of the text (according to my analysis), the attributes and nature of 'Rother', that is, of the system of government distinguished by the name of the King Rother, are established. This system then acts, in disguise. In the final part of the text, the system reacts to events it cannot control, namely the capture of the princess and the invasion of Ymelot. It is striking that the protagonist acts as Dietrich and reacts as Rother, and that the two names mark out two different modes of behaviour. It is possible to suggest, as demonstrated in the first part of the text (according to my analysis), that kings are static and stable figures who represent an order or an institution, in this case the institution we see put to the test in this latter part of the text. Yet in order to act with cunning, it is therefore necessary *not* to be a king. Obviously the adoption of the Dietrich-disguise is all part of a cunning plan, and is logically tactical, but the all-consuming nature of the disguise is striking. Paradoxically, even though we (the audience) know that Dietrich is Rother, it would be impossible for Rother to do what Dietrich does, and the disguise, by moving away from the system of kingship, paradoxically clarifies that system in all its institutional stability. By the end of the text, this stability has been ensured and the order affirmed thanks to the finality of the battle and the birth of an heir, and as a result of this affirmation the text can make statements about historical longevity. Instead of being simply one idealized system of ruling, 'Rother' now designates *the* idealized system of ruling, continued by Pippin and Charlemagne.

Continuation is assured with the accession of his son, to whom all Rother's men swear allegiance to Pippin (ll. 5061–64). This act demonstrates that he will keep the same men and so, with them, will maintain the same attributes of kingship; it is striking that the king himself ages, but the vassals (with the exception of Berchter) remain the same, in clarification of their primary symbolic role. Thus, Rother can withdraw from the world, and his story can end. Worldly power is only ever loaned from God, so a turn, with his wife and Berchter (noticeably the only vassal with sons to assume his role), to a spiritual life is understandable. The humility of the ruler is symbolized in the Claugestian stone, worn by Berchter when he comes to advise Rother to make this withdrawal (ll. 4951–58).[93] As Berchter says, *daz dinc nemac immer niht sin!* (l. 5122), stressing not only the evanescence of worldly power, but also the need for succession.

Conclusion

König Rother is usually interpreted as a 'nicht mehr' or 'noch nicht' text, looking back at an earlier form or oral conception of the bridal-quest schema or forwards towards courtly romance. Both lines of interpretation are based on often tenuous premises and prevent a reading of the text for what it is. Even those studies that do concentrate on the contemporary resonance of *König Rother* usually argue for a particular source or patron, so are prone to guesswork and assumption themselves. Although this is to a degree inevitable in the study of medieval texts, it seems misguided to concentrate on the search for a single and defined meaning or purpose to a text, whilst ignoring its complexities and what it actually says and does. The reading of *König Rother* offered here shows, I hope, that searching for a single meaning of the text is unnecessary and perhaps artificial. Instead of focusing on a self-reflexive double-structure, it has divided the text into three, demonstrating a pattern of introduction (or establishment), recontextualization, and restoration. Norms of behaviour, in this instance those of a king, are serious literary themes in their own right and do not require any developmental framework in order to be made visible. The exploration of the roles in society played by literary characters is also a central feature of the following chapter, on *Salman und Morolf*, although in that case they are rather less clearly delineated.

Notes to Chapter 1

1. *König Rother* is transmitted in one (almost) complete manuscript (H) and five fragments (M, E, L, N and B), three of which come from the same manuscript. H and M can be dated to the end of the twelfth century, E, L and N — all from the same manuscript — to the end of the thirteenth century and B, important because it contains sixteen lines from the otherwise lost conclusion to the text, to the fourteenth century. For further details, see Karin Schneider, *Gotische Schriften in deutscher Sprache*, I: *Vom späten 12. Jahrhundert bis um 1300* (Wiesbaden: Reichert, 1987), pp. 52–53; 113–14 and Thomas Klein, 'Ermittlung, Darstellung und Deutung von Verbreitungstypen in der Handschriftenüberlieferung mittelhochdeutscher Epik', in *Deutsche Handschriften 1100–1400*, ed. by Volker Honemann and Nigel F. Palmer (Tübingen: Niemeyer, 1988), pp. 110–67. I thank Nigel Palmer for sending me his as yet unpublished article on the fragment L, which he found in the Charles E. Young Research Library, Los Angeles.
2. On the importance of structure to early literary texts, see in particular Markus Stock, *Kombinationssinn: Narrative Strukturexperimente im Straßburger Alexander, im Herzog Ernst B und im König Rother* (Tübingen: Niemeyer, 2002), pp. 8–9. Stock argues that pre-courtly texts do not reflect on poetology or fictionality, but react to different structural forms and frameworks, which enables them to be literary:

    '[S]elbst wenn keine Poetologie formuliert wird, kann in den frühen Epen das Strukturexperiment neue Dimensionen des Literarischen aufschließen; selbst wenn von Fiktionalität nicht die Rede sein kann, bleibt dennoch die Möglichkeit freier Strukturierungen des Stoffes, die einen literarischen Gestus verraten und im Verarbeiten des Hergebrachten individuelle Dispositionen und Sujetfügungen zeigen. Wir sind bei der Bestimmung des Literarischen in der Epik dieser frühen Phase auf die Struktur der Texte verwiesen.' (p. 9).

3. This phrase is borrowed from Jan-Dirk Müller, *Spielregeln für den Untergang: Die Welt des Nibelungenliedes* (Tübingen: Niemeyer, 1998), p. 50, who in setting out the terms of his study (pp. 48–51), discusses and problematizes the trend of such an interpretation of the *Nibelungenlied*.
4. Frings, 'Die Enstehung der deutschen Spielmannsepen'.
5. Contrary to this trend, see Thomas Klein, 'Zur Thidreks saga', in *Arbeiten zur Skandinavistik: 6. Arbeitstagung der Skandinavisten des deutschen Sprachgebietes*, ed. by Heinrich Beck (Frankfurt a. M.: Lang, 1985), pp. 487–565 (pp. 487–512), who argues that the first part of *König Rother* and the Osantrix story had a shared source and that the first part of *König Rother* was composed from this in Northern Germany. He posits that the second part was then added in Bavaria at a later date, accounting for the shift in emphasis and considerable difference between the two parts. For the story of Osantrix, see *The Saga of Thidrek of Bern*, trans. by Edward R. Haymes (New York and London: Garland, 1988), pp. 25–30.
6. The interpretation of *König Rother* as a largely interpolated text persisted until the middle of the twentieth century; the first person to attempt a reading of *König Rother* as a deliberately unified text was Walter Johannes Schröder, 'König Rother: Gehalt und Struktur', *DVjs*, 29 (1955), 301–22, repr. in *Spielmannsepik*, ed. by Schröder, pp. 323–50,

who argues that, although the second half is a Christianized version of the first, the theme of the whole text is the nature and limits of worldly power and the necessity of securing this power through the production of an heir. A more recent argument for the separation of the two parts is given by Ingo Reiffenstein, 'Die Erzählervorausdeutung in der frühmittelhochdeutschen Dichtung: Zur Geschichte und Funktion einer poetischen Formel', in *Festschrift für Hans Eggers zum 65. Geburtstag*, ed. by Herbert Backes, *Beiträge zur Geschichte der deutschen Sprache und Literatur*, 94 (Sonderheft) (Tübingen: Niemeyer, 1972), pp. 551–76, who argues that the larger amount of narrative 'Vorausdeutung' in the first part of the text demonstrates that the parts do not belong together.

7. Curschmann, *Der Münchener Oswald und die deutsche spielmännische Epik*, pp. 101–14.
8. Haug, 'Struktur, Gewalt und Begierde'. See also Walter Haug, 'Die geistliche Umformulierung profaner Typen: *Rolandslied*, Brautwerbungsepen, *Alexanderroman*', in Haug, *Literaturtheorie im deutschen Mittelalter: Von den Anfängen bis zum Ende des 13. Jahrhunderts*, 2nd edn (Darmstadt: Wissenschaftliche Buchgesellschaft, 1992), pp. 75–90 (pp. 80–83), for a simpler argument about how the second half of *König Rother* provides a contrastive variant of the first, a more religious outlook that is qualifying and reflexive.
9. Hugo Kuhn, 'Erec', in Kuhn, *Dichtung und Welt im Mittelalter* (Stuttgart: Metzler, 1959), pp. 133–50 (p. 147).
10. Ibid., p. 150: 'Der gleiche Grundton geht durch alle vier Epen Hartmanns: Wer sich in dem Dasein, das ihm geschenkt ist, genießend abschließt, oder, mit Gregorius zu reden, wer im *zwîfel* lebt, der neutralisiert es, der macht seine Kräfte unwirksam; wer aber durch freiwillige Preisgabe, wer durch Buße lernt, es von oben zu empfangen, der erst kann auch seine irdischen Kräfte recht benutzen: als Aufgabe und Dienst zur Ehre in der Welt wie zum Lohn bei Gott.'
11. The link between the double-structure of *König Rother* and that of the Arthurian romances has also been doubted by Hans Fromm, 'Doppelweg', in *Werk-Typ-Situation: Studien zur poetologischen Bedingungen in der älteren deutschen Literatur*, ed. by Ingeborg Glier and others (Stuttgart: Metzler, 1969), pp. 64–79.
12. The basic premise of Haug's argument, that orally transmitted narratives cannot be reflective, is criticized fundamentally by Deutsch, 'Die Einführung der Schrift'.
13. Christian Kiening, 'Arbeit am Muster: Literarisierungsstrategien im *König Rother*', in *Neue Wege in der Mittelalter-Philologie: Landshuter Colloquium 1996*, ed. by Joachim Heinzle, L. Peter Johnson, and Gisela Vollmann-Profe (Berlin: Schmidt, 1998), pp. 211–44 (p. 220), states that emphasis on the double-structure 'führt auch dazu, Intertextualität als primär genetische zu denken und die Frage nach der Sinnkonstitution des Textes auf das Prinzip der Doppelung zu verengen'.
14. Ibid., esp. pp. 221–22, describes how *König Rother* reaches a new level of distance from the oral schema (and from Lugowski's 'mythic analogue') by making the construction of the narrative visible. This is particularly apparent in the way in which individual figures take control of the logic of the schema and narrative alternatives are posed, as well as in the presence of 'final motivation'. Kiening goes on to expand this point by considering three points of discussion: the play between presence and absence; the tension between violence and the avoidance of violence; the fluidity between history and the present.
15. Silvia Schmitz, '*War umbe ich die rede han ir hauen*: Erzählen im *König Rother*', in *Situationen des Erzählens: Aspekte narrativer Praxis im Mittelalter*, ed. by Ludger Lieb and Stephan Müller (Berlin: de Gruyter, 2002), pp. 167–90.
16. Stephan Fuchs-Jolie, 'Gewalt, Text, Ritual: Performativität und Literarizität im *König*

Rother', *PBB*, 127 (2005), 183–207 (p. 192). A lengthier problematization is offered by Deutsch, 'Die Einführung der Schrift'.
17. Fuchs-Jolie, 'Gewalt, Text, Ritual', esp. pp. 203–07. A similar argument is put forward in a later article: Fuchs-Jolie, 'Rother, Roland und die Rituale: Repräsentation und Narration in der frühhöfischen Epik', in *Deutsche Königspfalzen: Beiträge zu ihrer historischen und archäologischen Erforschung*, VII: *Zentren herrschaftlicher Repräsentation im Hochmittelalter: Geschichte, Architektur und Zeremoniell*, ed. by Caspar Ehlers, Jörg Jarnut, and Matthias Wemhoff (Göttingen: Vandenhoeck & Ruprecht, 2007), pp. 171–96.
18. Stock, *Kombinationssinn*, p. 243.
19. Ibid., p. 254.
20. Ibid., p. 275. See also Christa Ortmann and Hedda Ragotzky, 'Brautwerbungsschema, Reichsherrschaft und staufische Politik: Zur politischen Bezeichnungsfähigkeit literarischer Strukturmuster am Beispiel des *König Rother*', *ZfdPh*, 112 (1993), 321–43, who offer a schema-dependent synchronic reading that focuses on longevity and stability, but that is focused on contemporary politics to the extent that they describe *König Rother* as 'ein propagandistisches Werk' (p. 322).
21. Klein, 'Ermittlung', p. 132.
22. Ibid., pp. 120–22. See also his illustrations on p. 116.
23. Ludwig Wolff, art. 'Heinrich von Veldeke', *VL*, III, cols 899–902.
24. Klein, 'Ermittlung', p. 121.
25. See Joachim Bumke, *Mäzene im Mittelalter: Die Gönner und Auftraggeber der höfischen Literatur in Deutschland 1150–1300* (Munich: Beck, 1979), pp. 91–96, for an overview of potential patrons (Bumke favours the idea of a Welfish patron) and Kerth, pp. 34–36, for a concise summary of the critical position.
26. For a thorough discussion of possible sources and historical models for Rother, including the Langobard kings Authari and Rothari, Roger of Sicily, and Friedrich Barbarossa, see Kerth, pp. 21–31.
27. See in particular Stock, *Kombinationssinn*; Jan-Dirk Müller, 'Ratgeber und Wissende in heroischer Epik', *Frühmittelalterliche Studien*, 27 (1993), 125–46; and Fuchs-Jolie, 'Rother, Roland und die Rituale'.
28. All line numbers and quotations are from *König Rother: Mittelhochdeutscher Text und neuhochdeutsche Übersetzung*, ed. by Ingrid Bennewitz and trans. by Peter K. Stein (Stuttgart: Reclam, 2000).
29. Some studies of *König Rother* have, however, challenged its double structure. Gudula Dinser, *Kohärenz und Struktur: Textlinguistische und erzähltechnische Untersuchungen von König Rother* (Cologne and Vienna: Böhlau, 1975) suggests a tripartite structure for the plot, the first part (ll. 1–1900) consisting of wooing expeditions, the second (ll. 1901–3260) of winning and losing the bride, the third (ll. 3261–5197) of winning her back and returning home. This division would, according to her, be more suited to the oral delivery of the text. Christian Gellinek, *König Rother: Studie zur literarischen Deutung* (Bern: Francke, 1968), pp. 11–39, offers a more complex interpretation, with five sections within three acts ('Auftakt' within the first act, 'Brautwerbung und Eheschliessung', 'Gewinn und Verlust der Frau', and 'Wiedererringen der Frau' within the second, and 'Ausklang' within the third), although he does maintain the idea of two plot cycles.
30. Müller, *Höfische Kompromisse*, pp. 179–224. See also Caroline Walker Bynum, 'Did the Twelfth Century discover the individual?', *Journal of Ecclesiastical History*, 31 (1980), 1–17, who argues that the discovery of individuality in the twelfth century is linked with choice and conscious identification with a social class or religious order, rather than a sense of personal 'uniqueness' in the modern sense.

31. Müller, *Höfische Kompromisse*, p. 172.
32. Ibid., pp. 29-34, for a detailed explanation of the term 'Erzählkern'.
33. Ibid., pp. 195-204, on these two texts.
34. Stock, *Kombinationssinn*, p. 280: 'Die Zweiteiligkeit des *König Rother* bleibt einem Prinzip des Erzählens verpflichtet, das nicht an Korrektur oder gar Verunsicherung der Adelidentität interessiert ist. Der zweite Teil ist nicht die Alternative, die den Spielraum für neue Sinnstiftungen eröffnet, sondern im wesentlichen Affirmation des bereits im ersten Teil dargestellten Programms.'
35. Müller, *Höfische Kompromisse*, p. 178.
36. Ibid., p. 182.
37. The number seventy-two appears frequently in medieval texts, referring to the seventy-two descendants of Noah's sons, who populate the whole of the earth after the flood (Genesis 10:1-32). In this case it seems to point to the vast extent of Rother's kingdom.
38. Rolf Bräuer, *Literatursoziologie und epische Struktur der deutschen Spielmanns- und Heldendichtung* (Berlin: Akademie-Verlag, 1970), pp. 52-67, and Maria Dobozy, *Full Circle: Kingship in the German Epic; Alexanderlied, Rolandslied, Spielmannsepen* (Göppingen: Kümmerle, 1985), pp. 67-89.
39. Stock, *Kombinationssinn*, p. 274.
40. Müller, 'Ratgeber und Wissende', p. 125. See also Schröder, 'König Rother', pp. 331-32, who argues that Rother's marriage is a 'staatspolitische Unternehmung des Regenten'. On 'Fernliebe' in general, see Horst Wenzel, 'Fernliebe und Hohe Minne: Zur räumlichen und zur sozialen Distanz in der Minnethematik', in *Liebe als Literatur: Aufsätze zur erotischen Dichtung in Deutschland*, ed. by Rüdiger Krohn (Munich: Beck, 1983), pp. 187-208; Rüdiger Schnell, *Causa Amoris: Liebeskonzeption und Liebesdarstellung in der mittelalterlichen Literatur* (Bern: Francke, 1985), pp. 275-86; and Müller, *Höfische Kompromisse*, pp. 364-66.
41. Müller, 'Ratgeber und Wissende', pp. 129-30.
42. Peter K. Stein, '*Do newistich weiz hette getan. Ich wolde sie alle ir slagen hanc*: Beobachtungen und Überlegungen zum *König Rother*', in *Festschrift für Ingo Reiffenstein zum 60. Geburtstag*, ed. by Peter K. Stein and others (Göppingen: Kümmerle, 1998), pp. 309-38 (pp. 319-21), discusses this passage through the notion of 'Relativierung'. He suggests that the ideal 'types' of character presented in the text are difficult to realize, so must be relativized in order to increase their believability; the wise Berchter therefore here undergoes a process of 'Vermenschlichung'.
43. Fuchs-Jolie, 'Gewalt, Text, Ritual', pp. 184-86, understands this scene as an instance of the necessary paradox of quelling violence with violence in a ritual situation (in this case the council scene). We are made aware of the option of using violence (in Berchter's suggestion of attacking Constantinople), but in order to prevent the use of it and maintain an ideal ritual situation, violence must be employed. See also Schmitz, pp. 177-80, who uses this scene as an example of the way in which the characters, rather than the narrator, extract meaning from the action. In this case, Berchter's 'failed' judgement stresses the importance of the council and his use of violence — which *is* beneficial to the general good — allows the reader to realize that his previous 'violent' suggestion was not.
44. Other examples of the same technique include Witold (ll. 759-73), Wolfrat (ll. 3476-79), and Berchter (ll. 3496-511; ll. 5080-88).
45. Stock, *Kombinationssinn*, p. 258: 'Die auf der römischen Herrschau auftretenden Riesen können [...] als Signale dafür gelten, daß der Herrscher und sein Verband kein gründsätzliches Defizit haben, das zu bearbeiten wäre; sie haben alles, was sie zur Idealität brauchen, und können sich nun einzig um die generationsübergreifende Dauer dieser Idealität Sorgen machen.'

46. Kiening, 'Arbeit am Muster', p. 231, cites the giants as an example of a remaining trace of oral, 'archaic' storytelling, arguing that they primarily represent archaic violence, not yet entirely overcome: 'An ihnen wird eine rudimentäre Form hierarchischer Ordnung und eine untere Schwelle 'höfischer' Sozialisation sichtbar, mit ihrer Fixierung auf das Physische zugleich die Grenze einer höfischen Gewaltreglementierung markiert, die ihrerseits die 'archaische' Gewalt noch nicht völlig überwunden hat.'
47. Schröder, 'König Rother', p. 330, states that the giants 'funktional die ungeheuere militärische Macht Rothers bedeuten'. See also Hubertus Fischer, 'Gewalt und ihre Alternativen: Erzähltes politisches Handeln im *König Rother*', in *Gewalt und ihre Legitimation im Mittelalter: Symposium des Philosophischen Seminars der Universität Hannover vom 26. bis 28. Februar 2002*, ed. by Günther Mensching (Würzburg: Königshausen & Neumann, 2003), pp. 204-34 (pp. 213-14).
48. Rita Zimmermann, *Herrschaft und Ehe: Die Logik der Brautwerbung im König Rother* (Frankfurt a. M.: Lang, 1993), pp. 15-21, whose study focuses on the historical reality of medieval kingship, discusses the importance of 'Gewaltfähigkeit' for medieval rulers, the violent potential imperative for maintaining power.
49. Kiening, 'Arbeit am Muster', pp. 234-35, argues that Ymelot is a 'deus ex machina' figure who allows the conflict between Rother and Constantin to be solved without violent aggression towards one another. On a compositional level, he is the scapegoat who enables 'das Aggressionsmoment, das jede gefährliche Brautwerbung enthält' (p. 235).
50. See in particular Kiening, 'Arbeit am Muster', pp. 229-35, Fischer, pp. 213-19, and Fuchs-Jolie, 'Gewalt, Text, Ritual'.
51. Fischer, pp. 210-11.
52. Müller, 'Ratgebende und Wissende', pp. 133, 137, discusses the usual absence of the king during decision-making in institutionalized orders of government.
53. The only occasion when the disguise slips is not long after it is assumed, when Dietrich is unexpectedly referred to as 'Rother' by Asprian (l. 941), presumably as a moment of comedy or suspense for the audience; Constantin notices nothing and Asprian never has any problem dissimulating again. Kiening, 'Arbeit am Muster', pp. 230-31, interprets the giants as a kind of latent uncourtliness threatening to break through, and argues that Constantin does not notice the inconsistency of disguise here because that would not fit into the compositional motivation.
54. For a discussion of Iwein's loss of name, see Müller, *Höfische Kompromisse*, pp. 195-99.
55. Contrary to this, see Ortmann and Ragotzky, p. 328, who argue that Rother's honour is damaged by the capture of the messengers; hence the princess cannot be won and Rother's supremacy asserted without their being freed.
56. Schröder, 'König Rother', pp. 333-34, Fischer, pp. 216-17.
57. Kiening, 'Arbeit am Muster', pp. 225-26.
58. She comments similarly in ll. 1466-68; ll. 1175-97; l. 1805. On the queen as narrative commentator, see Schmitz, pp. 180-84. She is usually considered to be a positive figure; see Kerth, pp. 71-73 and Kiening, 'Arbeit am Muster', p. 226, who states that she is a voice of reason. It also reflects particularly badly on Constantin's kingship and masculinity that he has a wife who criticizes him constantly; Schröder, 'König Rother', p. 330, uses the example of the queen to provide a constrast between Rother's practice of advice and Constantin's lack of it: 'was er [Constantin] hätte tun sollen, erfährt er immer erst hinterher, wenn er durch sein unkluges Verhalten in Not geraten ist, aus dem Munde seiner Gattin'. See also Ferdinand Urbanek, *Kaiser, Grafen und Mäzene im König Rother* (Berlin: Schmidt, 1976), pp. 130-32, who argues that the prominence and behaviour of the queen might reflect the historical reality of Byzantine empresses.

59. We know from the *Kaiserchronik* that Dietrich was already the subject of worldly stories in the twelfth century: *Die Kaiserchronik eines Regenburger Geistlichen*, ed. by Edward Schröder (MGH, Scriptorum qui vernacula lingua usi sunt, vol. 1) (Hannover: Hahn, 1892), ll. 14176–87, uses chronology to reject the truthfulness of stories about Dietrich and Etzel. On the possibility of a connection between *König Rother* and epic stories of Dietrich, see Elisabeth Lienert, *Die 'historische' Dietrichepik: Untersuchungen zu 'Dietrichs Flucht', 'Rabenschlacht' und 'Alpharts Tod'* (Berlin and New York: de Gruyter, 2010), p. 37: '[O]b *König Rother* [...], dessen Held als angeblicher Exilant *Thi[e]derich* in Konstantinopel um Kaiser Konstantins Tochter wirbt, als Zeugnis der Dietrichsage gelten kann, ist fraglich; auffällig ist allerdings die Verbindung des Namens Dietrich mit dem Exilmotiv'. The name Thidrek is also taken by the disguised Osantrix in the *Vilcinasaga*, but the direct influence of one text on the other is impossible to prove. See *The Saga of Thidrek of Bern*, pp. 28–29, and Klein, 'Zur Thidreks Saga'.
60. Fuchs-Jolie, 'Rother, Roland und die Rituale', p. 172: 'Er ist höfisches Symbol für die Herrschaft des Königs über den König der Tiere, allein, daß er nicht Beherrschung und kultivierte Zähmung der Naturgewalt repräsentiert, sondern tatsächlich agiert als Drohinstrument eines Despoten, und als dann tatsächlich handelnde Figur gerade Nicht-Beherrschung der naturhaften Gewalt am sich doch sonst zivilisiert gerierenden Hof anzeigt.'
61. Dagmar Neuendorff, 'Kaiser und Könige, Grafen und Herzöge im Epos von König Rother', *Neuphilologische Mitteilungen*, 85 (1984), 45–58, makes the point that all dukes in *König Rother* are portrayed negatively, possibly indicative of a negative treatment of a potential patron of the text in the twelfth-century process of territorialization, which benefited dukes. Problematically, however, Berchter is sometimes referred to as a duke, something that Neuendorff attempts to solve (pp. 54–55).
62. Fear of the giants also causes Constantin to lie rather transparently earlier in the text. When Dietrich and his men arrive at his court, he crows over his treatment of Rother and his messengers, causing Asprian to reach for his armour; Constantin excuses himself by claiming that his men have made him drunk (ll. 1016–29).
63. Stock, *Kombinationssinn*, pp. 262–63, also points out that this scene causes damage to Constantin's honour, as it demonstrates that he does not understand the importance of status etiquette and how to perform effectively the 'event' of 'herrscherliche Repräsentation'.
64. Schröder, 'König Rother', p. 341: 'die Macht Rothers bleibt gegenüber Constantin und den Seinen immer eine bloße Macht in potentia. Eine Reihe von Szenen, so vor allem die der Riesen, erhalten von dieser Funktion her ihren possenhaften Charakter. Man sieht die Riesen nicht im Kampf, sonder immer nur wie im Schauspiel.'
65. Ortmann and Ragotzky, p. 329, argue that this use of *milte* signals a 'Zielsituation'; see also Fuchs-Jolie, 'Rother, Roland und die Rituale', p. 181. On the function of generosity, see Hartmut Kokott, *Literatur und Herrschaftsbewußtsein. Wertstrukturen der vor- und frühhöfischen Literatur: Vorstudien zur Interpretation mittelhochdeutscher Texte* (Frankfurt a. M.: Lang, 1978), p. 111.
66. Kokott, p. 113, also notes that this cunning prevents the death of any of Dietrich's or Constantin's men.
67. On the parallels between this scene and Dietrich's cunning, see Stock, *Kombinationssinn*, pp. 267–68. See also Jan de Vries, 'Die Schuhepisode im König Rother', *ZfdPh* 80 (1961), 129–41 (p. 133), who argues that the Spielmann-episode is based on the same model as the 'Schuhprobe' scene.
68. Wenzel, pp. 190–92, suggests that in cases of 'Fernliebe' the ear replaces the eye as the door to the soul and therefore the means of falling in love.

69. Monika Schulz, 'Iz ne wart nie urouwe bas geschot': Bemerkungen zur Kemenatenszene im *König Rother*', in *Literarische Kommunikation und soziale Interaktion: Studien zur Institutionalität mittelalterlicher Literatur*, ed. by Beate Kellner, Ludger Lieb, and Peter Strohschneider (Frankfurt a. M. and Oxford: Lang, 2001), pp. 73–88. She argues that there is no possibility that the princess is an unwitting party, tricked by Dietrich into trying on the shoe (an 'Ehepfand') and thus becoming betrothed to him; her very act of sending Herlint back to him for the shoe for her second foot should be read as an acceptance of marriage. The mutuality of the betrothal and the active role of the princess are stressed to a greater extent by Kerth, pp. 120–42, who argues that she carries out her own 'bridal quest'. See also Hans Fromm, 'Die Erzählkunst des *Rother*-Epikers', *Euphorion*, 54 (1960), 347–79 and de Vries, 'Die Schuhepisode'.
70. Stock, *Kombinationssinn*, pp. 263–64.
71. See Schröder, 'König Rother', p. 334, on the princess's love for Rother: 'Die Liebe entzündet sich ja nicht an der Person des Mannes, sondern ist eine Wirkung von dessen Macht, die auf *tugend* ('Tüchtigkeit') beruht. So genügt das bloße Wissen um Rothers Herrschermacht, die Liebe zu entfachen: die Schönste liebt den Stärksten.'
72. Clemens Lugowski, *Form, Individuality and the Novel: An Analysis of Narrative Structure in Early German Prose*, trans. by John Dixon Halliday (Norman: University of Oklahoma Press, 1990), esp. pp. 19–21.
73. Kiening, 'Arbeit am Muster', pp. 224–25, states that the messengers' illogical lack of recognition means that the moment of recognition is made more dramatic and public: 'Rothers Präsenz wird nicht einfach effektvoll hergestellt, sondern zugleich in einem immanenten Schauraum vorgestellt'.
74. Armin Schulz, *Schwieriges Erkennen: Personenidentifizierung in der mittelhochdeutschen Epik* (Tübingen: Niemeyer, 2008), p. 205.
75. On Arnolt's appearance, see Kokott, p. 166.
76. The negative portrayal of the Dießen house in *König Rother* is one reason for assuming a Welfish patron for the text; the enmity between the two families is well-attested. See Bumke, *Mäzene im Mittelalter*, p. 94.
77. See for example ll. 3644–49; ll. 4263–68; ll. 4617–19.
78. Stein, '*Do newistich weiz hette getan*', p. 326, argues that holding an advice scene under the table is comic, taking the motif one step too far; I see no reason why this should be the case, given that asking advice is an inescapable part of the system.
79. Schröder, 'König Rother', p. 343. See also Stein, '*Do newistich weiz hette getan*', p. 326, who discusses the constant implied (or 'erzählerisch') presence of Rother's army, ensuring his security even in their physical absence.
80. Stock, *Kombinationssinn*, p. 273: 'Die Gefangennahme Rothers ist nicht ein Sich-Gefangennehmen-Lassen als ein weiterer Ausweis des Listhandelns Rothers. Vielmehr ist sie Folge der neuen Weltsituation, in der Rother nicht mehr — wie im ersten Teil — aufgrund seiner *liste* innehat; die Aufgabe, die Rother und sein Verband zu bewältigen haben, ist umso schwieriger; in dieser neuen Situation gerät Rother in konkrete Todesgefahr.'
81. Ibid., p. 272: 'im ersten Teil war das Erzählen entweder protagonistenzentriert, oder wo es das nicht war, erschien die Handlung von der List des Protagonisten determiniert beziehungsweise zumindest planend abgedeckt. Mit dem zweiten Teil des retrospektiven *recken*-Berichts wird nun ein der Kenntnis und dem Einfluß des Protagonisten entzogener Strang der Erzählung nachgereicht.' Stock has contradicted this opinion in a more recent essay: Stock, 'Sich sehen lassen: Die Visibilität des Helden und der höfische Sichtraum in *König Rother*', in *Sehen und Sichtbarkeit in der deutschen Literatur des Mittelalters*, ed. by Ricarda Bauschke, Sebastian Coxon, and Martin Jones

(Berlin: Akademie, 2011), pp. 228–39. Here, he argues that Rother's revealing himself is the final part of a process of making himself publically visible and acts therefore as a demonstration of power and legitimacy.
82. Kiening, 'Arbeit am Muster', p. 228: 'das Spiel mit Präsenz und Absenz schafft ungleiche Wissensverhältnisse und mit diesen die Möglichkeit, die Machtverhältnisse sukzessive zu verändern'.
83. On Rother's prospective death by hanging, see Stock, 'Sich sehen lassen', pp. 236–37.
84. Schröder, 'König Rother', p. 329: 'Rother kämpft nicht, er regiert. Es soll nicht der Held, sondern der König und Kaiser dargestellt werden'.
85. Stein, '*Do newistich weiz hette getan*', pp. 329–30: 'die religiöstranszendentale Dimension ist abgebaut, indem Innerweltlichkeit an die Stelle der Überweltlichkeit, Rother an die Stelle Gottes gesetzt wird'.
86. Ortmann and Ragotzky argue that *König Rother* acts as political propaganda, reflecting the ideals and challenges of the Hohenstaufen era, particularly the feud between Friedrich I and Manuel I of the Byzantine Komnenus dynasty. See also Schröder, 'König Rother', pp. 346–47, who discusses the problem of unifying the worldly and religious, which he sees as particularly symptomatic of the reign of Friedrich I (1152–1190).
87. None of the religious emphasis in this section of the text is at odds with what has come before. Schröder, 'König Rother', p. 339, discusses the seeming incongruity of the pious speeches of the giants (ll. 4398–4458): 'die Analyse geht falsche Wege, wenn sie etwa das Ungeschlacht-Groteske der Riesen und ihre zuweilen sentimental-erbaulichen Reden für einen inneren Widerspruch hält. Die Riesen sind die militärisch stärkste Kraft Rothers, aber natürlich sind sie auch Christen. Und so erscheinen sie ja nach der Funktion als dies oder das — aber nie beides zugleich. Es wird nicht ein starker und frommer Mensch dargestellt, sondern Stärke und Frömmigkeit bei einem Menschen.'
88. Ibid., pp. 348–49, points out that the lands Rother divides between his men were those controlled by the Staufen dynasty in the twelfth century. They did, however, lose Bavaria in 1156 to Henry the Lion, which could indicate that *König Rother* was composed before this date; Schröder thinks the opposite, and that Rother's empire suggests an ideal, unified world picture.
89. Neuendorff, pp. 49–50.
90. See Reiffenstein, p. 563, on how these two passages about Charlemagne frame the second bridal quest. On the way in which Charlemagne is used to demonstrate the validity of *König Rother*, see Rüdiger Schnell, 'Zur Karls-Rezeption in *König Rother* und in Ottes *Eraclius*', PBB, 104 (1982), 345–58. Schnell draws a connection between the text and Gottfried of Viterbo's *Speculum regum* (1183), which also suggests Byzantine ancestry for Charlemagne, albeit through his mother Bertha.
91. Uwe Meves, *Studien zu König Rother, Herzog Ernst und Grauer Rock (Orendel)* (Frankfurt a. M.: Lang, 1976), pp. 69–99, and Urbanek, pp. 216–22, have made a case for the Tengelingen as the patrons of *König Rother*. The fact that the Tengelingen split in the twelfth century into the houses of Peilstein-Hall and Burghausen-Schala, losing much of their influence, has proved problematic for this argument, as well as for the dating of the text.
92. In this respect Kiening, 'Arbeit am Muster', p. 237, discusses the strategy of historicization, which turns to a past that related to the present in both its alterity and modernity, 'die Vergegenwärtigung der als historisch Ausgewiesenen in einer sich darauf beziehenden Jetztzeit'. References to the Tengelingen and other families and the various associations of the name 'Rother' provide an aura of semi-referential, vague historicity: 'Indem das Epos mit obskuren und multiplen Referenzen auf die historische Wirklichkeit operiert, kann es einen Ursprungsmythos begründen, der im Spannungsfeld von Kontinuität und Diskontinuität die erzählte Welt und eine zeitgenössich erfahrene überblendet'

(p. 239). The timeless nature of Rother's kingship is also discussed by Ortmann and Ragotzky, p. 333, who state that the 'lehensrechtlich definierte Idealität der Rother-Herrschaft reich bis in die mythische Vorzeit zurück (vgl. die Riesen). Die expansiven Möglichkeiten der Rother-Herrschaft sind so unbegrenzt wie ihre über die historische Zeit hinausreichende Geltung'.

93. This stone also appears in Herzog Ernst, ll. 4456–65, where it is called *der weise* and said still to shine in the imperial crown. In Pfaffe Lambrecht, *Alexanderroman*, ed. and trans. by Elisabeth Lienert (Stuttgart: Reclam, 2007), l. 6484f., Alexander is also given such a stone when he reaches the gates of paradise; it is here also a symbol of the humility of man.

CHAPTER 2

Salman und Morolf: Salme and Morolf

In the mid-nineteenth century August Koberstein admitted in his *Grundriß der Geschichte der deutschen National-Litteratur* that he was at a loss to know what to do with *Salman und Morolf*:

> Endlich ist hier noch des seinem Inhalte nach mit keinem der übrigen Sagenkreise zusammenhängenden strophischen Gedichts von Salman und Morolt zu gedenken, das von einem Volksdichter oder Fahrenden herrührt und diesen Ursprung weniger als irgend ein anderes Werk des zwölften Jahrhunderts in seinem Inhalt, seiner Behandlung und seiner Form verleugnet.[1]

As the genre of *Spielmannsepik* subsequently developed as a literary historical category, the sense of confusion about *Salman und Morolf* disappeared. It came to be regarded as the most 'spielmännisch' of the *Spielmannsepen*, thanks to its humorous content and mixture of material from Orient and Occident;[2] furthermore, it came to be considered by some as the oldest of the texts, thanks to its supposed influence on the second half of *König Rother*, an opinion now discounted.[3] But then, as the notion of *Spielmannsepik* came under increasing suspicion, the difficulty of the classification of *Salman und Morolf* again became apparent. De Boor attempted to understand the so-called *Spielmannsepen* by dividing them into more adventurous, 'spielmännisch' texts (*König Rother* and *Herzog Ernst*) on the one hand and 'Legendenromane' (*Salman und Morolf, Der Münchner Oswald, Grauer Rock*) on the other, and his terminology was also adopted by several subsequent literary histories. Such terminology is hardly satisfactory, however, and even de Boor admitted that *Salman und Morolf* is short on religious motifs.[4] Indeed, its relationship to biblical tales of Solomon is very slight and it cannot be read as an example of the medieval understanding of the biblical king.[5]

When scholarship turned to the bridal-quest schema in order to interpret the former *Spielmannsepen*, a new way of reading *Salman und Morolf* developed: it came to be seen as a text that 'plays' with the schema and inverts it, overturning or overstepping expected norms. The bridal-quest is turned upside-down, with heathen kings coming for Salman's baptized wife, Salme, herself a negative character; religion is arguably parodied; the comic-grotesque aspect is emphasized; the expected role of king and hero is upset in the figure of Morolf. This principle characterizes one current trend of scholarship on the text. Haug, developing his idea that the writing down of oral forms necessarily brings about reflection upon them, argues that the 'upside-down' bridal quest in *Salman und Morolf* does not create positive reflection on the bridal-quest schema, but rather allows enjoyment in brutality, obscenity, and magic.[6] The idea of the 'upside-down' quest is taken further by Bachorski, who demonstrates how the text upsets a large number of expected norms, of both story-type and character; he argues that this is a characteristic of all *Spielmannsepen*, written at a time before the formation of the main genres of the 'Blütezeit'.[7] For Neudeck, the overstepping and overturning of boundaries is the founding narrative principle of the text, constituting its fictionality and suggesting that the version of the story we have can be dated to the later Middle Ages; Schulz's reading depends on the 'Umcodierung' of the bridal-quest 'Erzählmuster' and the numerous 'Irritationen' of the text, highlighted in the corrective epilogue added to its printed editions.[8]

Another, counterposed, trend in current scholarship is to insist on a harmonious moral principle behind the text, namely the importance of faithful worldly *minne* not founded on blind lust and sexual desire; according to this interpretation Morolf restores harmony by doing away with Salme, the epitome of the 'unfaithful woman' who has reduced Salman to a 'Minnesklave', replacing her with Afra, *ein getruwes wip* (str. 781a, 5).[9] Such an argument is reminiscent — even if rarely explicitly — of Curschmann's study of *Spielmannsepik*, which argues that the fundamental principle of all the texts is an attempt to construct an ideal kind of love in the world, which is pleasing to God; this attempt, Curschmann asserts, finds its culmination in the works of Wolfram.[10] Critics who put forward such interpretations tend to suggest a twelfth-century dating, or at least a relationship between *Salman und Morolf* and courtly love literature. For Griese, Morolf's conscious wooing of Afra is of the utmost importance, something also stressed by Haug, in whose opinion the text is saved from degeneracy by this new bride and Morolf's love for his brother.[11] Miklautsch argues against the validity of the bridal-quest schema as a generic model, yet returns to the Curschmann-influenced line of interpretation, arguing that *Salman und Morolf* consists in a discussion of the potential dangers of love.[12] Bornholdt goes one step further, asserting that *Salman und Morolf* is a didactic text for lay people.[13]

I shall return to both of these lines of interpretation later in this chapter, but it is important to discuss first the possible origins of *Salman und Morolf* and the medieval Solomon tradition. These are complex and — as we have already seen for *König Rother*, and will see for the *Münchner Oswald* and *Grauer Rock* — unique and independent from the supposed generic model of the bridal quest. *Salman und Morolf* is part of a literary tradition, related to stories in which the wisdom of Solomon is pitted against the irreverent wit of the peasant Markolf in dialogue form. Stories about King Solomon and a Markolf-figure are first explicitly attested by Notker in the late tenth century, who condemns Markolf's undermining responses to Solomon's proverbs as heretical lies,[14] and such stories are frequently mentioned throughout the Middle Ages.[15] The very number of references to arguments between Solomon and Markolf indicates the popularity of such stories in Western Europe and Lambert of Ardres's *Historia comitum Ghisnensium* of 1194 makes this explicit, pointing to a specifically lay and courtly milieu for their reception.[16]

The earliest extant manuscripts of the dialogue between Solomon and Markolf, in both Latin and German, are, however, from the fifteenth century. There are at least twenty-eight manuscripts and a large number of printed editions of the *Dialogus Salomonis et Marcolfi*, which consists of two parts, a verbal argument between Solomon and the ugly, cunning peasant Markolf, and a series of comic episodes playing out the difference between wisdom and cunning, with cunning always gaining the upper hand.[17] The *Dialogus* was adapted into the vernacular as the so-called *Markolfs buch* (or *Spruchgedicht*), transmitted in four extant (and one burnt) fifteenth-century manuscripts;[18] there are also a fifteenth-century prose redaction and *Fastnacht* plays.[19] The epic *Salman und Morolf* does not follow the same principle as these other texts: Morolf is now the brother of Salman, the king of Jerusalem, and uses his considerable *list* to twice recapture Salman's wife, Salme, who has been kidnapped by heathen kings. It is transmitted in three full fifteenth-century manuscripts (E, S, and P) and three fragments (D, M, and the privately owned Gü); another manuscript, Cod. b 81 of the Strassburg Johanniterbibliothek (St), was burnt in 1870. There are also two prints, both from Strassburg, the first (d) made by Mathis Hüpffuff in 1499, the second (d') in 1510 by Johannes Knoblauch.[20]

It is difficult to get to the bottom of the dependency of epic and 'Spruch' on one another. Both traditions distort and adapt various Solomon legends in different directions; legends which, based on Oriental, Arabic and Hebrew myths, arrived in the medieval West via Byzantium.[21] 'Bridal-quest' themes can be found in the Oriental myth of Solomon winning the foreign queen Balqis, and there is also the widespread myth of his battles with the demon Aschmedai (in the Hebrew tradition) or Schamir (Arabic) who steals the magic ring or stone in which all his power is contained, which can be considered the origin of the magic rings used to seduce Salme. Equally, traces of Aschmedai, Solomon's 'opponent', can be found in the characters of Salme and Markolf. Other myths circulate about Solomon's heathen wife, the daughter of the Pharaoh — mentioned in I Rg. 3:1 — through whom he becomes a slave to love and is made to worship idols. Solomon's weakness for women is also intimated in the bible: *rex autem Salomon amavit mulieres alienigenas multas [...] cumque iam esset senex depravatum est per mulieres cor eius ut sequeretur deos alienos nec erat cor eius perfectum cum Domino Deo suo* (I Rg 11:1/4).[22] He appears frequently in medieval literature — both didactic and otherwise — as an example of a slave to love or to the charms of women.[23]

Yet the main focus in both the epic and 'Spruch' is the relationship between Solomon and Markolf/Morolf. In both, he is a figure against whom King Solomon is pitted, and who outdoes the king with his wit and cunning (although this only occurs in direct competition in the 'Spruch' tradition). There are some direct parallels: the 'Ofenschwank' episode, where Markolf/Morolf exposes his bottom at Solomon, is found in the *Dialogus* (p. 43, ll. 22–24) as well as the epic (str. 140); moreover, some manuscripts of the *Dialogus* and all of the *Spruchgedicht* have an epilogue-section containing a shortened version of much the same course of events as the first half of the epic.[24] In the *Dialogus*, the (unnamed) wife is punished by having her nose and lips cut off,[25] whereas in the *Spruchgedicht* she is murdered in the bath by Markolf, without objection from Salman (ll. 1870–74). Older criticism argued either that the 'Spruch' epilogue bore the traces of a story older than the epic, thanks to its simpler form, or that it was an abbreviated version of the epic,[26] but current scholarship is now unanimous that the nature of the dependency between the epic and the Spruch tradition cannot be asserted. It is possible that they may have had the same original source, but development cannot be traced and respective dating is highly uncertain.[27]

Dating *Salman und Morolf* itself is also very difficult. The traditional twelfth-century dating is no longer regarded as a certainty, particularly if we are sceptical about either *Spielmannsepik* or *Brautwerbungsepik* as a generic category. The strophic form is unique to the text and is no longer regarded as evidence of oral, early medieval origins — perhaps even the opposite. The so-called 'Morolfstrophe', consisting of five verses with a rhyme scheme of aabcb, is found nowhere else in medieval poetry, its closest relative being the so-called 'Lindenschmidtstrophe' (4a4a3b4x3b), mainly used for historical and political songs in the fifteenth and sixteenth centuries.[28] Chrétien de Troyes's romance *Cligés*, written in 1176, gives proof of the existence of some kind of story thematically similar to *Salman und Morolf* when it refers to the pretend death of the wife of Solomon: *Lors lor sovint de Salemon, | Que sa fame tant le haï, | Qu'an guise de mort le trahi*.[29] Stories of Solomon's wife were therefore presumably circulating in twelfth-century France, but there is nothing to suggest they would have been written down — there is nothing extant — or would have borne a great deal of similarity to the fifteenth-century manuscripts of *Salman und Morolf*. There is also a reference to Morolf's murder of the Jew in the fourteenth-century 'Märe' *Frau Metze* by Arme Konrad, which shows that some version of the story must have been current at this time, but we do not know how it may have changed.[30] All we know for certain is that *Salman und Morolf* was popular in the fifteenth century and read by members of the nobility, but otherwise the transmission tells us little.[31] MSs E, S, P, and D and both prints are all either illustrated or have space left for illustrations — not unusual for manuscripts of this period — and MS E also contains the text of *Markolfs buch*. The burnt MS St was a 'Heldenbuch' manuscript, in which *Salman und Morolf* was found (perhaps curiously) between *Rosengarten* and *Ortnit*. MS S also contains *Wilhelm von Orlens*, but the texts were bound together from two different manuscripts in the sixteenth century.

Intertextual connections also tell us little. *Salman und Morolf* certainly shares motifs with *König Rother* — the capture of the bride by a cunning minstrel and the gallows rescue scene, when the king blows a horn to summon his hidden army — but it shares just as many motifs with other stories. In *Cligés*, Fenice, the wife of the emperor of Constantinople, fakes her own death so she can be with her lover and molten lead is poured through her palms by doctors doubting that she is dead; in the same way, Morolf pours molten gold through Salme's palm. Chrétien also states that Fenice's actions led all future emperors to keep their wives locked in a sea-bound tower, reminiscent of the tower Salme is kept in by Princian to keep her safe from Morolf.[32] It is impossible to tell whether Chrétien was influenced by already extant stories of the wife of Solomon, but it is clear that *Salman und Morolf* may have developed from a variety of models. There are also references to the *Nibelungenlied* in the description of Salme, which bears similarity to that of Kriemhild, and her 'Falkentraum', as well as to Tristan stories with the drinking of a magic potion to cause love and the mention of a King Isolt, a character otherwise unattested. Yet none of the above is direct intertextuality — other texts or stories are never mentioned explicitly and most connections could be attributed to shared topoi or story motifs.

Perhaps Koberstein was right to be perplexed by *Salman und Morolf*. I do not want to attempt to date the text for, although the story-matter is almost certainly very old, it is impossible to tell how it was changed and developed as it was written down, and when any of these changes may have occurred. Instead, through close readings of its two main characters (or rather, the characters who constitute the drive and action of the narrative), I hope to understand the inner workings of the text. As I have said, most scholarship on *Salman und Morolf* either concentrates on describing the individual work's deviations from a presumed generic norm or attempts a harmonious, moral reading, according to which the author is promoting an ideal form of love in the world. In this chapter, I intend to take these two ways of reading — which I find valid yet simultaneously limited — as a springboard for my discussion of the text. First, I will discuss the dangerous love personified by Salme, which I will argue constitutes the drive of the narrative and therefore undermines any potential moral purpose; second, I will examine the character of Morolf, who plays by rules that are different from those of anyone else, and who always succeeds in restoring harmony even as he disrupts it. If there is a moral to the story, then it is often difficult to find; and if boundaries are crossed, then they are always restored.

Salme, the Danger of Love, and the Drive of the Narrative

For a text often thought of as 'odd' and heterogeneous, *Salman und Morolf* has a remarkably uncomplicated style. Nothing is ever marked up as unusual and there is hardly any narrative commentary; the text is stylistically very simple and direct, with a good deal of direct speech.[33] There is no allegory, hardly any simile, and — other than the lengthy introductory description of Salme and one strophe on the subject of a chessboard — no ekphrasis or descriptive asides. Very little is taken for granted — we are told exactly how Morolf effects his disguises, for example (this is discussed in more detail below) — and causality is generally made very plain. Even if some matters, such as Salme's responsibility with regard to her own kidnapping and the effectiveness of the magic rings, are ambiguous, the style of the narrative makes it very clear that one thing leads to another without confusion; this is also the case in passages of direct speech, in which one speaker always speaks most definitely in response to what the other has just said. The narrative can be accelerated and slowed down — battles, for instance, are described fleetingly — but never changes in its straightforward directness and lack of complication.

Salman und Morolf is a narrative of movement. I discussed in the introduction the futility of the idea of the bridal-quest schema as a generator of a specific meaning and the nature of the bridal quest as a loose and flexible story-motif that can be used in a variety of contexts. Here, questing for a bride constitutes the motive of the narrative, by which I mean that the entire text consists in movement towards one (moveable) goal: Salme. There are many different quests: Salman's original quest for Salme, completed before the story begins, but violent in its execution (str. 3); Fore's quest for Salme, the already-married potential bride; Morolf's quest to find Salme (but not bring her back), followed by a second quest to bring her back, this time accompanied by Salman. The process is then roughly repeated: Princian comes after Salme, Morolf goes to find her and then, this time unaccompanied by Salman, returns to fetch her. In the midst of this is another partial bridal quest, in which Morolf brings Fore's sister back to Jerusalem, who eventually marries Salman. A minstrel also travels across the sea after Fore's escape from Jerusalem to collect Salme for him and a king, Isolt, travels to Fore's kingdom after his death in an attempt to win Salme, making a total of nine journeys (including Salman's initial one, and not including return trips), eight of which are explicitly across the sea (Isolt's journey may not be), in one direction or another, with Salme as the target.[34]

With this in mind, it is striking that the story begins with a detailed description of Salme — the only such description in the text — and ends fairly abruptly after her death. The first strophe introduces Salman, briefly, and the second turns to his winning of a bride:

> Er nam ein wip von Endian,
> eins heiden dochter her und lobesam.
> durch sie wart manig helt verlorn.
> es war ein ubel stunde,
> das sie an die welt wart geborn. (str. 2)

The end of the description of Salme returns to this omen, framing all other details with the certainty of forthcoming trouble: *umb das vil wonder schone wip | muste manig stolczer ritter | verlieren sinen werden lip* (str. 20, 3–5). This introduction corresponds very closely to that of Kriemhild at the start of the *Nibelungenlied*:

> Ez wuohs in Búrgónden   ein vil édel magedîn,
> daz in allen landen   niht schoeners mohte sîn,
> Kríemhílt geheizen: si wart ein schoen wîp.
> dar umbe muosen degene   vil verlíesén den lîp.[35]

In both cases we are given 'Hinweise auf die Nicht-Idealität der Situation [...], die diese Ausgangslage unter ein Negativ-Vorzeichen setzt'.[36] In the *Nibelungenlied*, however, it is Kriemhild's love that brings about the downfall of so many, whereas in *Salman und Morolf* danger is posed by the love that others — Salman, Fore, Princian, Isolt — have for Salme, or rather Salme's power to make men fall madly in love with her.[37]

In the introductory description, the narrator first gives details of her Christian education as Salman's wife — she has been baptized, taught the psalter and how to play chess, a courtly activity prefiguring her central chess scene with Morolf, (str. 4) — then moves to her external appearance, which is described in conventional topoi. Her throat is white as snow (str. 5, 1), her mouth as red as a ruby (str. 5, 3), her eyes are bright (str. 5, 5), her hair as golden silk (str. 6, 1), her body well-formed (str. 6, 3). The description then moves to her attire: she is wearing white silk (str. 7, 2), a narrow golden belt (7, 3–5) and a robe covered with precious stones (8, 1–3). The culmination is a wondrous crown:

> die luchte recht als der sonnen schin.
> dar inne lag der liechte karfunckl stein.
> rechte als der morgen sterne
> ir antlitz [uz den] frauwen schein. (9, 2-5)

The sudden shift in this final line from the carbuncle back to the woman, resplendent above all others, inevitably draws a parallel between Salme's face and the precious stone, both glowing and radiant; it is as if she herself were a precious stone of the utmost beauty. This is a pertinent comparison, because Salme is, for almost every other character in the text, irresistibly alluring, a beautiful object to be possessed. The carbuncle is used metaphorically in many contexts in the literature of the Middle Ages; as a stone of the highest value, it always describes someone or something unusually precious.[38] It is often used as a metaphor for Mary — as is the morning star, to which the carbuncle in Salme's crown is compared — usually because of its particular glow, a true light in the darkness of sin.[39] Another interpretation, and one that is certainly valid here, is of the carbuncle as a metaphor for a lover or someone seeking love.[40]

The effects of Salme's appearance confirm the impression that she is an alluring object, even an alternative Mary to be worshipped. The static description is rendered active — *Das beschach* [...] (str. 10, 1) — and the reader's reaction to Salme (presumably s/he has envisaged her in his mind's eye) is repeated by the characters in the text who stare at her, entranced, and forget themselves. She is described entering church at Whitsun, holding a gold-lettered psalter in her white hand (str. 13), listening to the gospel, and donating a gold ring as her *opffer* (str. 14).[41] The effect she has at the banquet after mass is then depicted:

> Vor ir vil manig ritter saß,
> der siner sinne vil gar vergaß.
> in was zu schouwen also not.
> sie vergassent inn den henden
> beide win und brott. (str. 16)

Although we are no longer in the church, the mention of *win und brott* cannot help but be reminiscent of the Eucharist;[42] the knights forget their wine and bread in favour of a more worldly object of worship. Salman reacts in the same way — *Salmon selber nit enwuhst, | was geberden er von freuden solt han* (str. 18, 4-5) — and spends a good deal of time in his chamber, taking pleasure in his wife's snow-white arms (str. 19).

The treatment of Salme as an object of religious devotion continues throughout the text. She remains in her coffin after her fake death for three nights — a possible parody of the resurrection of Christ[43] — and the church, both Christian and heathen (they are described in exactly the same terms), is always the locus of actions involving her. The church would admittedly have been the place where noble ladies were most accessible to the public eye, but it is striking that Salme is seen either in or outside church so many times. Fore's minstrel meets her as she enters church (str. 121) and it is there that she consumes the magic herb that brings about her fake death (str. 124), rather like a perverse eucharist. Morolf first sees her in Fore's kingdom when she is entering the church (strs 196–99) and Princian meets her for the first time as she leaves it (str. 601).

The tone is set for the rest of the text: '[F]aszination durch sinnliche Schönheit'.[44] The heathen kings Fore, Princian, and Isolt have only heard about Salme's beauty, rather than seen her, yet are still desperate to possess her.[45] In each case, the result is disastrous, and the king in question dies along with many of his men. Salman, too, is unable to realize that Salme's outer beauty could pose a danger and not reflect inner virtue; he cannot understand why Morolf is against leaving the captured Fore in Salme's care (strs 84–90), refuses to believe that she is not really dead (strs 128–42), and accepts her pleas for forgiveness after she is caught with Fore, refusing to allow Morolf to hang her (strs 530–39). He is even distraught when Morolf kills her at the end of the text after she has been retrieved from her second heathen husband, Princian (str. 779). In each of these situations, Salman appears blinded by love and is unable to accept the explanations of Morolf, the only man to remain unaffected by Salme's beauty. It is made clear in the first of these instances that he is displaced from the role of the biblical Solomon when Morolf assumes it, judging the situation correctly and quoting a proverb to justify his statement:

> Morolff sprach: 'here, das duncket mich nit gut.
> wer strohe nahe bi fuwer dut,
> villicht entzundet es sich an.
> also beschicht dir mit konig Fore,
> wilt du ine bi diner frauwen lan.' (str. 85)[46]

The brothers argue; Salman cannot understand what Morolf has against Salme (str. 86) and Morolf says that Salman will bring *laster und schande* upon himself (str. 87, 3). The narrator sums up Salman's decision to place Fore under Salme's care: *da endet er nit wißlich an!* (str. 90, 3). Solomon is renowned for his wisdom; here Salman has lost his.

It is understandable why many scholars should argue that *Salman und Morolf* is about the dangers of love, for in this text, obsessive love for a woman brings about only disaster or shame. Some have gone so far as to suggest that it even offers a form of courtly critique, ridiculing courtly love and undermining the ideal portrayal of the woman.[47] Love in the world is not, however, depicted as hopeless, as Salman is offered a replacement wife in Fore's sister, whom Morolf brings to Jerusalem and baptizes. She remains nameless until the very end of the text when she is given the name Affer (Afra), presumably after the third-century martyr, daughter of the king of Cyprus and patron saint of Augsburg —

a name, therefore, with very different connotations to that of Salme (Salome).[48] Fore's sister, who is never described in detail (we know only that she is the most beautiful of Salme's ladies-in-waiting), is struck by Salman, rather than the other way about, thinking him the most beautiful man she has ever seen: *Es ist der aller schonste man, | den ie kein frauwe ie gewan* (str. 405, 1–2). After Salman is recognized and captured by Salme, she begs her brother to allow her to care for the prisoner and there follows a 'Kemenatenszene' of the kind common in Middle High German literature, in which the lovers sit together, talk, and play music (strs 463–76).[49] Salman forgets his sorrows (str. 467) and Fore's sister suggests to Salman that he escape (strs 471–72), despite promising her brother otherwise on pain of death (strs 456–57). The reader is aware by this stage that she is the suitable partner for Salman, not only because of this 'Kemenatenszene', which also echoes Salme's care for the imprisoned Fore, but also because Morolf has already 'won' her in his game of chess against Salme. This fact is of great importance to Griese, who argues that Morolf consciously sets out to find a replacement bride for Salman, one more suitable and in possession of *triuwe*.[50]

There are two ways of viewing Fore's sister as a corrective figure — either as the *getruwes wip* in comparison to the unfaithful Salme, or as the embodiment of a different kind of marital love, one that does not blind the male partner with lust and turn him into a slave to love. In this sense we can talk about her — and Salme — either in active or in passive terms, as women who have motivation or as women who provoke reactions in men. A simple reading along either of these lines is, however, problematic. First, there is almost no commentary by the narrator. The faithfulness of Fore's sister is mentioned only once (str. 781a, 5) and the only other narratorial comment is a strophe on the importance of *huote*:

> Da von so sol ein iglich bider man
> sin frouwe selber hutten lan.
> wan es wart nie kein hut so gut,
> wan die ein ieglich biderb wip
> nun ir selber tut. (str. 578)[51]

If this is meant to be the moral purpose of the text, then it is not hammered home. The end of the story is also curious in that it finishes very abruptly after Salme dies in her bath at the hands of Morolf, and we are told only the following about the marriage between Salman and Afra:

> Die was zu Jherusalem, das ist war,
> ein gewaltige kunigin
> vollenclichen dru und drissig jar,
> bitz das der edele kunige lobesam
> und auch sine werde minne
> gottes hulde da gewan. (str. 783)

The mention of *werde minne* — which could refer to Afra herself or to Salman's love for her — and the love of God does imply a superior relationship to that between Salman and Salme, but any comparison seems cursory and something of an afterthought. This could be one explanation for the rhyming-couplet epilogue to the text found in its printed editions, which describes in more detail — and in ideal terms — the marriage between Salman and Afra, their devotion to God and their children, as well as Morolf's repentance and acceptance into heaven.[52] The epilogue is usually considered a reaction to the 'irritations' of the preceding narrative, which it hopes to normalize and, most importantly, christianize: the negative presentation of love and marriage, the lack of dynastic succession, and the needless brutality of Morolf.[53] It is important to remember, though, that the epilogue does not give a complete picture of how *Salman und Morolf* was received in the fifteenth century, as it only appears in the prints and not the manuscripts. Moreover, it is striking that the redactor chose to add a distinctly separate epilogue — even in a different poetic form — rather than alter the main body of the text itself. Yet it does give us a good idea of contemporary opinions, and points, amongst other things, to the fact that Fore's sister is not established as a corrective replacement to Salme in the main body of the text with a sufficient degree of obviousness. It therefore draws into question the success — even the existence — of a didactic or moral purpose.

Furthermore, the motivation of both the women is ambiguous. Fore's sister is not an unquestionably ideal figure, agreeing only to be baptized after Morolf promises her she can marry Salman (strs 580–90), and the baptism scene itself is depicted rather comically, with the *juncfrouwen meister* lifting Fore's sister on to her lap and attempting to lift her to the font, complaining about her weight (str. 589). Salme's ambiguity is also discussed frequently, particularly with respect to her responsibility in her kidnap by the two heathen kings.[54] On the one hand, she is lured away by magic by both Fore and Princian; on the other, she appears to have a share of responsibility, unsatisfied as she is after Fore's death until another heathen comes after her with magic: *so mocht si kume fröude gehan, | biß das sie aber ein ander heiden | mit großem zouber ouch gewan* (str. 577, 3–5). She also conveniently blames her love for Fore on magic after he is captured, reasserting her love for Salman in order to save her own life, and is referred to later in the text as a *mortgrime wip*.

Salme's responsibility is, I would argue, essentially irrelevant. The point is rather that men fall obsessively in love with her, losing all reason — they become slaves to love. The idea of the 'Minnesklave' is set out in the seminal essay by Maurer, who argued that love is problematized differently throughout the course of the literature of the Middle Ages; the challenge to find the correct form of worldly love develops into a discourse concerning relinquishing worldly love altogether in favour of the love of God.[55] Schnell offers a critique of this definition of the 'Minnesklave', and finds Maurer's programme too simplistic, arguing instead that there is no clear developmental process. Moreover, he thinks it of vital importance to distinguish between the 'Minnesklave' and the 'Frauensklave' — the man who is conquered by love and the man who is conquered by woman — the latter of which is usually described in much more negative and misogynist terms. Solomon, as well as David and Samson, is used as a typical example in both contexts. The topos of the 'Frauensklave', he argues, is derived from Genesis exegesis and is usually found in didactic theological contexts, whereas the 'Minnesklave' is found in more courtly contexts and depicted in a more positive light. Here, it is a personified 'minne' that is the cause of the behaviour of the man, not the cunning of women, and there is no direct line of development from the more misogynistic 'Frauensklave' topos; instead of a 'realistic', flawed woman, the 'Minnesklave' topos centres around the abstract, idealized, fictional power of 'minne', who is also a narrative determinant.[56]

The distinction between the personified 'minne' and women (or a woman) is a useful one, but the problem with attempting to fit *Salman und Morolf* into this programme is that the text is neither primarily didactic nor courtly, although it does deal with the sort of themes discussed by Schnell.[57] The men in *Salman und Morolf* are certainly enslaved by a woman rather than by a personified 'minne', but, problematically, she appears only sometimes to be a human agent, the rest of the time an objectified 'thing' of the potential sexual lures of the female sex rather than anything specifically or personally evil. Thus the question of her guilt is largely irrelevant; it is more important that men want her and that she provokes lust, than that she wants men, and the very fact that men want her to such an extent makes her a negative figure. She certainly seems at times entirely objectified; she is the fire that will cause the straw to set alight (str. 85), later even an object so precious and desirable that she must be kept enclosed out of sight and reach in a *steine* in the sea, lest Morolf capture her. It is striking that the word used to describe her presence in this *steine* is *verwircket*, usually used of objects being 'worked in' to something and used in *Salman und Morolf* only of Salme (who is also *verwircket* into her coffin, str. 143) and of the *groß heiltum*, which is *verwircket* into Salman's ring (str. 653).[58] Salme is most active in her dealings with Morolf — unsurprisingly, as he is the only man in the text for whom she is not an object of desire.

If *Salman und Morolf* wants to offer a warning against the dangers of love, then it fails to do so, for three reasons. First, the narrative offers very little commentary and is mainly taken up with Morolf's own adventures and tricks when in pursuit of Salme, as will be discussed below. Second, the ambiguous construction of Salme as, on the one hand, a human agent and, on the other, an objective 'thing' that provokes reactions, makes it impossible to say unequivocally that Salme is a bad person or personifies a negative principle. This leads to the third reason: Salme — desiring her, wooing her, winning her — is the framing device for the whole text. We can return here to the enthralling description of Salme at the start of the text, to her being the goal and drive of the narrative and to the abrupt end of this narrative after her death. She is a fascinating object, the occasion of actions which are represented by stories, and being enthralled by her is much the same as being enthralled by the story. The great paradox of *Salman und Morolf* is that it takes a negative example and makes it desirable. Salme's desirability makes the story itself desirable and the reader *wants* people to go after her, *wants* Morolf to chase after her because it is entertaining. And as soon as she dies, so does the narrative. Paradoxically, by *being about* the dangers of enslavement to a woman or sexual desire, *Salman und Morolf* does not act as a polemic against it.

Morolf, Practical Knowledge, and Normative Behaviour

Within the framework of movement towards Salme, most of the action is carried out by Morolf; he is the main actor of the story and controls its outcome. Yet he has posed difficulties of interpretation because his character is difficult to pin down and thus seems to exemplify the overturning and overstepping of boundaries that so many scholars argue to be typical of the text. The important difference to the 'Spruch' tradition is the change in the relationship between Salman and Morolf; Markolf the peasant has become Morolf the king's brother. The narrative is not founded on antagonism or competition between the two men, as Morolf helps, rather than challenges his brother the king.[59] Nonetheless the way in which Morolf's character is interpreted is influenced by the way in which he makes Salman appear. Does he make Salman seem foolish by realizing what will happen with Salme and therefore undermine the supposed wisdom of the king? Does he make him appear impotent by achieving everything himself? Does he challenge received authority and undermine the social system? Hence the usual interpretation of a 'mixed', flexible character, the king's brother and wisest and most trusted adviser, yet also a character of Schwank, comic and anarchic, coarse and violent at the same time as he is noble.[60]

Bachorski argues that the relationship between lord and servant ('Herr' and 'Knecht') is challenged in *Salman und Morolf*, for Morolf does not only help his brother but also challenges received authority. Furthermore, his chameleon-like identity — expressed in his multiple disguises — goes against the courtly ideal, relegating conventional courtly habitus to the background in favour of the freedom provided by the 'Eigensinn' of the vassal.[61] Such an interpretation moves towards a reading of Morolf as someone who has his own conception of the world, different from that of others. According to Röcke, 'Eigensinn' is the defining characteristic of late medieval and early modern fools in literature and is expressed through fragmentation and contradiction in the fool's attitude to religion and society, an emphasis on the body and bodily drives rather than human *sapientia*, and an increased level of gesture and speech through bodily functions.[62] Although Morolf cannot be considered a fool or be equated with a character such as Til Ulenspiegel or the peasants of Wittenwiler's *Ring*, two of Röcke's main examples of this kind of behaviour, one of his often-cited character traits is 'Schwank', or folly. There is the Ofenschwank episode in which Morolf, having been told by Salman that he never wants to see his face again, leaps into an oven and bares his bottom instead (strs 137–40)[63] and other similar moments — Morolf farts when disguised as a cripple (str. 661) and during his chess game with Salme (str. 244), and shaves tonsures on Fore and his men, leaving Fore in bed with a young chaplain whom Fore presumes to be Salme (strs 290–333).[64]

The emphasis on the body and the bodily could suggest the applicability of Bakhtin's famous theory of the carnivalesque, which argues that popular humour and the world of the carnival played a vital role in the culture of the Middle Ages and the Renaissance. The 'grotesque realism' that had so large a part in this — the emphasis on the corporeal and primary bodily needs (eating, defecating, sex, and so on) — is a celebration of life, linked to birth and renewal. The carnivalesque itself is a symbolic destruction of societal norms and authority, but also renews and regenerates the whole system.[65] The final result of *Salman und Morolf* is certainly one of renewing the received order, with the death of Salme and the marriage of Salman and Afra; Salme's death — in a bath — could even be thought of as a ritualistic act of purging and cleansing, but such an interpretation cannot explain everything. The text is not pervaded by Schwank episodes and moreover its entire world is not turned upside-down and made bodily in order for it to be renewed. The rules of society are never destroyed and the majority of people function in an entirely conventional manner, even Morolf, who does not really invert or cross boundaries of social behaviour. Instead, he is a rather unusual character who understands *how* things could be done differently and is able to adopt different modes of behaviour in order to achieve something. The manner in which he does this then makes for a highly entertaining narrative.

What I hope to do away with is the idea — which appears in criticism a good deal — of Morolf as a composite and norm-breaking character, made up of many, often contradictory component parts. The problem here, I think, is a confusion between *being* and *doing*. Instead of asserting that Morolf *is* many different things, I would like to argue that he is able to *do* many different things. There is never any doubt that he is quite simply Morolf, the noble brother of the king of Jerusalem, but he also has a large quantity of practical knowledge that he is able to put to use to achieve his goals. Practical knowledge and its conscious application are explicitly made much of throughout the text.

The world of *Salman und Morolf* is not a topsy-turvy one. It is a world where everything follows the rules we might expect of serious medieval literature — beautiful women, kings who woo and fight — with one exception: Morolf. Even Salman does not behave in a particularly unusual fashion for a king and is always described in positive terms as a ruler, with emphasis on his beauty and wisdom. He may not appear to be wise or act wisely, but is never established as a negative example; if anything is at fault for his behaviour it is the woman as object of lust. *Salman und Morolf* is far removed from the biblical Solomon, and it is questionable whether we should think of him at all. The story is more concerned with practical knowledge and with Morolf, who functions like no-one else; he can change identity and social status at will, he has technical ability, he can do more and go further than anyone else, in mind and body. He can always, however, fit in to the rules of society. For what is striking about Morolf is that he understands how to play by more than one set of rules and how to adopt different roles (including that of the fool), and adopts these at will, suggesting an unusual kind of knowledge (and superiority) for a literary character. Morolf's understanding of how to behave in different ways has two main effects: first, it enables him to succeed in his endeavours, which are to return (and ultimately defeat) Salme and restore order, and second, it creates a highly enjoyable narrative. As is the case with the dangerous love embodied by Salme, which motivates the narrative and therefore paradoxically becomes desirable, so are Morolf's actions emphasized more strongly than their result, the restoration of harmony.

In comparison to the heathen kings, who use magic to win Salme, Morolf achieves everything with *list*, which can be understood in this narrative as a particularly practical kind of cunning. Although some of the techniques he uses are remarkably similar to those used by Fore in particular — a ring that has an effect on people (Fore's ring makes Salme fall in love with him; Morolf's ring distracts her during the chess game) and a herb to bring about the appearance of a change in health (Fore's herb makes Salme appear dead; Morolf's herb gives him the pale and sickly appearance of a cripple) — it is notable that the word *zouber* is only ever used of Fore and, indirectly, of Princian.[66] Although *zouber* does not necessarily imply a 'dark' or dangerous force and could suggest some sort of technical ability, it is noticeable that it is never clarified, in contrast to *list*, the technical workings of which are always explained clearly.[67] *zouber* and *list* appear to be two different kinds of skill, a notion that clarifies the fact that Morolf is unable to recognize the magic in Fore's ring when Salme shows it to him, a moment that may seem oddly out of character but is made understandable on closer consideration of the language used:

> Morolff es gein der sunnen bott,
> da was das golt also rot,
> das Morolff mit den listen sin
> den zauber nit kunde kennen,
> der da lag in dem vingerlin. (str. 98)

list and *zouber* are both 'artes', but Morolf's competence in the 'ars' of *zouber* is insufficient to allow him to recognize it in Fore's ring.[68] The ring that Morolf uses to distract Salme when they play chess has a nightingale worked into it *mit spehen listen* (str. 248, 4), however, and all his other tactics are, as we shall see, similarly described in detail so that we are made aware of how they work. One example is Morolf's 'submarine' escape from Fore's kingdom, which, unlike similar scenes in stories of Alexander, plays a functional role in the narrative, as do all other uses of technology.[69] Furthermore, Morolf's underwater boat is not made for him, but rather he knows how to make it himself:

> er det in siner liste kundt,
> vor ir aller angesicht
> sencket er sich an den grundt.
>
> Ein rore in das schifflin gieng,
> dar durch Morolff den atum enpfing.
> das hat er wol gemachet dar an
> mitt einem starcken leder
> Morolff der listige man.
>
> Ein schnür die lag oben dran,
> daz dem tugenthafftigen man
> das ror nit ließ brechen ab.
> er verbarg sich zu dem grunde
> vollichen vierzehen tag. (strs 342, 3–344)[70]

What is striking about this passage is that it appears to want to make the underwater boat as believable as possible, showing in detail the practicalities of breathing and thus the extent of Morolf's *list*.

Morolf's knowledge of how to act in different ways and how to assume different roles is exemplified in his use of disguise, through which he is able to manipulate his own personal identity with consummate skill and ease. There are six main disguises: he travels to Fore's kingdom in the skin of an old Jew, over which he then dons the clothes of a pilgrim and appears in Princian's kingdom as, variously, a cripple, pilgrim, minstrel, butcher, and pedlar. Morolf's disguises are strikingly different to the Dietrich-disguise in *König Rother*, where there is no physical change. He gives himself an alternative name only once — in disguise as a pilgrim, he says to Salme he used to be a minstrel named Stoltzelin (str. 254) — instead preferring to adopt a social role without specific personality. Whereas Rother, as argued in chapter I, seems to change personal identity with his name, we are always aware in *Salman und Morolf* that it is Morolf acting out some form of cunning plan beneath the skin of the disguise he uses to help him. His first disguise involves, quite literally, the wearing of a new skin: he visits an old Jew, ostensibly for advice about his journey to fetch Salme, then stabs him through the heart, skins him, preserves the skin and wears it as a disguise. We are not just told that Morolf disguises himself as a Jew, but are told exactly *how* he does it:

> Er nam ine balde bi der hant,
> er furte in inn ein kamennate
> und wolt im raten da zu hant.
> Morolff zoch uß ein messer scharff und lang,
> er stach es dem juden durch sin hertz,
> das es im an der hende wider want.
>
> Morolff Salmons drut
> oberthalb dem gurtel
> loste er dem juden abe die hut.
> er balsamte sie und leite sie an sinen lip.
> er sprach: 'nu wil ich nimmer erwinden,
> ich finde dann das wunder schone wip.' (strs 161–62)

The reader is informed how the skin is made wearable, and even told about the kind of knife with which the Jew is killed, long and sharp presumably so that his skin is damaged as little as possible.[71] Outlandish as this scene may seem — to the modern reader it could be something from a comic book — the narrator appears to want it to be as realistic and as plausible as possible. Morolf is taking disguise to a new level and we are encouraged to believe what he does. It is not enough for Morolf just to wear the disguise, however, for a degree of skill is involved in realizing it successfully, as emphasized by the fact that he wears the skin of the Jew as if it were his own: *in der hute ging der ritter lobesan | in allen den geberden, | als were sie im gewachssen an* (str. 163, 3–5). We should note here that he is still referred to as a *ritter lobesan*. A similar skill in disguise is achieved later in the text when he wears the clothing of one of Fore's manservants and makes himself look just like him: *sin antlitz was glich dem kemerer uber al* (str. 318, 2).

The detailed description of Morolf's disguises is characteristic of the wider text. When he travels to Princian's kingdom, he disguises himself as a cripple or fool, shaving his hair and piercing his ears and neck (str. 617), as well as eating a herb to make him turn pale (str. 618). He leaves Jerusalem on hands and feet, then rides a donkey to the sea (strs 622–23). The text does not simply say that Morolf disguises himself as a cripple, but gives the reader details of how he does it, and Morolf himself seems concerned for authenticity, given how difficult the disguise makes his journey. It is notable that he suffers in his quests for Salme; the verb *wallen* is used for his journeys and the fact that he travels at least partially on hand and foot increases the sense of similarity to a pilgrimage. This enacts the metaphor of Salme as a religious object to be venerated, but it is curious that *wallen* is applied most commonly to Morolf, the only man who does not see her in this way. At the end of the text, he makes it explicit that he has suffered, saying to Salman that he had to kill Salme to save himself from future *arbeit* (str. 780). Although this language is never allowed to dominate the narrative, it offers a reminder that Morolf's actions, despite their entertaining nature, have at their root a positive purpose.

Perhaps it is not surprising that the cripple Morolf comes prepared with clothing for another disguise — a *wallender man*. Again, the text gives details of this clothing and associated objects (strs 665–67), but the pilgrim disguise is only the first of a series in a comic episode. Having managed to obtain Princian's ring (given to him by Salme after she was given it by Salman), Morolf predicts correctly that Salme will recognize him by description.[72] He sheds his cripple disguise and dons the clothes of a pilgrim; when asked by Princian's men if he has seen the cripple, he sends them in the wrong direction (strs 678–82). When told of this, Salme realizes that the pilgrim was Morolf, but he has by this point disguised himself as a minstrel (str. 688 — as per usual, details of costume and attributes are given, as well as Morolf's capacity to wear them and behave appropriately). He sends Princian's men after the 'pilgrim' — again in the wrong direction (strs 690–96). The same thing happens once more, with Morolf disguised as a butcher; finally he disguises himself as a pedlar and leaves the country.[73] Such is Morolf's ability for disguise that Princian is led to exclaim: 'schone frauwe wol gethan, | sol niemant uff der strassen gan, | es si alles Morolff, | daz muß mich umer wunder han (str. 698, 2–5). For Neudeck, this is representative of the essential nature of both Morolf and the text itself, namely the constant overstepping of boundaries and overturning of norms:

> Wenn in letzter Konsequenz jeder Morolf und Morolf jeder sein kann, ist die eindeutige Zuordnung von außen und innen, ist die Identität von Zeichen und Bezeichnetem aufgehoben. Indem der einzelne beliebig mit diesen Zuordnungen spielt, setzt er sich nicht nur über die Konventionalität der Zeichen, sondern noch weitergehend über die Verbindlichkeit von gesetzten, sichtbaren Ordnungen hinweg.[74]

It is true that Morolf can adopt any social role, play the harp as well as he can fight, even survive in a boat underwater for fourteen days, but, contrary to what Neudeck suggests, the conventionality of signs and orders is not done away with. Indeed, Morolf's disguises — and the possibility of seeing through them — depend on maintaining the conventionality of signs. Furthermore, talking about a topsy-turvy distorted world is problematic, given that according to the Bakhtinian explanation, even the most carnivalesque situation has an order against which it is defined, something to return to, to be renewed and reconfirmed. Morolf's behaviour is not ritualistic and he does not specifically turn things upside-down in order to destroy authority, renew it, or reconfirm it. His unusual behaviour is either the conscious application of practical knowledge to help him achieve his ends, or a sign of his triumphant superiority. Importantly, he never actually leaves or distorts the conventional order. This is demonstrated in several ways, not least the fact that his nobility is always undisguisable.

When Morolf arrives in Fore's kingdom in the skin of the Jew, he sits on a stool under a linden tree that can be sat on only by members of the nobility (str. 188).[75] One of Fore's manservants wants to kill him, but Fore himself laughs it off, for, despite the disguise, he recognizes that Morolf is noble: *ich han an sinem libe uß erkorn | und prieff an sinen geberden, | er ist von hoher art geborn* (str. 195, 3-5). In a similar fashion, when Morolf is disguised as a cripple at Princian's court later in the text, a *kamerer* describes how ill his body looks apart from his noble brow:

> er sprach: 'durfftige, du hast war,
> du bist an dem libe nit gesunt
> als duer als umb ein cleines har.
>
> Din hende, din fuß und auch der munt,
> din augen in dem heubt sint dir ungesunt.
> hoffelich stant dir din brawen an.' (strs 649, 3-650, 3)

This latter example, with its catalogue of body parts, demonstrates the thoroughness of Morolf's disguise and his remarkable ability to manipulate his body, but it is striking that in both instances his nobility cannot be hidden entirely; indeed, the purpose of the first passage could be to demonstrate just that, as there is no narrative reason for Morolf to sit on the stool. It may seem that he is upsetting the ruling order — deliberately, flagrantly — but he is actually not upsetting it at all, as he still *is* a high-ranking member of the nobility and is recognized as such. Paradoxically, this does not hinder the efficacy of Morolf's disguise, which remains convincing; it is important that he should both be able to disguise himself skilfully and unnoticeably, but that his nobility should, despite the disguise, be in its essence undisguisable.

Morolf's noble status is further emphasized by the fact that he wears a breastplate between his false skin and pilgrim's clothes, noticed by a young noblewoman at Fore's court, who immediately tells Salme what she has seen: '*ich seite dir von dem bilgerin, | was ich in an dem libe sach haben, | ein pantzer, ist gut und stehelin, | es solt ein fromer ritter tragen.*' (str. 216, 2-5). Unlike Fore and Princian, who think nothing of a noble pilgrim or cripple, and take him unquestionably for a pilgrim or cripple because that is how he is dressed, Salme calls this pilgrim to her and the following day they play a game of chess. It is not made explicit whether she has recognized Morolf yet, although it is quite plausible that she has, given the nature of the following game and Morolf's fear of entering her company: *Morolff hette angst umb den lip, | er begunde sere furchten | Salome das mort grime wip* (str. 221, 3–5).[76] Griese wonders why Morolf is suddenly scared of her, as she has not yet actively done anything, a consideration that highlights a very important feature of the narrative, namely the relationship between Morolf and Salme.[77] Morolf is the only man in the story for whom Salme is not an object of desire and, following on from this, it is only in her dealings with Morolf that Salme has any agency. The narrative is — as we have seen above — motivated by her, but the movement in which it consists is carried out by men, all of whom desire her, other than Morolf. There exists, therefore, tension between the two kinds of relationships men have with Salme, between the desire of all other men and the enmity of Morolf. As a result of this, it is possible to discern two different aspects of Salme: on the one hand the object of desire without agency and on the other the *mort grime wip*, the only person who can come close to understanding how Morolf functions. It has already been shown in the first section of this argument with respect to Salme as an object of desire that *Salman und Morolf* is a narrative for narrative's sake, at the expense of a clear moral message; this is played out in the details of Morolf's chase too, as its excitement and tension depend on a foe who is, to an extent, his equal. Morolf and Salme rarely come face to face, but when they do, the result is highly decisive, such as the chess game or Salme's death at the end of the text. Moreover, she is the only person who can recognize him — even by hearsay — and the only person able to understand that he can behave in the way he does, that is, to accept his ability to assume different roles.

Morolf has already tested out his disguise as a Jew on Salman, asking him to give him his wealth and his ring *durch aller frauwen ere* (strs 164–68).[78] Salman does not recognize him and Morolf is delighted to reveal who he really is. When he finally returns from Fore's kingdom, he has greyed and no-one recognizes him, and Morolf takes advantage of the situation by pretending to be someone else and claiming that Morolf himself is dead (strs 347–59). Here, Morolf definitely has the upper hand; his tactics and unusual abilities cannot be seen through. We can compare this episode to the central chess scene with Salme, the tension and excitement of which is derived from the potential of recognition.

As mentioned above, Salme invites the disguised Morolf to join her after she has been told he is wearing a breastplate. She knows about Morolf's particular cunning, as she had told Fore about it earlier in the text (str. 101), but now she pits herself directly against it for the first time. Morolf suggests *kurtzewil* (str. 225, 1) and she brings out a golden chessboard, the object in the text described in the most detail after Salme herself (strs 226–27); much like her, it is beautiful and covered with precious objects.[79] They play for high stakes — Morolf's head and Salme's most beautiful lady-in-waiting — and the tension of the game is heightened by the uncertainty of Salme's recognition of Morolf. The style of the narrative furthers this tension, with lots of fast exchanges of direct speech, from which Morolf never emerges the victor, as he does in his conversations with Salman. Salme cannot be tricked with disguise or quick wit and Morolf cannot win the game through conventional skill at chess, but must resort to farting (str. 244, 2) and distracting her with a ring containing a nightingale (strs 248–50). It is possible to read this scene as a metaphor for the story as a whole, which can be seen as a big game for a precious object (Salme), and it can also be considered as a condensed version of the relationship between Morolf and Salme, one in which the balance of power is very precarious. Salme has the upper hand at the outset — she may have recognized Morolf, he is the outsider, and it is in her power to kill him — but Morolf appears to control the game, letting her take the lead (str. 238). He then insists they swap places (we could even think of the two halves of the chess game as the two halves of the story, the first of which is 'won' by Salme), enabling him to recognize her for certain by the hole he has burnt in her hand (str. 247). He eventually wins the game by distracting her with *ein alrot gulden vingerlin, | da was mit spehen listen | ein nachtegal schone verwircket in* (str. 248, 3–5). The use of the ring resonates with other motifs found in the text: first, Salman's ring, which he gives to Salme, who gives it to Princian, but which is eventually retrieved by Morolf; and, second, Morolf's use of *list* (as opposed to *zouber*) to achieve his ends. Morolf also wins Fore's sister by winning the game, who, as Afra, is his triumph at the end of the game of the story, the replacement wife for Salman. When he finds out the maiden he has chosen is Fore's sister, he offers to relinquish the game, but Fore's sister warns him against the queen and says she would gladly go with him if he were to win (strs 235–37). I would not go as far as Griese in stressing the utmost importance of the 'indirect' wooing of Fore's sister — the discussion above has shown that finding an improved replacement for Salme is not the main interest of the narrative, even if it is its end result — but it is notable that she speaks favourably of Morolf and unfavourably of Salme. Again, Salme is only 'false' in the eyes of (and the company of) those who do not view her as an object of desire. Yet Fore's sister is not the central factor in this scene, nor is it to her that any romantic connotations of the game of chess appropriate. This is not to imply a romantic relationship between Morolf and Salme, rather a particular cerebral closeness — the closeness of enemies — that is exposed and played out in a game of tactics and cunning.

Morolf does not, however, emerge the victor from this scene, as he is finally recognized for certain and imprisoned after he sings in triumph at winning the game (strs 251–60). Because he is disguised in the skin of the Jew, physical recognition would be impossible; instead, recognition is dependent on Salme's knowledge of the way in which he behaves and by Morolf performing an act that only he could perform, in this case singing a song she last heard in Jerusalem, sung by him (str. 257, 4).[80] Salme's later recognition of Morolf in Princian's kingdom is also dependent on knowledge of his behaviour and on hearsay, because she does not see him but is rather told about the cripple who deceives the king and his men. She asks Princian about his eyes:

> Sie sprach: 'wie warent im die augen gethan?'
> 'luter als ein spiegel',
> sprach der kunig Princian,
> 'hoffelich stundent im sin brawen an.'
> da sprach die kunigin edele:
> 'es ist Morolff kunig Salmons man.' (str. 673)

Princian doubts this, because the Morolf he saw in Jerusalem wore *eine zohen mantel* (str. 674, 3) instead of the clothes of a beggar, but Salme responds that *siner liste erkennest du nit* (str. 675, 1). Her ability to recognize him depends on an understanding of his characteristic mode of behaviour, confirmed by familiarity with his physical appearance.

It is striking that Salme is able to recognize both Morolf and Salman from a description of their eyes, the body part linked most directly to the soul, which can give an understanding of the whole person.[81] The description of their eyes also provides an interesting point of comparison between the two brothers: Morolf's eyes are brighter than mirrors, whereas Salman's burn brighter *als einem wilden felckelin* (str. 405, 4). The metaphorical description of eye as mirror is used widely in medieval literature, the possibilities of reflection offering a wide range of poetic interpretation. In a theological context, the mirror can be used as a metaphor for seeing God inside oneself, for simply seeing God, or for the act of creation; in a more worldly context it is often used to describe the closeness of lovers, whose souls can look into each other as if into a mirror.[82] In the case of Morolf, the comparison of his eyes to mirrors most probably indicates his ability to see well, to understand the motivations of others and perceive the complexities of a situation.[83]

Salman, on the other hand, is compared to a falcon, usually a symbol of a hero or lover.[84] This motif is assumed again later in the text when Salme speaks of a dream in which two falcons fly to her hand (strs 534–35), interpreted by her to signify Salman and an unborn son, a clear allusion to Kriemhild's dream in the *Nibelungenlied* in which two eagles attack a falcon. This dream is interpreted by Kriemhild's mother as a bad omen, the falcon signifying a noble man whom Kriemhild will lose unless God intervenes.[85] In the case of Salme's dream, Salman is a 'false' falcon, as her interpretation is followed by an alternative — and correct — one by Morolf, who says that the two falcons represent Salme's two heathen husbands, one now dead and one yet to come (str. 536). It is noticeable that it is Fore's sister, who loves Salman, who describes his eyes as being brighter than a falcon; Salme can recognize him from this description but describes (or dreams of) only her own lovers in these terms.

Perhaps more important than a comparison of the description of their eyes is the relative speed at which Morolf and Salman are recognized. When Salman, as advised by Morolf, enters Fore's court in disguise as a pilgrim (as Morolf has already done), he is recognized almost immediately by Fore's sister as being noble, indeed she says that *Es mag vil wol sin der kunig von Jherusalem* (str. 406, 1). Salme realizes that this pilgrim is Salman, summons him to her, and hides him behind a curtain while she dines with Fore, thus drawing out his agony before she reveals him and has him imprisoned (strs 409–27a). Salman may be beautiful and noble, but he does not have Morolf's unusual ability to disguise himself well and behave appropriately in another role; he is not only recognizably noble, but recognizably the King of Jerusalem.

Salme may be the only person who can see through Morolf's disguises, but he is equally able to recognize her, both in person and by hearsay. When he arrives in Fore's kingdom, he asks an old man about the queen; this old man describes her complexion and superlative beauty before Morolf kills him so that no-one will be aware of his arrival (strs 181–84). Much the same happens when he arrives in Princian's kingdom, this time without the murder (strs 632–34). In the first case, however, Morolf needs additional proof that Fore's queen is indeed Salme. He watches her going into church and is almost certain of her identity (strs 197–98), but is not convinced until (as mentioned above) he has seen the one mark that distinguishes her — the hole in her hand he made with molten gold when she appeared to be dead. After he insists they swap places during the chess game, the sun shines through her glove, enabling him finally to recognize her:

> Aller erst sach er ir durch die hant,
> da er sie mit dem golde hette durch gebrant.
> da ir die sunne durch den hentschuch schein,
> aller erst bekante er sie rechte. (str. 247, 1–4)

As we have seen in *König Rother*, the ability to recognize someone *for certain* depends not so much on facial or indeed bodily appearance, but rather on one distinguishing mark (which may or may not be bodily) that could belong to no-one else — a hole in the hand, an eye, a song known only by that person.[86] Otherwise the entire perception of the person depends on how he is dressed, that is, the role he assumes with his dress, which as this story demonstrates in the figure of Morolf, can often be deceptive.

It is intriguing that Morolf himself has created the mark by which Salme is made recognizable, branding her for this very purpose:

> 'ich muß baß versuchen die edele kunigin,

> das sie mir werde baß bekant.
> entrinnet sie mir von hinnen,
> so muß ich nach ir kunden fremde lant.' (str. 132, 2-5)

He exerts this control upon her by altering her body, which is otherwise an unchangeable, almost totemic entity, a symbol of desire drawing potential husbands from far and wide (it is striking that Morolf, whose bodily in endlessly manipulable, ages to the extent that he is unrecognizable, but Salme's appearance remains stable). Morolf marks her irreparably, leaving a physical reminder of her false death and of him, in particular his ability to know what she is up to. His superiority and success in the world of the text is marked out by an ability to alter and manipulate his own body, so it is striking that he extends this in the manipulation of the bodies of others: by branding Salme and by shaving tonsures on Fore and his men. In this sense, it is possible to understand how the 'Schwank' moments fit in: we should not think of them as simply the irruption of another literary form or as moments of pure anarchy and mockery, but notice how they resonate with the way in which Morolf is able to behave. He can achieve his ends through his practical knowledge of how to manipulate his body, so it makes sense that he asserts his triumph by manipulating the bodies of others. It is the same with his farting, which is not an involuntary physical action, but something that Morolf can do on demand and with a particular aim in mind.

In the end, however, Morolf turns to an unexpected source to get Salme out of her tower: a mermaid, to whom he is related, and her dwarfs.[87] The fact that he is able to call for the aid of such beings is another instance of his practical ability, eliciting the help of others who may help him practically, but also clarifies the difficulty of vanquishing Salme. The turn to the mermaid for help is prefigured in the central chess scene, in which Morolf uses an external object — a ring — to distract Salme; something unexpected is necessary in order finally to break the deadlock of their rivalry. The use of mermaids and dwarfs demonstrates the very extent of this rivalry, for Morolf must resort to something beyond his usual cunning, even something seemingly beyond the world of the text, in order finally to triumph.

Salme is brought back to Jerusalem and Morolf insists to Salman she is bathed, *niit me dan vor fremde minne* (str. 776, 3). Morolf kills her in her bath:

> er dette ir laßen an der median,
> daz sage ich uch nit nach won.
> er druckte sie also susse,
> das ir die sele lachende von irem munde schiet.
> sie wuhste nit, wie es geriet. (str. 777, 3-7)

It is no surprise that Morolf must kill Salme. She is the impetus for the narrative, as discussed above, so her death is the only way of bringing it to an end. Death is also the only way that Morolf can finally conquer her; she has already used death as a tactic (the fake death), and now he triumphs by making the death real.[88] There are, however, two notable points about the way Salme dies: first, her death takes place in a bath; second, she feels nothing, *sie wuhste nit, wie es geriet*. The location reminds us of the suicide of Seneca or perhaps the murder of Agamemnon, but I am unconvinced that Salme's death is supposed to be directly referential.[89] Perhaps more important is the reason Morolf gives for her bathing, to rid her of *fremde minne*. His speech might amuse the audience, but it points to both the reasoning behind her death and its method. It was discussed above that Salme sometimes appears to be an objectified 'thing' that drives men to desire, leading to an ambivalence about her guilt that is perhaps the reason behind the painlessness of her death. Her death is gentle (*er druckte sie also susse*) and free from torture, with the air of ritual rather than punishment; in this sense, we can think of it as a ritualized cleansing away of the objectified thing, which is a lure to *fremde minne*. Washing Salme away in the bath — killing her — is to be equated with washing away *fremde minne*.

Conclusion

Neither of the conventional interpretations of *Salman und Morolf* is entirely satisfactory. The story cannot be interpreted unproblematically either as a narrative about the potential dangers of love or women or as a narrative that constantly overturns conventions, breaks boundaries, and distorts genre norms. Salme, the woman who drives men to insatiable desire, is ambiguously constructed and desire for her is the impetus for the whole narrative, with multiple quests after her across the sea. Paradoxically, there is too much enjoyment in the desire for Salme to render her a negative model. Morolf, the supposed epitome of the boundary-breaking character, understands well the appropriate codes of behaviour in society (and stays to a degree within them, never losing his appearance of nobility, for example), using his particular practical knowledge to achieve his ends. If *Salman und Morolf* can also be considered to be an 'inverse' bridal-quest epic, distorting the conventions of the genre, then there must be a genre and a norm to comply with in the first place. The existence of such a norm has already been doubted in the introduction; if the bridal-quest motif is simply a story-motif that can be used flexibly and in a variety of contexts, then *Salman und Morolf* cannot upturn conventions, because there are none to be upturned.

Notes to Chapter 2

1. August Koberstein, *Grundriß der Geschichte der deutschen National-Litteratur*, 4th edn, I (Leipzig: Vogel 1847), p. 198.
2. Ehrismann, p. 139: 'Das Spielmannsgedicht von Salman und Morolf stellt unter den verwandten Dichtungen die spielmännische Art am reinsten dar. Hier ist der niedere, volksmäßigere Geschmack am besten getroffen. Ergötzt und belustigt will dieses Publikum werden, es hat seine Freude an derberer Kost.' See also Ebenbauer, 'Andere Großepen', p. 287.
3. The connection with the second half of *König Rother* caused many older scholars to assert that *Salman und Morolf* was the older text, the original Byzantine-influenced bridal-quest story. See Curschmann, 'Spielmannsepik', pp. 456–58 and *Der Münchener Oswald und die deutsche spielmännische Epik*, pp. 97–98. Frings, 'Die Entstehung der deutschen Spielmannsepen', pp. 208–09, argues that *Salman und Morolf* is the first double-structured *Spielmannsepos* and that the second half of *König Rother* is derived from it. On this, see de Boor, p. 250.
4. de Boor, p. 253.
5. Sabine Griese, *Salomon und Markolf: Ein literarischer Komplex im Mittelalter und in der frühen Neuzeit* (Tübingen: Niemeyer, 1999), p. 84: '[H]ier kann man höchstens das Aufgreifen biblischer Motive bei Salomon oder auch Salome beobachten, darüber hinaus finden sich jedoch keine weiteren Anhaltspunke, den *Salman und Morolf* als "Legendenepos" zu bezeichnen'.
6. Haug, 'Brautwerbung im Zerrspiegel'. For Haug's earlier ideas about oral and written story forms and the necessity of reflection, see Haug, 'Struktur, Gewalt und Begierde'.
7. Hans-Jürgen Bachorski, 'Serialität, Variation und Spiel:. Narrative Experimente in *Salman und Morolf*', in *Heldensage, Heldenlied, Heldenepos: Ergebnisse der II. Jahrestagung der Reinecke-Gesellschaft, Gotha, 16.-20. Mai 1991* (Amiens: Université de Picardie, Centre d'études médiévales, 1992), pp. 7–29.
8. Otto Neudeck, 'Grenzüberschreitung als erzählerisches Prinzip: Das Spiel mit der Fiktion in *Salman und Morolf*', in *Erkennen und Erinnern in Kunst und Literatur: Kolloquium Reisenburg 4.-7. Januar 1996*, ed. by Dietmar Peil, Michael Schilling, and Peter Strohschneider (Tübingen: Niemeyer, 1998), pp. 87–114; Armin Schulz, 'Morolfs Ende: Zur Dekonstruktion des feudalen Brautwerbungsschemas in der sogenannten Spielmannsepik', *PBB*, 124 (2002), 233–49.
9. *Salman und Morolf*, ed. by Alfred Karnein (Tübingen: Niemeyer, 1979). All quotations will come from this edition.
10. Curschmann, *Der Münchener Oswald und die deutsche spielmännische Epik*, esp. pp. 156–66.
11. Griese, pp. 107–32; Haug, 'Zerrspiegel', p. 188.
12. Lydia Miklautsch, '*Salman und Morolf* — Thema und Variation', in *Ir sult sprechen willekomen: grenzenlose Mediävistik: Festschrift für Helmut Birkhan zum 60. Geburtstag*, ed. by Christa Tuczay, Ulrike Hirhager, and Karin Lichtblau (Bern: Lang, 1998), pp. 284–306.
13. Claudia Bornholdt, '*in was zu schouwen also not: Salman und Morolf* bildlich erzählt', in *Visualisierungsstrategien in mittelalterlichen Bildern und Texten*, ed. by Horst Wenzel and C. Stephen Jaeger (Berlin: Erich Schmidt, 2006), pp. 226–47. Bornholdt's largely unconvincing reading relies entirely on the premise that *Salman und Morolf* was composed in the twelfth century; she compares the narrative solely to courtly romances and relies heavily on Bumke's reading of *Parzival* in his *Blutstropfen im Schnee*. See also Wolfgang Spiewok, 'Vom Salman zum Salomon, vom Morolf zum Markolf', in *Schelme*

und Narren in der Literatur des Mittelalters: XXVII. Jahrestagung des Arbeitskreises Deutsche Literatur des Mittelalters (Greifswald), Eulenspiegelstadt Mölln, 24.-27. September 1992 (Greifswald: Reinecke, 1994), pp. 151-60, who argues that *Salman und Morolf* is programmatically concerned with the dangers of *minne* and can be read as anti-courtly and anti-heathen propaganda.

14. Notker der Deutsche, *Der Psalter*, III, ed. by Petrus W. Tax (Tübingen: Niemeyer, 1983), 118, 85: 'Vuaz ist oih anderes daz man marcholfum saget sih éllenon uuider prouerbiis salomonis? An diên allen sint uuort scôniû. âne uuârheit.'
15. Griese, pp. 298-340, provides a detailed overview of all sources mentioning some kind of Solomon and Markolf/Morolf story up to the nineteenth century.
16. Ibid., pp. 1-3; 303. Lambert describes Arnold of Guînes's love of literature, stating that he enjoys *chansons de geste* and stories about King Arthur, Tristan, Merlin, and Markolf.
17. An annotated list of all known manuscripts and prints is given by Griese, pp. 31-73.
18. Ibid., pp. 140-47. All references to the *Dialogus* are from *Salomon et Marcolfus*, ed. by Walter Benary (Heidelberg: Carl Winter, 1914) and to *Markolfs buch* from *Salomon und Markolf: Das Spruchgedicht*, ed. by Walter Hartmann (Halle: Niemeyer, 1934).
19. All are discussed by Griese in her comprehensive handbook to the Solomon and Markolf tradition.
20. See Griese, pp. 86-93, for a full discussion of the manuscripts and printed editions, a more up-to-date (although less detailed) survey than that of Karnein (pp. xix-xliv).
21. For a full description of Solomon myths, see Samuel Singer, 'Salomosage in Deutschland', *ZfdA*, 35 (1891), 177-87, repr. in *Spielmannsepik*, ed. by Schröder, pp. 72-84.
22. 'But king Solomon loved many strange women [...] For it came to pass, when Solomon was old, that his wives turned away his heart after other gods: and his heart was not perfect with the Lord his God'. This and all subsequent bible quotations are from the Vulgate, with the Douay-Rheims translation.
23. Many such examples are offered by Schnell, *Causa Amoris*, pp. 475-505.
24. This epilogue is found in MS Kra of the *Dialogus* (see Griese, pp. 42-43; 78), referred to by Benary as MS S, a Bohemian MS from c.1453-77. The text is included in Benary's edition, appendix III, pp. 48-51. Such an epilogue is also found in MSs B, D, E, and H of *Markolfs buch*, all dated to the mid-fifteenth century. See Griese, pp. 78; 140-44.
25. *Dialogus*, p. 51, ll. 26-28.
26. Curschmann, 'Spielmannsepik', p. 454.
27. Griese, p. 8, suggests that it is impossible to form a 'literarische Reihe' from the different traditions. See also Curschmann, 'Spielmannsepik', pp. 454-55. It is impossible to trace the *Dialogus* and *Markolfs buch* to the same source, particularly as regards the epilogue section, which in *Markolfs buch* is more similar to *Salman und Morolf*. Less brief than the *Dialogus* epilogue, it is here Solomon rather than Marcolfus who must escape the gallows, for Markolf's first journey to the heathen kingdom is merely to ascertain the whereabouts of the lost queen, rather than to bring her back straightaway. The most striking difference, however, is the punishment of the wife; in the *Dialogus* she is maimed, in *Markolfs buch* killed by Markolf in her bath.
28. On the form of *Salman und Morolf*, see Carl Colditz, 'Über die Anwendung der Morolfstrophe im Mittelalter und im deutschen Lied', *Modern Philology*, 31 (1933/34), 243-52, and Griese, pp. 102-06, who argues that the strophic form marks the text out as one designed to be sung and read out loud. Scribes of late fifteenth-century manuscripts tend towards writing the strophes out as couplets, combining the 'Waisenzeile' with the previous verse, and thus attempting a transformation to 'Buchliteratur' (p. 103). Griese thinks, however, that *Salman und Morolf* is an example of 'fictive orality'. Contrary

to this, see Armin Wishard, *Oral Formulaic Composition in the Spielmannsepik: An Analysis of 'Salman und Morolf'* (Göppingen: Kümmerle, 1984), who examines the text according to the theory of oral formulaic composition.
29. Chrétien de Troyes, *Cligés*, ed. by Stewart Gregory and Claude Luttrell (Cambridge: Brewer, 1993), ll. 5854–56.
30. *Der arme Konrad, Frau Metze die Käuflerin*, in *Neues Gesamtabenteuer*, I, 2nd edn, ed. by Werner Simon (Dublin and Zurich: Weidmann, 1967), pp. 70–83 (ll. 1–7): 'Wa man von wunderlisten seit, | da gedenket man der listikeit, | wie Marolf einen juden schant | und sich in sine hut verwant, | daz man in niht erkande. sust vuor er in dem lande | unz daz er aventiure vernam'.
31. See Curschmann, 'Spielmannsepik', pp. 452–53.
32. On the connection to *Cligés*, see Griese, p. 77, and Miklautsch, '*Salman und Morolf*', pp. 294–95.
33. Griese, p. 136.
34. Neudeck, p. 106, argues that the dangerous sea separating Christian and heathen kingdoms and the constant crossing of it is a metaphor for the way in which the text itself oversteps boundaries and is therefore — following the theories of Lotman — a sign of its fictionality.
35. *Das Nibelungenlied*, ed. by Helmut Brackert, 27th edn (Frankfurt a. M.: Fischer, 2001), str. 2.
36. Griese, p. 107. Joachim Heinzle, *Das Nibelungenlied: Eine Einführung*, 2nd edn (Frankfurt a. M.: Fischer, 1996), pp. 74–76, argues that str. 2 of the *Nibelungenlied* is inconsistent with the narrative — Kriemhild's beauty *per se* does not bring about the death of many — and may be an attempt to associate Kriemhild with Helen of Troy and the topos of perilous beauty.
37. This difference is of great importance for Bornholdt, '*in was zu schouwen also not*', pp. 228–29, for whom Salman's particularly sensual — indeed visual — love for Salme is key to understanding the text. It is difficult to tell quite what the relationship is between *Salman und Morolf* and the *Nibelungenlied*. It is highly likely that *Salman und Morolf* was written (down) after the *Nibelungenlied* and that the text intends to draw some kind of connection between Kriemhild and its female protagonist. Further comparative study could be fruitful here.
38. Ulrich Engelen, *Die Edelsteine in der deutschen Dichtung des 12. und 13. Jahrhunderts* (Munich: Fink, 1978), pp. 328–29.
39. Ibid., pp. 324–27. See also Griese, p. 108. The morning star can also be used to refer to Venus, a symbol of sexual love; see *Handwörterbuch des deutschen Aberglaubens*, ed. by H. Bächtold-Stäubli (Berlin: de Gruyter, 1927–42), 10 vols, IX, cols 17–20. Links between the morning star and Christ are discussed in Chapter 4 of this study.
40. Engelen, p. 329. He mentions the description of Salme explicitly in this context. Griese, p. 107, also argues that the brightness of Salme's eyes demonstrates her readiness for love.
41. Contrary to the usual reading of the description of Salme — that it is highly conventional — Kraß argues that the language of excess in the church scene (the golden psalter and golden ring) and physical description results in a more ambivalent, negative characterization; she could even appear to be a 'Dämonin'. See Andreas Kraß, *Geschriebene Kleider: Höfische Identität als literarisches Spiel* (Tübingen: Francke, 2006), pp. 263–65. Arguments for the 'conventionality' of the description of Salme are offered by Haug, 'Zerrspiegel', pp. 182–83 and Griese, p. 107.
42. Regina Schiewer, 'Riskante Theologie? Minnegrotte, Engel und Eucharistie: Eine rezeptionsgeschichtliche Untersuchung', in *Exemplar: Festschrift für Kurt Otto Seidel*,

ed. by Rüdiger Brandt and Dieter Lau (Frankfurt a. M.: Lang, 2008), pp. 243–61 (pp. 249–53), shows that the references to *lebende brôt* in the prologue of Gottfried's *Tristan* would, according to contemporary vernacular sermons, have been automatically recognized as a reference to the Eucharist.
43. Neudeck, p. 104.
44. Haug, 'Zerrspiegel', p. 183.
45. On the phenomenon of 'Fernminne', discussed in Chapter 1, see Wenzel, 'Fernminne und Hohe Liebe'. The fact that hearing is sufficient for the heathen kings undermines Bornholdt's argument about the priority of sight in the text.
46. The proverb in question is derived from Isaiah 5:24: 'propter hoc sicut devorat stipulam lingua ignis et calor flammae exurit sic radix eorum quasi favilla erit et germen eorum ut pulvis ascendet abiecerunt enim legem Domini exercituum et eloquium Sancti Israhel blasphemaverunt' ('Therefore as the fire devoureth the stubble, and the flame consumeth the chaff, so their root shall be as rottenness, and their blossom shall go up as dust: because they have cast away the law of the Lord of hosts, and despised the word of the Holy One of Israel').
47. Spiewok, pp. 155–56.
48. On St Afra, see Erhard Gorys, *Lexikon der Heiligen*, 5th edn (Munich: dtv, 2004), p. 21.
49. Griese, p. 123.
50. Griese argues that this is central to the interpretation of the whole text, the goal of which is Morolf's restoration of harmony through a suitable, faithful wife: '[M]orolfs Fahrt in das Heidenland war eine Kundschafter-Fahrt in zweifacher Hinsicht: Einmal sollte er Salme, die bisherige Königin finden, zum anderen gewinnt er (im Spiel) eine neue Frau für Salman. Damit stellt sich dieser Ausflug sowohl als Einleitung der Rückeroberung als auch einer neuen Brautwerbung dar.' She argues (pp. 116–17) that chess, a game traditionally played by lovers, does not reflect the relationship between Morolf and Salme, but rather points to Morolf's 'verdeckte Werbung' of Fore's sister.
51. This strophe is strongly reminiscent of the discourse on *huote* in Gottfried von Strassburg, *Tristan*, ed. and trans. by Rüdiger Krohn, 9th edn (Stuttgart: Reclam, 2001), ll. 17867–78. Both instances are proverbial; see Griese, pp. 126–27.
52. This epilogue is included in Karnein's edition, pp. 259–65.
53. Schulz, 'Morolfs Ende', pp. 244–45. He argues that the epilogue essentially fails in its task, as it paradoxically highlights the 'Irritationen' it aims to correct. Neudeck, p. 103, suggests that the purpose of the epilogue is to make the text comply to the genre conventions it has broken: 'Zu konstatieren bleibt jedoch, daß ein solcher Kunstgriff anscheinend für notwendig erachtet wurde, um — im Rückgriff auf die Tradition — den unkonventionellen Umgang mit der Gattungskonvention zu korrigieren'.
54. Schulz, 'Morolfs Ende', p. 242; Neudeck, p. 98.
55. Friedrich Maurer, 'Der Topos von den "Minnesklaven": Zur Geschichte einer thematischen Gemeinschaft zwischen bildender Kunst und Dichtung im Mittelalter', *DVjs*, 27 (1953), 182–206.
56. Schnell, *Causa Amoris*, pp. 475–505.
57. Bornholdt, '*in was zu schouwen also not*', falls prey to this, relying heavily on Schnell and treating *Salman und Morolf* as both didactic and a courtly product.
58. On the use of *verwirken*, see *Mittelhochdeutsches Handwörterbuch von Matthias Lexer*, <http://germazope.uni-trier.de/Projekte/WBB2009/Lexer/wbgui_py?lemid=LA00001> [accessed 13 September 2010] 'verwirken verwürken swv. part. adj'.
59. It is true that Markolf does help Salomon recover his adulterous wife in the epilogue to *Markolfs buch* (ll. 1631–1902), but the fact remains that Markolf is still a peasant

and the text consists mainly of aphorisms. As I have said, it is impossible to suggest with confidence a chronology or correlation of influence for the epic and the Spruch tradition.

60. Henning Wuth, 'Morolfs Tauchfahrt: Überlegungen zur narrativen Bedeutung von "Technik" im *Salman und Morolf*', *Archiv für das Studium der neueren Sprachen und Literaturen*, 235 (1998), 328-44 (p. 328): 'Morolf zeichnet sich wesentlich dadurch aus, daß er seine geistigen Fähigkeiten in Handlungen münden läßt, die sich nur schwer mit höfischer Zucht und ritterlichem Verhalten in Einklang bringen lassen, obwohl er zweifellos als adliger Charakter inszeniert ist'. Schulz, 'Morolfs Ende', pp. 241-42: 'Morolf, die männliche Hauptfigur, tritt einmal in höfischer Vollkommenheit, Feinheit und Großzügigkeit auf, das andere Mal als rasender Heros, listiger Ränkeschmied, furzender Derbling und sogar als feiger Mörder'.

61. Bachorski, pp. 13-17. On the 'Eigensinn' of the servant in Hegelian thought, see 'master/slave morality', *The Oxford Dictionary of Philosophy*, ed. by Simon Blackburn (Oxford: Oxford University Press, 2008), *Oxford Reference Online* <http://www.oxfordreference.com> [accessed 13 September 10]: 'On emerging from the state of nature, there is a 'moment' of consciousness in which one party enslaves the other. The slave, involved in production and activity, is conscious of ends in his or her life, whilst the master retreats to a meaningless state of leisure and consumption. Neither can give the other the recognition and acknowledgement that is required if a person is to have value in his or her own eyes. An initial response to this impasse is a retreat to Stoicism, and then to the 'unhappy consciousness' of religion. However, the slave at least achieves a selfconsciousness through his or her own activity. The inner freedom thus acquired allows an overthrow of the master [...]'

62. Werner Röcke, 'Schälke — Schelme — Narren: Literaturgeschichte des "Eigensinns" und populäre Kultur in der frühen Neuzeit', in *Schelme und Narren in der Literatur des Mittelalters: XXVII. Jahrestagung des Arbeitskreises Deutsche Literatur des Mittelalters (Greifswald), Eulenspiegelstadt Mölln, 24.-27. September 1992* (Greifswald: Reinecke, 1994), pp. 131-49.

63. This episode also appears in the *Dialogus*, pp. 43-44 and *Markolfs buch*, ll. 1487-1552.

64. Griese, p. 120, shows that shaving tonsures as a joke is a Neidhart-topos, appearing for instance in the *Großes Neidhartspiel*, ll. 1341-1601. It is also one of the tricks played by a wife on her husband in Heinrich Kaufringer's *Drei listige Frauen*, in *Novellistik des Mittelalters: Märendichtung*, ed. and trans. by Klaus Grubmüller (Frankfurt a. M.: Deutscher Klassiker Verlag), pp. 840-71 (ll. 306-10).

65. Mikhail Bakhtin, *Rabelais and his World*, trans. by Hélène Iswolsky (Bloomington: Indiana University Press, 1984).

66. *zouber* or *zouberhaft* are used of Fore's ring in strs 92, 93, 94, 96, 99, and the herb he gives to Salme in strs 110, 120, 121, 122, 123, 126, 129, 133. In str. 532 Salme refers to the *zouber* with which he won her and in str. 577 she is described as waiting for another heathen to win her with *zouber*. Other than this there are no occurrences.

67. *zouberlist* is used by Blanscheflur in Gottfried's *Tristan* (l. 1003), who wonders if Riwalin has learnt some kind of 'magic skill' by which he makes women fall in love with him, most probably referring to some technical ability rather than 'dark art'. The use of the compound *zouberlist* shows that each word need not imply something opposed to and incompatible with the other.

68. Maria Dobozy, 'The Function of Knowledge and Magic in *Salman und Morolf*', in *The Dark Figure in Medieval German and Germanic Literature*, ed. by Edward R. Haymes and Stephanie Cain Van D'Elden (Göppingen: Kümmerle, 1986), pp. 27-41 (pp. 29-30) also notes that *zouber* is limited to heathens, but views it as 'dark magic'. She suggests

in the rest of her essay that *list*, too, is an ambiguous characteristic and causes Morolf to appear to be a 'dark figure'. Her argument is marred by her undefined use of the terms 'knowledge' (which she claims Morolf and Salme have) and 'dark figure', both of which apparently highlight the ambivalence of Morolf.
69. On this episode in stories of Alexander, see Wuth, pp. 330-31.
70. Wuth compares this episode to similar scenes in stories of Alexander, arguing that the fact that Morolf makes his underwater boat himself is of great importance, as it suggests a breaking down of the boundaries between design and application of *artes mechanicae*. This leads him to suggest that *Salman und Morolf* should be considered a product of the later Middle Ages owing to its interest in technology and its 'Bauplanmentalität', characteristic of an era increasingly interested in how the world works.
71. The language of str. 161 is also used for Morolf's killing of the heathen doorkeeper in str. 183.
72. On the motif of rings in the text see Miklautsch, '*Salman und Morolf*', pp. 301-04.
73. Kraß, p. 261, refers to this disguise episode as a 'Serienmodell' in comparison to the 'Schichtenmodell' of disguise in the first part of the text, which is built up of different layers: Morolf's own skin, then the skin of the Jew, then a breastplate (noticed by a young *hertzogin*, str. 213), and finally the clothes of a pilgrim.
74. Neudeck, p. 111. His analysis of this passage occurs as part of a reading through Iser's 'Akt der Entblößung' of what he considers to be the 'fictional' nature of the text; in *Salman und Morolf*, the text displays its own fictionality not just through staged narrative or similar, but within the story itself in Morolf's disguises, which demonstrate how the behaviour of others can be manipulated by the telling of stories. Neudeck's complicated argument essentially boils down to an attempt to understand the complexities of the text by showing that it is fiction through various signs such as Morolf's disguises. In this instance, he seems to confuse the intention to speak in the fictional mode (that is, suspending the usual truth and sincerity commitments of a speech-act) with the intention to deceive, which is an abuse of standard communicative commitments, not their suspension.
75. Griese, p. 114, notes the similarity of this scene to *Willehalm*, strs 126-30, and *Wigalois*, ll. 1477-91.
76. This is the first time the epithet *mort grime* is used of Salme; it reoccurs throughout the text and is eventually assumed by Morolf when he kills Salme.
77. Griese, p. 115.
78. Miklautsch, '*Salman und Morolf*', pp. 302-03, argues that the main purpose of this test is to mock Salman's gullibility and that the formulation *durch aller frauwen ere* picks up on his weakness towards women and his blind worship of Salme.
79. On the game of chess in the Middle Ages, see Griese, pp. 115-17.
80. This act of recognition resembles the one in *König Rother*, where Rother's disguise is uncovered after he plays songs of the lyre that only he could play. The situation is, however, very different, as Rother's recognition is staged — his men have been told explicitly how they are to recognize him — and he is not physically concealed, but looks the same as he ever did, whereas Morolf does not want to be recognized and is disguised to such an extent he is wearing the very skin of another man. In *König Rother* it is striking that appearance does not play a role at all.
81. Wenzel, p. 190. Schulz, *Schwieriges Erkennen*, pp. 195-96, argues that eyes are 'Körpersynekdochen bzw. -metonymien' and that this is particularly pertinent for Morolf, who can alter all parts of his body and his clothes, by which a person can usually be recognized. Unfortunately, this completely contradicts his later argument concerning Morolf shedding the skin of the Jew after Salme recognizes him: '[D]as

akustische Gnorisma, das Lied, ist nur ein vorläufiges. Den endgültigen Beweis liefert die sichtbare Oberfläche. An diesem Basismuster kommt man nicht vorbei. Wo die Wahrheit nicht sichtbar ist, weil sie unter einer falschen Oberfläche verborgen liegt, muß man sie nur aufdecken.' (p. 206). In this case it makes more sense to interpret Morolf's shedding of the skin as a sign of his capitulation to Salme; it is not a contributory factor to the process of recognition.

82. For a detailed description of the different metaphorical uses of the mirror in medieval German literature, see Gudrun Schleusener-Eichholz, *Das Auge im Mittelalter*, 2 vols (Munich: Fink, 1985), II, 863–83.

83. Griese, p. 130: 'Die Eigenschaften des Spiegels von Helligkeit und Glanz, als Attribute angewandt auf Morolfs Augen, zeichnen diesen aus als Inbegriff des Sehens und des Sehers. Seine Augen übertreffen die Strahlkraft eines Spiegels noch. Seine Sehfähigkeiten und damit seine Erkenntnis, seine vorauskalkulierende Klugheit (List) machen ihn zum Protagonisten der unbesiegten Intelligenz.'

84. 'Falke', *Handwörterbuch des deutschen Aberglaubens*, II, cols 1156–58. See in particular Kriemhild's 'Falkentraum' in the *Nibelungenlied*, str. 13, and Der von Kürenberg's 'Falkenlied' (MF 8, 33–39, 5). See also Griese, pp. 122–23, who interprets the falcon as a symbol of the freedom and *hohen muot* of the ruler, and Bornholdt, '*in was zu schouwen also not*', p. 234, who argues that it symbolizes the untamed beloved and therefore Salman's untamed, unchaste love for Salme.

85. *Das Nibelungenlied*, strs 13–14.

86. Schulz, *Schwieriges Erkennen*, pp. 194–95, argues that the narrative arrangement of this passage of *Salman und Morolf* demonstrates that a 'Gnorisma', or recognizable mark, is a more reliable means of identification than the general appearance of the person, verifying the first impression. This is, he states, not unusual for medieval German epic (p. 193): '[G]ewöhnlich focussiert sich die Wahrnehmung nicht auf die Physiognomie, sondern auf bestimmte Einzelheiten oder singuläre körperliche Markierungen. Über solche Metonymien wird das Verhältnis zwischen dem Helden und den Zeichen, an denen er identifizierbar wird, nicht als ein willkürliches oder zufälliges, sondern als ein wesentliches gefaßt. Offenbar scheint dem die Vorstellung zugrunde zu liegen, daß sich in solchen metonymischen Zeichen die körperliche Präsenz des Heros dinghaft und sinnlich wahrnehmbar materialisiert. Die Kleidung scheint hierbei, anders als im höfischen Roman, die geringste Rolle zu spielen, weil sie am leichtesten manipulierbar ist.'

87. Neudeck, p. 104, suggests that the mermaid and dwarfs are a parody of the religious helpers usually found in bridal-quest narrative.

88. Griese, p. 132, argues that Salme is the embodiment of faithlessness and can therefore only be conquered by death.

89. Ibid., p. 131, suggests her death is a parody of the 'Philosophentod'.

CHAPTER 3

The *Münchner Oswald* Saint and King

The *Münchner Oswald* is particularly difficult to categorize. It tells the story of a historically attested saint, which places it firmly within the scope of classification as a hagiographical *vita*, and also negates the conventional result of a bridal quest by ending with a chaste marriage. On the other hand, it could — along with *König Rother* — be considered as one of the purest representations of the so-called bridal-quest schema, fitting the prototype almost exactly. All the 'necessary' elements are present: the advice scene; the messenger (with preternatural powers); objection to the marriage; cunning; a chase. Moreover, the characteristics applied to *Spielmannsepik*, the 'spielmännisch' style — comedy, a touch of burlesque, 'rough' poetics, and so on — could fit here, particularly in the character of the raven, who acts as Oswald's messenger. Even if these characteristics are dismissed as vague, the presence of comedy in the *Münchner Oswald* remains an important and not unproblematic question for its understanding. One of the particular aims of this study is to demonstrate the irrelevance of the bridal-quest schema as a useful explanatory structure, that is, its lack of pertinence as a symbolic structure or generator of specific meaning. Yet it cannot be denied that, thanks to its necessary subject matter — wooing — the bridal quest naturally lends itself to the literary exploration of worldly concerns. Here, the wooer is a saint and the marriage chaste. Equally, it is possible that the text may be funny, which might not be appropriate for saintly themes. These are the problems that face the reader of the *Münchner Oswald*, but, as I hope to show, they need not be problems at all.

Lives of St Oswald

St Oswald (*c.* 605–642) was king of Northumberland. The earliest written sources are found in the *Life of St Columba* (*c.* 700) written by Adomnán, abbot of the monastery of Iona, as well as in various other contemporary annals and, in most detail, in Bede's *Ecclesiastical History of the English People*.[1] Here, he is portrayed as a missionizing Christian king, killed on the battlefield by his heathen enemy, Penda.[2] His cult spread to continental Europe from the tenth century, but all the vernacular German Oswald stories are transmitted in manuscripts of the later Middle Ages.[3] There are a number of short *vitae*, all of which contain baptism miracles, Oswald's bridal quest (with the raven present), chaste marriage, battlefield martyrdom, and posthumous miracles: these lives are found in *Der Heiligen Leben* (often referred to as zn), *Das Märterbuch*, *Dat Passionael*, and (included because it has been shown to derive from a no longer extant MHG source) in the *Reykjahólabók* (the Icelandic *Ósvalds saga*).[4] For the sake of simplicity, I shall frequently refer to this group of *vitae* as the *Heiligen Leben* strand. The *Wiener Oswald*, transmitted in four fourteenth- and fifteenth-century manuscripts, and the *Münchner Oswald*, transmitted in six fifteenth-century manuscripts, are both verse texts, with a bridal quest, chaste marriage, and confessor death.[5] There are four prose versions of a similar story, all in fifteenth-century manuscripts: s, u (*Budapester Oswald*), b (*Berliner Oswald*) and the East-Swabian prose Oswald,[6] and the fourteenth-century fragment of the verse epic *Linzer Oswald*, the story of which is impossible to reconstruct.[7] Common to all German Oswald stories (with the possible exception of the *Linzer Oswald* fragment) are Oswald's chaste marriage and the presence of the raven as messenger and proxy wooer, although he is characterized differently in different stories. Scholarship has focused almost exclusively on the *Münchner Oswald*, the longest and most developed Oswald story, as well as perhaps the most problematic; the *Heiligen Leben* strand is made up of short texts with a clear hagiographical function in collections of *vitae*, the prose versions are generally argued to be redactions of the *Münchner Oswald* and the *Wiener Oswald* is generally considered to be much more 'serious', so less problematic. This latter text is usually discussed only in light of the *Münchner Oswald*, either as a later 'correction', a revision of its light-heartedness, or (for the same reasons) as an earlier work, closer to the archetypal vernacular Oswald story, with the *Münchner Oswald* as its more deviant descendant.[8]

The expansiveness of the *Münchner Oswald*, its comedy (particularly the raven), and the problem of a saint undertaking a bridal quest have led to particular trends in scholarship. Grouping the text with the other *Spielmannsepen* results in a determination to date it to the twelfth century to form a community with *Herzog Ernst* and *König Rother*. This desire for concurrency persists when the texts are classed as 'bridal-quest epic' and also suggests the secularization of the Oswald story in its integration into the popular, lay form of the bridal quest, which would result in a splicing of religious and secular genres, affecting the success of the text as a coherent whole. A short overview of some landmarks in scholarship is enlightening on this point.

For Georg Baesecke, who prepared the first critical edition of the *Münchner Oswald*, the late dating of the extant manuscripts provided scope for theories of interpolation. Dissatisfied with the transmitted text, he isolated a large number of interpolated passages, or even lines. He was particularly unsettled by the religious elements of the text, and therefore implied in his argument an uncomfortable meeting of lay and secular; the entire chastity motif, for instance, was considered an interpolation.[9] Using the evidence of the *Wiener Oswald* and the life of Oswald in *Der Heiligen Leben*, he attempted to reconstruct stages in the development of the German Oswald story tradition, with the aim of establishing the contents of the true archetype, which he dated to 1170 and located in or near Aachen.[10] Baesecke's style of interpretation is particularly characteristic of his age, directed at peeling back layers of interference to find the 'true' original text; although this style is now usually regarded as a futile exercise, the problem of finding the 'real' Oswald story has persisted in criticism.[11]

Walter Haug, for instance, maintains Baesecke's theory that the chaste marriage is a later addition: 'Baesecke hat in ihr gewiß zu Recht eine jüngere Zufügung gesehen'.[12] For him, the *Münchner Oswald* fits into the 'Doppelweg' structure he argues is characteristic of bridal-quest epic, but the chaste marriage alters the structure, providing a coda to the normal ending. This coda then forms the basis of his argument for the gradual literarization of the Oswald story; literary structures become old, their possibilities are used up, and people become aware of the structure and conscious of how it works. This enables the onset of a critical approach.[13] In the case of the *Münchner Oswald*, the addition of the chaste marriage at the end of the text works as an inversion of the principles of the bridal quest, a surprising final turn that does not destroy the traditional structure, but steps in a critical manner beyond its rules to change its perspective.[14] The core of this interpretation is again the apparent disparity between the bridal-quest structure and a religious emphasis.

Michael Curschmann also enters into the question of the emergence of the text, although he claims to attempt a reading of it as a coherent whole. He dates the *Münchner Oswald* to c. 1170–80, although he believes that the version we read today was written down in Regensburg at the start of the fourteenth century, the story having been brought from Weingarten by the Welfs at the highpoint of the Oswald cult in Southern Germany. It was then, he argues, disseminated fairly widely in the hundred years before the extant manuscripts were written.[15] Much of his argument is based on his excursus on the history of the cult of St Oswald and its iconography, which has many fascinating findings, particularly with regard to the translation of the Oswald cult to the continent, the Welfs, and Regensburg, but does not prove the dating of the *Münchner Oswald* in any way. His suggestion that the early dating of this version can be shown by its particularly accurate relationship to the historical facts — in the *Münchner Oswald* Oswald is king of Northumbria, whereas in the *Märtyrerbuch* and Linz fragment he is king of Norway, in the *Wiener Oswald* king of Germany, and in *Der Heiligen Leben* chosen to be king of an unnamed country by God because of his faith — seems particularly tenuous.[16] Moreover, the main argument for a twelfth-century origin of the *Münchner Oswald* is based on what Curschmann interprets as its use of a secular form (the bridal-quest schema) to discuss religious possibilities, namely the question whether worldly love (*minne*) can be justified in the eyes of God. This problem, he argues, as well as the fact that it seems embryonic and slightly unsuccessful in its execution, dates the text to before the *Blütezeit*; the theme, the 'Sanktionierung der minne durch Gott', finds its culmination in the works of Wolfram von Eschenbach.[17] Such an interpretation nonetheless implies a clear distinction between the religious and secular within the text, the combination of which Curschmann argues is not entirely successful. He finds a particular problem in the lack of cohesion between 'Thema' and 'Tiefenstruktur', suggesting that the bridal-quest schema insists on a clear structure which here has to be manipulated according to the theme (the sanctioning of worldly love in the eyes of God). The marriage of structure and theme is, he argues, not always a happy one.[18]

Curschmann's theory of reconciling religious and worldly affairs does not necessarily situate the text in the pre-*Blütezeit* period, for it is a theme that persists past the time of Wolfram and in this case, as we shall see, stems from the fact that Oswald has always been saint and king, rather than from the trend of any particular age. Moreover, his iconographic discourse does not help his argument; none of the early examples of iconography insist on the existence of this kind of Oswald story and the first instance of the raven is from the very late thirteenth century on one of the statues made for the so-called Dollingersaal in Regensburg.[19] The raven is also not only present in the *Münchner Oswald*, but also plays a part in the *Wiener Oswald* and *Der Heiligen Leben* strand; indeed, he is a fixed feature of Oswald stories in the vernacular.

It is not surprising, therefore, that attempts have been made to impose a late dating on the *Münchner Oswald*. De Boor stresses the popularity of the cult of St Oswald in the later Middle Ages and argues that the joy of storytelling, as well as the primitive nature of religion and the miraculous in the *Münchner Oswald* are characteristic of this period. He also finds it unconvincing that the form and freedom of rhyme in the text suggest a twelfth-century original, and finds similarity instead to late medieval religious drama.[20] Bräuer also argues that the *Münchner Oswald* has late medieval characteristics, resembling in particular literature produced in towns in the fifteenth century, and he even suggests that its redactor was a goldsmith. In a detailed comparison of each episode of the story, he aims to show that the *Wiener Oswald* is the older text and the closest to the original twelfth-century source, mainly by exploring its comparative 'seriousness'.[21] More recently, Marianne Kalinke has argued for the priority of the *Ósvalds saga*, transmitted in the Icelandic *Reykjahólabók* in the first half of the sixteenth century. She believes this to be the translation of a long Middle Low German Oswald legend, the High German source of which was the earliest vernacular Oswald legend, composed shortly after the canonization of Henry II in 1146. The Oswald stories in *Der Heiligen Leben* and the Low German *Dat Passionael* are condensed versions of this source, she argues, meaning that *Ósvalds saga* is the closest reflection of the original. The *Münchner Oswald* and *Wiener Oswald* cannot be a source for the other lives as they lack the coronation legend, *passio*, and miracles, which are unlikely to have been added at a later stage.[22]

Unfortunately, the arguments for dating the *Münchner Oswald* to the later Middle Ages are no more convincing than those in favour of a twelfth-century composition. It is clear only that the cult of St Oswald was translated to Germany in the twelfth century and there were almost certainly German Oswald stories at this time, but we cannot know what form they took, or which of the current extant versions they most resembled. The raven seems to become part of the story from the late thirteenth or early fourteenth century (at the latest), but again, we do not know what kind of role he played. Equally, the motif of marital chastity and the water bath to ensure this were an established part of the Oswald story by the mid-fourteenth century, as evidenced by Rulman Merswin's *Fünfmannenbuch*, in which the second lay brother discussed calls on the examples of Sts Elisabeth and Oswald to help him live chastely with his wife, who then taunts him into suffering a cold-water bath in the mode of St Oswald.[23] Again, this does not help us, however, to establish an exact date for the version of the *Münchner Oswald* we have today; all we can say for certain about this text is that it is in the form in which it was read in the fifteenth century.

It therefore seems advisable to consider the *Münchner Oswald* in a different light and return to the earlier discussion of different versions of the Oswald story. Two of the 'problems' with the *Münchner Oswald* — the bridal quest and chaste marriage — are common to all German vernacular versions of the Oswald story, and there is no reason to suggest that these were all influenced by the *Münchner Oswald*. It is clear that no contemporary readers had any difficulty with the religious status of these stories, as all versions (including the *Münchner Oswald*) are transmitted solely with other saints' lives or theological texts.[24] These versions were all transmitted contemporaneously, albeit in different geographical areas, so there is no proof that they directly influenced one another or (perhaps more importantly) that there could only be one canonical version of a saint's life at any one time. It seems more likely that saints' lives could develop in the manner of heroic epic or oral tales, changing details slightly to comply with specific functional needs, creating a web of strands that could influence one another and exist contemporaneously. I am not convinced that what matters in saints' lives is a particular historical truth (in the modern sense), but rather a compliance to certain models and traditions of sanctity, which may change in the course of time.

Chastity and Kingship

St Oswald has always been both saint and king, never a monk or an ascetic. He is a historically attested Christian warrior king, a battlefield hero-martyr.[25] He is not chaste, for, as Bede tells us, he has a wife and child and has assisted in the conversion of his wife's father.[26] Details of Oswald's life and emphases change in later *vitae*. Kalinke suggests that Drogo (d. 1084), who wrote a Latin *vita* of St Oswald in the late eleventh century in the abbey of St Winnoc in Bergue, placed more emphasis on Oswald's proselytizing efforts,[27] but of arguably more importance in this instance is Reginald of Durham's *Vita S. Oswaldi regis et martyris*, dated to 1162.[28] In this work, the motif of marital chastity has been introduced, although only after Oswald and his wife have had a son:

> Et quia, rege sancto Dei flagellis castigato, quicquid hactenus in aliquo excessit totum sedule emendare curavit, factum est ut Kyneburgam sponsam suam, regis Kynegulsi filiam, post hanc visionis gloriam ab unius thori communione sejungeret, et deinceps castitatis illibatae munditiam conservaret. Prius tamen de ea sobolem procreaverat, quem unicum tantum in terra filium possidebat.[29]

The importance of the conversion of Kyneburga (Oswald's wife) and her father before the marriage is also emphasized and Kyneburga takes the veil after Oswald's death.[30]

The most useful way of considering Reginald in the context of the German vernacular Oswald stories is not as a direct source (which cannot be proven), but rather as an example of the awareness of the problem of combining the roles of saint and king. Oswald is a king, so it is necessary for him to produce heirs and thus ensure the stability of his land (and his son is mentioned by Bede); yet he is also a saint, so should be chaste. Reginald provides a compromise by introducing chastity after the birth of a son. In the vernacular stories, this is taken one step further: there is no child, and the marriage is chaste from the start.

It is easy to see how and why the life of Oswald changed to comply with the demands of the time: the proselytizing purpose of Oswald's marriage is retained, but chastity is added, to fit the demands of the reforming movements of the eleventh and twelfth centuries.[31] The idea of an unchaste saint is almost unthinkable by the twelfth century. So why keep the marriage in the story at all? First, it must be remembered that Oswald is a king, and kings get married (this will be discussed in more detail below) and second, the marriage enables a demonstration of Oswald's sanctity; it allows him to convert heathens, perform miracles and, in his final test by Christ, shows that he is prepared to relinquish all his worldly life for the sake of God.

The twelfth century also saw the first instances of canonized kings who had apparently lived in chaste marriages: Edward the Confessor (d. 1066, canonized 1161) and the Holy Roman Emperor Henry II (d. 1024, canonized 1146).[32] Claims of chastity in both cases may have been motivated politically, for, as Elliott states in her study of chaste marriage ('spiritual' marriage, as she prefers to call it): '[C]learly the phenomenon of the virgin king is a convenient explanation for a disruption in succession — be it an awkward interregnum or the end of a dynasty. It also has the advantage of concealing disagreeable personal problems'.[33] It is important that the veneration of a monarch is posthumous and does not increase his worldly power, for a monarch canonized for his chastity and asceticism would most likely be considered in life to be shirking his most vital responsibilities of ensuring succession, but this form of posthumous veneration was certainly not detrimental to the church in the light of the reform movements. As Elliott suggests:

> The cult of the virginal king [...] conveyed a distinct political message to the lay world on behalf of the reformed papacy. The message was twofold: first, that in order for a layperson to be considered truly holy, he must attain a monastic level of purity, and second, that the monarchy was in no way exempt from this imperative. In other words, kings, who had more of a responsibility to reproduce than the average person since a country's stability depended on a regular succession, were commended and elevated for becoming eunuchs for God.'[34]

Kings canonized for their chastity are an extreme example of the contemporary demands of sainthood, relinquishing the world and retaining virginity at all costs. They could be considered to 'underline the level of asceticism that the laity was coming to expect from their saints'.[35]

The geographical proximity of the cult of St Oswald to that of Henry II, a Bavarian monarch, may well suggest the influence of the latter on the development of the former; Kalinke argues that the ultimate source of the vernacular Oswald stories was composed in the light of Henry's canonization, providing the motif of chaste marriage.[36] Ebernand von Erfurt's vernacular life of Henry (c. 1220) also contains certain motifs common to stories containing a bridal quest: the council scene, in which the king's advisers urge him to take a wife; the communal choice of wife; an exogamous marriage (albeit not a particularly exotic one).[37] Although these motifs are so widespread that direct influence in either direction cannot be inferred, it seems plausible that the cult of Henry and Kunegunde could have provided a model for the development of the Oswald story, which most likely reached Southern Germany at around this time.³⁸ This is made more likely by the fact that Oswald had always been saint and king, was attested to have married, and was involved in the conversion of his father-in-law to Christianity. Given the contemporary views on marriage, a chaste marriage would appear to be the most appropriate compromise of the story — perhaps even its natural development. We may therefore suggest that these circumstances point to the probability of the introduction of a chaste marriage to the Oswald story during this period, probably from the outset rather than after the birth of a successor, as in Reginald of Durham's *vita*. Yet this says nothing for the dating of the *Münchner Oswald*, especially given that the chaste marriage is present in the *Wiener Oswald* and the *Heiligen Leben* strand.

These contemporary models can also help to illuminate the change in the manner of Oswald's death from martyrdom on the battlefield to a confessor's death in bed. The simple act of dying in battle would not prevent him from having previously entered into a chaste marriage and I would argue that the bridal-quest structure does not place demands on the end of a text. The direct influence of the cult of Henry II could be suggested, but it seems more likely that a confessor death is symptomatic of the growing importance of saintly asceticism; it underlines a move from the heroic model of sainthood to the emphasis on the essential monasticism of the king. In the *Münchner Oswald*, withdrawal from the world seems to be the preferred means of gaining the approval of God and the narrator leaves us in no doubt of Oswald's place in the eyes of God after his death:

> also ist sand Oswald erstarben
> und hat gotes huld erwarben
> er und deu chun[i]gin:
> des sult ir sicher sein! (ll. 3555–58)

Oswald's death just two years after his marriage (l. 3511; ll. 3535–42) corresponds with a general preoccupation in this text with early death. The converted heathens also die as soon as they have been converted; having experienced hell after their death in battle, they are terrified, when miraculously resurrected, of living longer in the world for fear of committing more sins (ll. 3151–68). Oswald says that they will all die within a year, but this does not satisfy them, for they demand to die immediately, and this wish is granted. In the *Münchner Oswald*, therefore, there seems to be a sense that conversion is as far as one need go, and that after conversion we are saved, so have no more need of life. After Oswald's final test from Christ, it is clear that he has reached a state of saintly perfection and has achieved as much as he can, so there is no reason to delay death any longer.³⁹

A confessional death also makes the life of the saint more plausible for imitation. Note the bath, recommended to Oswald and Paug by Christ in order to quell temptation:

> merk, wie du den sunden solt widerstan:
> wasser soltu vor deinem pet han;
> wann dich dein manhait wil betwingen,
> so soltu in daz wasser springen.
> also tuo auch deu frau dein (ll. 3515–19)

It is possible to suggest — if hesitantly — that this could be read as a recommendation for the general audience. It brings chaste marriage into the sphere of the everyday; not an otherworldly state reserved for saint, but a challenging, practical solution for any man.[40] Not all versions of the Oswald story adopt a confessional death, however; the *Heiligen Leben* strand of lives retains the battlefield martyrdom, suggesting the flexibility of saints' lives and the likelihood of the possibility of concurrent (and different) strands of development.

The above discussion should have provided a plausible notion of how and why Oswald stories may have developed, although very little has been discussed that is specific to the *Münchner Oswald*. Nikolaus Miller's interpretation of this text, that the whole course of the bridal quest has a religious purpose, its end complying with the principle of negation common to saints' lives and God acting as its agent at every stage (expressed in advice or miracles), is highly attractive in its simplicity, particularly given the emphasis of our discussion up to now. He argues that the final scene of the text exemplifies the successful fusion of both bridal quest (marriage) and saint's life (relinquishing all worldly goods; test; death and ascension to heaven). In this sense, Oswald's final test from Christ works as a revision (or even negation) of the bridal quest, in which Oswald relinquishes its product (his wife): 'das Brautwerbungsschema ist also Mittel einer Heiligengeschichte, die ihren religiösen und letzlich kultischen Zweck als göttliches Wirken zugleich *verdeckt* und *exekutiert*: Oswalds Weg aus der Welt (Heiligkeit) wird als Weg durch die Welt (Brautwerbung) erzählt'.[41]

Yet the simplicity of Miller's argument is where its problem lies, as it could function just as effectively for the *Wiener Oswald* or the Oswald stories of the *Heiligen Leben* strand, given its result as essentially an explanation of how a bridal quest with a chaste marriage can be religiously motivated and demonstrative of sanctity. As is often the case with a largely structural argument, it divides the text into large blocks of plot, concentrating on *what* is told in large-scale — sending a messenger, wooing the princess, conversion, and so on — without considering *how* these scenes are told. Yet the specific narrative characteristics of the *Münchner Oswald* are to be found not in its objective structure, but in its subjective intention. It is here that we find the insertion of comedy or particular narrative oddities, moments that I believe have often led to interpretations of the text as incoherent, or an awkward splicing of secular and sacred. The *Wiener Oswald*, however, which has much the same objective structure, is rarely considered problematic, or even considered at all unless as a 'serious' foil to the *Münchner Oswald* (which I may be guilty of myself).[42] The next step, therefore, is to investigate these narrative 'oddities' and this potential humour, or rather how the particular narrative world of the *Münchner Oswald* is created. Attention will be focused on the way in which things in this world (which may seem odd or under-motivated) are made intelligible, and how (or indeed if) they affect the 'religious' purpose of the text. The raven merits specific consideration and will be discussed by himself at the end of the chapter.

Before moving on, however, it may be helpful to explain the treatment in this chapter of other versions of the Oswald story, particularly the *Wiener Oswald*. I mentioned above that I may be guilty of using it as a foil, but I hope that this is only because I do not have time or space to pay it more consideration. The specific fruit of the *Wiener Oswald* in this instance is its contrasting similarity to the *Münchner Oswald* — by which I mean that it tells largely the same basic story (the two texts could have much the same synopsis) but with different narrative modalities. I shall therefore be exploiting the former text when a contrast — a different way of telling the same episode — helps to illuminate the narrative world of the latter. I do not mean to suggest direct intertextuality, nor to suggest a common archetypal source or argue for the primacy of either version. My interest is rather in the different ways a similar story can be told, an exercise I believe is more interesting and valuable. Perhaps, at a later date, effort will be expended on the *Wiener Oswald* as a text in its own right.[43]

Problems of Interpretation in the *Münchner Oswald*

Oswald, young and orphaned, thinks constantly about how he may please God, and in this context decides he should take a wife:

> er sprach: solt ich mich sein nicht schämen,
> so wolt ich geren ain frauen nemen.
> nun pin ich ain kindischer man:
> herr, wie sol ich ez greifen an?
> ich näm geren ain magedein,
> möcht ez nür an sund gesein. (ll. 35–40)

Despite the mention of *scham* and *sund*, there is no explicit statement of intended chastity, unlike in the *Wiener Oswald*, where Oswald asks his men if they know a suitable woman:

> eine juncfrouwen so ho geborn,
> di im zu nemen tochte,
> da her mit bliben mochte
> kusche biz an sin ende
> ane alle missewende. (WO ll. 54–58)[44]

The sense of l. 35 of the *Münchner Oswald* refers to Oswald's intention to marry a woman of whose status he would not be ashamed (as in l. 54 of the *Wiener Oswald*) and *ez* in l. 40 of the former text refers back to the *magedein*, insisting that the bride, not the marriage itself, be without sin. The main motivation for marriage in the *Münchner Oswald* seems to be succession; when Oswald is sleeping, his *herz* advises his *sinnen* what he should do:

> 'Oswalt, sullend deineu land an ein frauen stan?
> treun, daz ist nicht guot getan!
> zweu sullen dir weiteu kun[i]kreich,
> du hiets[t] dann ain frauen tugentleich?
> sturbstu, so wurd ez erblos:
> nim dir aine die sei dein genoß!' (ll. 45–50)

It is unclear whether this 'dream' constitutes a message from God, but a similar instance of inspiration occurs later in the text, when the plan of the golden stag comes to Oswald in his sleep (*do was im in dem schlaf fur chomen* (l. 2331)), and given the agency of God in this part of the text (which will be discussed later), it seems likely that this 'dream' would be divinely inspired.[45] Probably of greatest importance, however, is that the statement about the necessity of succession is never contradicted, even when an angel appears and gives Oswald's bridal quest a crusading slant (ll. 60–70). The angel's speech is the first explicit introduction of the conversion function of Oswald's wooing, which seems its equal motivation from this time on; conversion and marriage become one and the same thing, dependent on one another and perhaps even mutually representative.[46] Yet the motivation of succession is never mentioned again, nor negated until the very end of the text in Christ's instigation of a chaste marriage. Why should it be mentioned at all?

The answer is simple: kings marry because they want progeny. Oswald is a saint and a king; his office dictates that he marry and this marriage can be used to offer a demonstration of his sanctity. There must be a reason for him to marry and for the story to begin, which has to be the desire for descendants, simply because it is the reason kings marry. Other motivation can then be introduced — in this case, conversion — and the original motivation of descendants forgotten; it is noticeable that the *erbe* is never mentioned again.[47] At the end of the text, when Oswald is tested by Christ disguised as a beggar, the last thing demanded of him is his wife, in exactly the same wording as ll. 46–47 cited above:

> '[Oswalt,] so gib mir auch die frauen dein!
> zweu solten mir weiteu kun[i]kreich,
> ich hiet dann ain frauen tugentleich?' (ll. 3440–42)

It is true that the *erbe* is not mentioned here, but the parallel use of language is still noticeable and drives home the fact that great kings must have wives.[48]

Following this reasoning, it could even be suggested that the *Münchner Oswald* makes more sense than the *Wiener Oswald*, which makes explicit the intention of chastity from the outset.

The intention to marry is formulated similarly to the *Münchner Oswald* in *Die Hochzeit*, an allegorical poem from the mid-twelfth century, transmitted solely in the so-called Millstätter Sammelhandschrift (Klagenfurt, Landesarchiv, Cod. GV 6/19, c. 1200), which uses a bridal quest as the basis for its exegesis.[49] After an introduction about the way in which a *zeichen* can be extricated from a *spel* and the duty of those with a good understanding to teach others, as well as a discussion of the importance of *reht* and baptism for the afterlife, a *spel* ('story') is told about a king who lives on a high mountain and woos a bride who lives in the valley below. The rest of the poem consists of an exegesis of this wooing and marriage, as well as the bridal procession, dress, and so on, and this exegesis often steps beyond the confines of the story in the strictest sense. The *spel* provides an impetus for the discussion of two themes central to Christian theology: life and death, and the birth of Christ and the history of salvation.[50] Noticeably, the king wants to marry to ensure succession:

> do wolde do der guote chneht
> gehiwen umbe daz reht,
> daz er einen erben verliezze,
> den nieman sines riches bestiezze,
> der mohte sin ein chunich ane sorgen
> ubir dei telir unde ubir die berge. (ll. 210–15)[51]

The marriage here is an allegorical union between Christ and the soul, the result of which will not be offspring, and this statement is never interpreted allegorically in the exegesis of the story.[52] *Die Hochzeit* seems to offer the same kind of 'false' motivation as the *Münchner Oswald*; marriage is initially motivated by succession, even if this seems logically out of keeping with the rest of the text, because it is the reason kings get married. In each case the product or symbolic value of the marriage is very different, and *erbe* is forgotten after it has fulfilled its introductory function.

Oswald's journey to Aron and the princess's escape is another example of odd motivation; here, the problem is more one of contradictory causality within the scene, of constant false starts and solutions. The princess gives the raven instructions for Oswald's wooing expedition, which include bringing a gilded stag and not forgetting the raven. Oswald duly follows her wishes, but spends so much time with the stag that he forgets the raven. When the raven finally arrives, however, having been summoned by an angel, he is sent immediately to the princess for yet further instructions — indeed, this seems to be his primary function and the role he must play in order that the expedition succeed.

The princess then suggests to the raven that Oswald and one hundred of his men disguise themselves as goldsmiths who have come to honour her father; goldsmiths, however, formed no part of her original plan, and the stag seems quite forgotten. Oswald panics at the lack of goldsmiths (ll. 2100–04), but, coincidentally, there are twelve among his men who happen to have brought their tools with them (ll. 2105–28). The goldsmith plan works insofar as it allows Oswald successfully to ingratiate himself with Aron, but has no larger effect for the plot and does not fulfil its aim of rescuing the princess, as the goldsmiths remain outside the castle walls for a year without achieving anything (ll. 2311–12). It does not even ensure his safety in an enemy land, for the men other than the hundred supposed goldsmiths remain undisturbed in their hiding place (ll. 2631–36).

The goldsmith episode is of great importance to Bräuer and central to his argument that the *Münchner Oswald* was written in a town in the latter half of the thirteenth century or the start of the fourteenth century; he also finds this episode somewhat contradictory, which he believes demonstrates that the goldsmiths first appear in this version of the Oswald story.[53] The seemingly unnecessary presence of the goldsmiths, as well as the prominence of the earlier goldsmith episode (ll. 435–564), lead him to argue that the redactor of this text may well have been a goldsmith himself.[54] Bräuer's argument, supported by the mid-fifteenth-century Strassburg manuscript of *Laurin*, which was written out (if not reworked) by *diebolt von hanowe der goltsmider*, is plausible but tenuous, and can only remain unproven.[55] Rather than any specific contextual significance, perhaps what is more important here is the way in which the narrative always seems to reach a dead end before being re-established in a new direction. This is further evidenced by the next solution, which is also largely unproductive.

Oswald dreams — the dream is probably (but not explicitly) divinely inspired — that he should cover his stag in gold to lure the heathens to a hunt. This motivational process is again highly odd, for the princess had insisted he bring a gilded stag with him and preparing a stag (albeit 'un-gilded') for the voyage is strongly emphasized, to the extent that it causes Oswald to leave the raven behind. The stag is then forgotten and hitherto unmentioned goldsmiths enter the story. The goldsmiths have no effect and the idea of a gilded stag — already suggested as an object without purpose — occurs seemingly unprompted to Oswald in a dream.[56] In this instance narrative and motivation do not work concurrently and the princess's suggestion of a golden deer is completely unmotivated, functioning as a means of ensuring that Oswald bring the animal with him, but without any purpose or premeditation on her part. In this sense, the prescribed deer is golden because at some point someone will decide to gild it, a future perfect golden deer, as it were. Equally, it could be argued that its function earlier in the plot is to cause Oswald and his men to forget the raven; in this sense, it is necessary for it to enter into the story earlier on. Nonetheless, motivation is still confused.[57]

In the *Wiener Oswald*, however, the stag is not mentioned in the princess's original plan — she merely suggests that Oswald come disguised as a merchant (WO, ll. 568-77) — but as part of her plan after Oswald has arrived in her father's land; the motivational confusion of the *Münchner Oswald* is not present. The stag in the *Wiener Oswald* is explicitly a religious beast, a solution for which Oswald can pray because, the princess claims, he is a saintly man (WO, ll. 1010-18). Oswald's prayers are successful:

> do her dise wort gesprach,
> einen hirz her do vor im sach
> uz dem pardise
> in alle der wise
> unde in alle dem gebere,
> obe iz ein engel were,
> von silber und von golde,
> also got von himel wolde. (WO, ll. 1058-65)[58]

In the *Münchner Oswald*, there is no explicit statement that the stag is a creature of God, and the animal is not miraculously golden, but gilded by the goldsmiths.[59] This process is described in Oswald's instructions to them in detail:

> und wurcht dem hirschen guldein clo,
> so wil ichs im mit schnüeren seidein,
> pinten zuo den füessen sein. [...]
> und mach mir zwai guldeiniu hirsch horen:
> macht mirs schon und innen hol,
> als si der hirsch auf dem haubt tragen sol.
> noch wil ich euch mer sagen:
> ein guldein dek muoß ich haben,
> das si neben des hirsch ge auf die erd. (ll. 2344-53)

Moreover, Aron believes the 'golden' stag to be a mechanical creation of the goldsmiths:

> daz geticht get von den goltschmiden her.
> die sind all sampt kunst vol
> und habent den hirsch innen gemacht hol,
> daz er lauft von den winden (ll. 2400-03)

This sense of the un-miraculous is continued by the stag itself: whereas in the *Wiener Oswald* and the Oswald stories of the *Heiligen Leben* strand the stag seems in some way aware of the role he has to play and enjoys leading the heathens a merry dance, this stag is scared by the sight of approaching huntsmen and dogs and runs away for this reason (ll. 2445-50).

In both cases, the stag only achieves a certain amount, for although it keeps Aron and his men away from the castle, they still lock the gates behind them so the princess is unable to escape. In the *Münchner Oswald*, she prays to Mary and the gates open miraculously (ll. 2543–68); in the *Wiener Oswald*, Oswald himself prays for the gates to open (ll. 1104–23). In both texts, as we have seen, there is a tendency for human action to achieve a certain amount and then reach an insurmountable obstacle, which can only be overcome with help from God. In the *Münchner Oswald*, however, this need for divine agency is made greater by the more complex causal process of wooing the bride — the goldsmiths, the unmotivated gilded stag — as well as the more 'worldly' nature of the stag himself. Perhaps the stag in the *Münchner Oswald*, a consciously 'man-made' object, cannot function as a 'Metonymie des Heils', as Kiening would have it for the *Wiener Oswald*, but this does not mean that a similar structure of divine intervention in the form of miracles is not present.[60] The stag may be more worldly, but is still miraculously saved when it reaches its own stumbling block at the top of a cliff, flying over it and landing on the other side by the sea (ll. 2455–68).

We should take a step back and consider how divine intervention functions in the rest of the text. Divine help is a constant from the start of the *Münchner Oswald*, when an angel advises Oswald to take a heathen bride (ll. 59–70), but the first direct intervention by one of the persons of the Trinity occurs when the raven is sitting on the top of a tall tower and cannot be called down:

> der himlisch hailant,
> den raben er schier her ab gesant,
> daz er kam geflogen pald
> fur den milten kunig Oswald. (ll. 395–98)

In all of these cases human action reaches a seemingly insurmountable obstacle and is saved by what I shall term a *miraculum ex machina*. The entire wooing episode consists of a series of miracula ex machina: the raven is forgotten, but fetched by an angel; the goldsmith tactic fails, but the idea of the gilded stag comes to Oswald in a dream; the stag is chased by the heathens and reaches the top of a high cliff, but miraculously flies over the top; the castle doors are locked but open miraculously for the princess.

Miracula ex machina persist after Oswald and the princess escape. The raven spies Aron and his men in pursuit, so Oswald prays for help (ll. 2795–812), promising to do whatever God asks of him and give him whatever he requests, if only he is freed from the heathens. His wish is granted, and a mist descends over the heathen boats. Yet, as is also the case for the miracles discussed above, this is only a temporary solution, as battle with the heathens is not avoided, but only delayed. The significance in this particular case is found in its later relevance, when Oswald's promise comes into play in his 'test' by the disguised

Christ. There is thus complexity in temporal cause and effect; Oswald's promise works in the short term, but the very short-term nature of divine help, as well as the inevitability of battle and overwhelming success of the Christians, make it seem irrelevant. The major significance of the promise is its long-term effect, namely the establishment of a framework through which Oswald can be tested and his sanctity finally proven.[61]

Haug makes the important observation that miracles in this form become a part of the literary structure of the *Münchner Oswald*; thus the audience's horizon of expectation comes to prescribe a major obstacle to each human action and a divine solution (the *miraculum ex machina*).[62] He develops this theory to argue that such a structure makes the hagiographical function of the text questionable, thanks to the inevitability and regularity of miracles, and that such a structured saint's life can only be thought of as comic.[63] Such a possibility brings us back to the earlier comparison with the *Wiener Oswald*, which raises the question of the seriousness of our text (even if we do not want to argue that the two versions are related or reacting to one another).

A lack of seriousness is also perhaps the impression gained from reading the conversion scene of the *Münchner Oswald*. Here, the demand is not for miracles as a solution to an insurmountable difficulty, but rather as a tangible sign of Oswald's faith and the power of Christianity. *What* happens — the conversion of heathens — is not problematic, but the question is rather one of *how* it happens and whether or not the miraculous is compromised in any way. As with wooing the princess, there is nothing challenging about the act of converting her father and the other heathens, but questions arise about the manner in which this is done.

Aron is the only heathen left alive after the battle, and agrees to be baptized if Oswald resurrects his slaughtered followers (ll. 2973–82). Yet after Oswald does this, Aron still refuses to convert, stating that even if he had seven heads, he would chop them all off before believing in the Christian god, before exhorting his resurrected men to renew the battle (ll. 3013–23). These men refuse; they have experienced hell and wish to convert. The emphasis here is therefore placed on the necessity of tangible experience for belief, not simply blind faith, although even this cannot satisfy Aron. He demands another miracle, that Oswald draw water from a rock, after which he agrees to be baptized (ll. 3052–60). Yet this conversion remains profoundly unsatisfying, for Aron only even considers baptism because Oswald has rid him of his military strength (ll. 3041–44) and is eventually scared into the process by Oswald threatening to behead him (ll. 3099–106). A comparison with the *Wiener Oswald* calls the seriousness of the episode into question. In the latter text, the princess's father is imprisoned and has a vision of heaven and hell; in hell, he sees a demented, disgusting she-wolf — his deceased wife — with an empty seat next to her, and in heaven he sees Mary and three empty thrones, two of which are destined for Oswald and his wife (WO, ll. 1252–305). The destiny of the heathen king (who is nameless in the *Wiener Oswald* until his conversion, but called Johannes afterwards, symbolic of his future converting efforts in his own land) is undecided — he can choose the empty chair in heaven or in hell.

The conversion scene, as well as the problematic motivation of the princess's escape, begs the question whether the *Münchner Oswald* is meant to be funny. If this is the case, then it must be asked whether comedy makes a mockery of the saint and the miraculous. One possibility is that events in the text are made irresolvable — ridiculous, even — in order to demonstrate that God can overcome anything, although this might be too naïve an interpretation of the thought-process of the reader. We must also be wary of enforcing a modern conception of comedy upon a medieval audience, particularly with regard to saints' lives and the miraculous, which often cannot help but seem ridiculous and overblown to our contemporary secular sensibilities. Haug admits this, but cannot accept that a medieval audience would have taken miracles such as these seriously. He attempts a compromising theory:

> ich glaube jedoch, man muß — so schwer es uns fallen mag, dies nachzuvollziehen — noch mit einer anderen Möglichkeit rechnen, mit der Möglichkeit nämlich, daß das Mittelalter das Wunder in seiner ganzen Unbegreiflichkeit, und das heißt in seiner ganzen Absurdität, akzeptiert hat und daß man sich deshalb nicht scheute, diese Absurdität unter dem Aspekt zu präsentieren, unter dem sie sich der menschlichen Vernunft darstellt, unter dem Aspekt des Komischen. [...] So paradox es klingen mag: weil das Mittelalter das Wunder ganz ernst nahm, konnte es komisch erscheinen.[64]

This argument falls down on its generalizing definition of 'menschliche[r] Vernunft' and the insistence on the absurdity of miracles; it is impossible to insist on such an argument for a society so strongly rooted in the Christian belief system, in which miracles surely held a significant (and serious) role. The theory posed by Ward seems more plausible:

> miracles were [...] inserted into discourses to arouse interest and attention, and thus became entertainment. As tales about human situations, often involving well-known people, they had the appeal of gossip. As tales about the mysterious otherworld of the saints, they had the appeal of the unexpected and novel. But they were not in themselves subjects for laughter.[65]

Yet this is not to discount the possibility of comedy in the *Münchner Oswald*; even if the miracles themselves are not funny, there is still comic potential in Aron's refusal to accept them, or Oswald's panic at his lack of goldsmiths or — most particularly — in the character of the raven. Haug suggests that comedy can enhance a serious argument, arguing that the most serious events and ideas, particularly those outside human possibility and understanding, require a relativizing lack of seriousness so that they do not become unintentionally comic. Thus:

> was jenseits menschlicher Möglichkeiten liegt, wird nur dadurch faßbar, daß man es ins Spiel eines interpretierenden Entwurfs einsetzt. [...] im Komischen dramatisiert und radikalisiert sich die Erfahrung von der spielerischen Setzung aller Entwürfe, in denen der Mensch sich selbst übersteigt.[66]

It is doubtful whether comedy need have such an active effect; equally, the purpose of relativization seems unnecessary, for surely comedy is not necessary to understand that human speech is incapable of adequately describing the divine.

More likely is the quite simple notion of 'prodesse ut delectare', the idea that something will be absorbed more easily and with more interest if it is also entertaining. Both Wehrli and Curtius speak of examples of comedy in a religious context in such light, Curtius discussing Latin hagiography and Wehrli entertaining tales of miracles, such as the *Dialogus miraculorum* of Caesarius.[67] In a similar fashion, Seeber bases his reading of the *Münchner Oswald* on the foundation of classical rhetoric and argues that insertions of comedy act as cognitive triggers, that is, 'they mark situations clearly and make it easier to remember the contents provided'.[68] His argument that the comedy of the text is dependent on its fictionality is more problematic. Following Kalinke's argument that the *Münchner Oswald* is to be distinguished from historical lives of Oswald as a fictionalized narrative, he states that:

> the Munich version of the Saint Oswald story shows the impact of fictionalizing a historical saintly figure and adapting his biography to a new literary context of transmission. It articulates the basic problem of how an already existing story can transgress given borders and enter the realm of a new genre, that of fictional narration, and it uses concepts of hagiography and comedy in combination to solve the task.[69]

The notion of 'fictionalizing' the life of a saint, which would imply that statements are made that are not objectively true, is perhaps a little extreme; moreover, the development of the narrative of the life of St Oswald has already been discussed, the aim being to show that there is no fundamental problem with the basic plot of the vernacular Oswald stories.

I would like to pose an alternative and suggest that the security of the Christian belief system may provide a kind of freedom of licence, an immovable framework of certainty within which risks can be taken and a certain amount of narrative and comic freedom allowed. So the *Münchner Oswald* is, in a sense, a more comic version of the Oswald story, but this does not compromise its seriousness (or increase it, if we follow Haug's argument). Furthermore, it is difficult to believe that the story of a saint would not have been taken seriously, and we only need to glance at the transmission of the *Münchner Oswald* to see that it was thought of as a religious work, transmitted solely with theological texts (see above). The *Münchner Oswald* is only one telling of the *vita* of St Oswald, whose cult was widespread in Southern Germany throughout the Middle Ages; the text was part of an established tradition. Tradition — the solidity of the cult of St Oswald and the framework of Christian belief within which it stands — gives a certain degree of freedom, namely a freedom of expansion and development. Note that the *Münchner Oswald* is over twice the length of the *Wiener Oswald* yet tells much the same basic plot; the difference is that the *Münchner Oswald* adds episodes, expands, and digresses. The 'fun' of the *Münchner Oswald* is had not in *what* happens, but *how* it happens. It does not matter, for example, if the conversion scene may be a touch ridiculous — what matters is that the heathens are converted and Oswald displays his sanctity in miracles, which can only be the work of God.[70] Equally, the earlier stumbling blocks in the narrative (the goldsmiths, the stag, and so on) simultaneously provide entertainment and demonstrate the presence of God; any comedy present in the text does not interrupt, derail, or call into question Oswald's sanctity.[71] Comedy exists in parallel to the religious narrative, but does not exert an adverse consequence upon it.[72] In this sense, it does not matter what the effect of the comic is: perhaps it might act as a 'cognitive trigger' and maintain for longer the attention of the audience, allowing them to learn more from the exemplary life of a saint; equally, perhaps it was possible to be entertained and to learn about a saint, and for these two actions to remain unconnected.

Following this line of thought, it may be fruitful to consider the conversion miracles in a little more depth. The miracles performed by God through Oswald are clearly located in a tradition with obvious precedents. The example of drawing water from a rock is discussed by Ward with reference to other saints, such as Sts Benedict (Gregory, *Dialogues* II.5), Dunstan, and Anselm, who in turn follow the example of Moses (Ex. 17:1–7).[73] This miracle, in turn, can be interpreted typologically with the blood and water flowing from the wound in Christ's side at his crucifixion (John 19:34) and the symbolic potential of Christ and the water he offers as life (John 4:5–15). According to Ward, it is of utmost importance that the saint, in his life and miracles, conform to the recognized patterns of sainthood, imitating Christ in particular, but also other saints.[74] In a discussion of common miracle topoi occurring while the saint is still alive, she demonstrates the importance of the saint's recognizable place in the patterns of sanctity:

> in the case of miracles in the *Lives* of the saints, the interest of the reader is focussed on the saint himself and his likeness to his predecessors. The life of a saint whose history was unknown could be entirely reconstructed

from hagiographical models. While the records of miracles at shrines in the medieval period were, generally speaking, a painstaking record of what people believed had happened to them by the power of the saint, miracles in saints' *Lives* cannot be taken at their face value in the same way; nevertheless, when this distinction has been made, they have a special and remarkable value in showing what mattered to readers in accounts of sanctity.[75]

If 'what mattered' was an assumption of common hagiographical topoi, a likeness to other saints and to Christ, then this is achieved successfully in the *Münchner Oswald*.

Drawing water from a rock is not the only instance of a widespread miracle in the *Münchner Oswald*; resurrection is also a very common miracle and, interestingly, particular communication with ravens is not rare. A biblical parallel can be found in the case of Elijah (1 Kings 17:4–6), who is brought food by ravens, and a raven brings food to St Anthony and St Paul in the desert.[76] Benedict (*Dialogues* II.8) feeds a raven daily with his own hands, and he also asks this raven (the act of speech, or communication, be it literal or spiritual, is of interest here) to carry away a poisoned piece of bread to where no-one might find it. Interestingly, the raven is at first hesitant to perform this task. Further to this, it is also notable that when Oswald prays for miracles in the conversion episode, he refers to the relevant episode in the life of Christ; he prays for resurrection in the memory of Christ's resurrection and salvation of mankind (ll. 2985–92) and for water from the rock in memory of Christ's baptism in the river Jordan (ll. 3071–78).

It seems that the clear patterns of hagiography in which these miracles stand and the immovable system of belief they represent allow a degree of freedom, a model so secure to allow movement and potential comedy within it. The *miraculum ex machina* structure of Oswald's wooing expedition allow an expansion of the scene and therefore more variety, more entertainment, more possibilities for 'exciting' plans and astounding miracles, as well as for an assertion of the constant presence of God. The theory of freedom within the plot can be continued in an interpretation of the role, character, and actions of the raven, who, on the one hand, is completely unproblematic for the plot, but on the other is the agent of seemingly superfluous detail, potentially undermining comedy, and actions that appear unmotivated and without symbolic meaning.

Oswald's Raven

Oswald's raven is the most obvious example of the mixture of the functional and the superfluous, the instance of where the freedom of expansion discussed above really comes to the fore, yet — importantly — without adversely affecting the course of the story or Oswald's sanctity.[77] The role of the messenger is particularly suitable for this, as it allows a certain amount of time away from the protagonist, enabling the progression of his cause (and the plot) but equally opening up space for individual behaviour and adventures. In this case, the very fact that the raven is a raven, not a human, will also become important.

The raven is introduced with a function: Oswald needs a suitable messenger, and the pilgrim Warmunt suggests a raven he has raised at his court for twelve years, who has been given the gift of speech by God. Oswald is surprised, because he has never heard the raven speak (ll. 360–66), but the raven is given speech at that very moment — another *miraculum ex machina*, a *zaichen* from God tied up with the raven's specific purpose in the plot:

> der himlisch trachtein
> tet da sein genad schein
> und gab dem raben an der stund,
> daz er alle sprach wol reden chunt. (ll. 391–94)

The raven's first appearance, just before he becomes a talking raven, sets the tone for his involvement in the story; he is sitting at the top of a tall tower and Oswald and his men panic at their inability to get him down, providing a sudden and unexpected injection of comedy (ll. 377–84). The problem is, naturally, solved by divine help, establishing the agency of God as a problem-solver in the text, but this solution nevertheless does not detract from the comic potential of the raven, whose presence is constantly accompanied by comedy or distraction from the narrative. He is demanding and obsessed with his appearance and food; on his way to woo the princess by proxy he is briefly captured by mermaids, a seemingly irrelevant episode; he refuses to tell Oswald the results of his wooing expedition until he is well fed and rested; when left behind, he sulks and must be forced into the air by an angel to join his master.

Being able to talk marks the raven out as different and as special, and he wants to extend this with physical decoration:

> wan ich kom under die haidmischen man,
> so wirt mich ein michel volk gaffen an,
> so mag ich desder paß einen frid gehaben
> (her, daz wil ich dir fur war sagen)
> fur vahen und fur schiessen. (ll. 445–49)

There is a practical side to this wish for decoration, for being marked out as 'no ordinary bird' will save the raven from the dangers commonly faced by birds, but this is qualified by people staring at him, suggesting a desire not only for protection, but also attention. There is no mention of how a richly decorated messenger might reflect well on Oswald.[78] To return to the *Wiener Oswald*, it is noticeable that the raven is decorated for largely the same reasons, but that it is the pilgrim — here called Tragemund — who suggests it (ll. 113–22; 202–16).[79] In the *Münchner Oswald*, it is the raven himself who makes these demands, entirely without modesty, and there is a relatively extensive description of his decoration. It is clear that appearance is important to him, a suggestion of vanity that ties in with his demanding love of food. Food plays a large part in the raven's adventures, and not entirely without narrative function: it gives him the wisdom to escape from the mermaids (ll. 707–10) and to plan how to tell Aron his message (ll. 901–04).[80] He perpetually demands food, and a lack of adequate nourishment is his primary complaint at being left behind by Oswald (ll. 1840–68). He is characterized as vain and demanding, concerned above all with his own comfort; as Haug suggests, '[D]er Rabe ist also als übersensibler Parvenu gezeichnet, wobei sich höfische Form mit mehr oder weniger kaschierter Gefräßigkeit mischt'.[81] Food plays no part in the *Wiener Oswald*.

Again, therefore, there is a mixture of the functional and the superfluous; an obsession with food helps the raven in his tasks, but at the same time seems rather gratuitous. It is an amusing tendency of this vain bird, but nonetheless a tendency that does not hamper the plot or Oswald's sanctity and even fulfils a functional role. On his first journey to Aron, the raven flies for ten days without food or rest, and so has to stop on a *stain* in the sea, exhausted and starving. The narrator implies that flying for so long without respite was foolish:

> sein craft was im entwichen,
> in het die müed erschlichen:
> daz lat euch nicht ein wunder dunken:
> er flog zehen tag ungaß und untrunken! (ll. 631–34)

It seems plausible that, through the figure of the raven, ascetic suffering and the topos of lonely saints on rocks are being mocked (there seems to be no doubt they are invoked in some way), particularly given that the raven encounters such an ascetic on his way back. This time, he stops on a *stain* because the ring the princess has given him has blown out from under his wing in a storm (ll. 1203–12). Noticeably, he has also been flying for ten days when this occurs (ll. 1199–1202), but neither hunger nor tiredness is mentioned. The *stain* he stops on to *trauren und clagen* (l. 1222; these words were also used when he stopped because of hunger, l. 642) is inhabited by an *ainsidel* who has been there *vollikleich zwai und dreissig jar* (l. 1226), which puts the raven's ten days of suffering to shame. It is notable that the raven's journey to and from the princess is framed by two adventures, at times similarly worded, which involve a figure sitting on a rock; the first — the moaning raven — catches a fish to eat and then becomes entangled with mermaids, and the second — the *ainsidel*, who has been told by God to pray for Oswald — catches a fish that has been bidden by God to eat the raven's lost ring. Both adventures — the mermaids and the lost ring — are unnecessary to the progression of the plot (surely the raven could fly to and from Aron uneventfully), but provide a framework to the raven's functional purpose within the narrative, namely wooing the princess for Oswald. On the way out, the raven makes a slight mockery of the topos of the lonely ascetic and then clearly steps outside the plot (as we shall see shortly) to have a possibly meaningless adventure with mermaids. On the way back, the ascetic trope is re-established as serious and meaningful, and the raven's status as a favoured being of God is restated; Christ is able, through prayer and the intercession of the *ainsidel*, to get his ring back for him.

The mermaid episode has been understood in many different ways.[82] If it is to be read symbolically, it seems most likely to prefigure the end result of Oswald's marriage: chastity. The mermaids, luring the raven to the depths of the sea, could symbolize the dangers of female bodily love and the raven escapes from them much as Oswald does from physical love in his chaste marriage. Yet this scene could equally (and concurrently) be an entertaining digression from the main course of the narrative. The raven, in stopping from hunger and exhaustion, leaves his functional role in the plot, for by sitting on the *stain* he explicitly stops travelling to Aron to woo the princess in proxy. He is captured by a mermaid who pulls him even further away from his purpose: *hin ein zuo des meres grunt* (l. 662). What happens next seems largely inconsequential; the mermaids demand the raven entertain them, but he demands food first, and when he has eaten, says that God will be appalled by the state of things at the bottom of the sea because everything is dead. The mermaids are shocked and distracted and the raven makes his escape, aided by God (notably, God is always on the raven's side — superfluous episodes such as this do not affect his favoured standing). Certain motifs are emphasized; not only the importance of food for the raven, but also his blurred status between wild animal and object of God, demonstrated when one mermaid argues he is an angel, another merely a wild bird (ll. 669–80). We are also made aware of his allure and status as an attribute to be possessed, not only by Oswald, but also by the princess (who takes him into her care at her father's court) and the mermaid, for whom he is *mein rabe* (l. 754). These motifs provide a sense of continuity and prevent this episode from being completely isolated from the plot (indeed, the raven does get the food he needs to continue on his journey), but are not consequential or emphatic enough to suggest anything more than an entertaining digression. Perhaps the episode is summarized most pertinently in the words of one of the mermaids: 'rab, kurtzweil uns ains, ez ist an der zeit!' (l. 682).[83]

After the raven escapes, a firm end is given to this short adventure. A mermaid bemoans the raven's departure and he makes it very clear that this episode was nothing more than a digression that will not be revisited; he explicitly re-enters the plot and his functional purpose within it:

> 'frau, nu laß nür dein[e] chlag,
> wann gult ez daz leben dein,
> ich chäm zu dir nicht mer hin ein.
> ich wil fliegen schon
> in daz land gen Aron
> und wil werben mit eren
> sant Oswalt meinem herren.' (ll. 764–70)

When Oswald and his men travel to Aron, they leave the raven behind, despite being told explicitly not to by the princess. Their departure is depicted as institutionalized and very much an action of the group, so the exclusion of the raven emphasizes his difference and 'special' nature outside of the normal confines of society.[84] The problem of his absence is solved quickly by another *miraculum ex machina*; Oswald prays, and an angel is sent to fetch him. Thus the presence of God and sanctity of Oswald is again displayed, but opportunity is also given for the raven to display more extreme, comic behaviour. He complains outrageously about his treatment and refuses to rejoin Oswald (*nu wie gar ist mein herr ain tor!*, l. 1817), so must be forced into the air by the angel (ll. 1879–92).

In the *Wiener Oswald*, however, problems are not solved so easily. On realizing he has forgotten the raven, Oswald sends messengers to fetch him, but the raven says he has been so badly treated that Oswald himself must come back (ll. 833–48). Here, the raven has not been established as a demanding or difficult figure, so it is clear that Oswald is in the wrong and it is necessary for him to return personally to atone for what he has done. Whereas the raven in the *Münchner Oswald* demands the execution of the cook and *chelner* who have treated him so badly, this punishment is suggested in the *Wiener Oswald* by Oswald himself. The situation is inverted so that not Oswald, but the raven himself rejects such an extreme punishment (WO, ll. 871–74). In the *Wiener Oswald* it is the raven who has moral superiority, emphasizing that leaving him behind is Oswald's mistake, a flaw for which he must atone on the path to ideal sanctity.

In the *Münchner Oswald*, it is hard to discern symbolic or motivational purpose behind the depiction and actions of the raven. The licence with which he is endowed is discussed by Haug, who argues that the raven's role as an object of God endows him with more comic potential, as this function provides a degree of freedom, both in the raven's own self-consciousness and in the respect that his status demands in the eyes of others:

> So komisch-untauglich [der Rabe] für seine Aufgabe ist, er taugt am Ende doch, da er als Werkzeug Gottes fungiert. Und das weiß er zwar selbst auch, aber das macht ihn nicht etwa einsichtig, sondern das steigert sein Selbstbewußtsein, was wiederum seine Komik erhöht. [...] Eine Figur also im Dienste Gottes, die komisch wird, weil ihr eine Rolle zugewiesen ist, die nach dem zugrunde liegenden Modell eine ganz andere Besetzung verlangte, eine Figur, die aber in ihrer Unzulänglichkeit trotzdem funktioniert und die sich darauf um so mehr einbildet, als sie von den übrigen dabei ernst genommen werden muß, was diese wiederum komisch erscheinen läßt: ein meisterhaftes Komödienkonzept.[85]

It seems more sensible to turn this argument away from the psychology of individual characters (which may be a misguided starting point for reading the text) towards the construction of the narrative itself. The peculiarities of the raven — his role as messenger, his role in Oswald's path to sanctity, the divine favour with which this role endows him, and also his 'otherness' as a bird, not a man — allow him to play a prominent part in the freedom of expansion characteristic of the *Münchner Oswald*. He is not self-aware; he is merely able to step outside the confines of the linear main plot of Oswald's *vita* without compromising his functional role as messenger.

It was mentioned above that the act of forgetting the raven emphasized his place outside the normal bounds of society, and the very fact that he is a bird, not a man, is important. The raven's physical form is emphasized in the text: the fact that he is able to fly is of great help, and he uses his wings to hide Oswald's letter and ring for the princess. His capture at Aron's castle is also explicitly that of a bird; Aron's men shut not only the doors but also the windows, because the raven is able to fly.[86] He is thus somehow 'removed' from the story because he is a raven. In the *Nibelungenlied* and *Tristan*, for example, the proxy wooer becomes a more prominent figure than the wooer himself, putting the bridal quest in great danger (if this is strong enough a formulation). In the *Münchner Oswald*, however, the raven seems at times in danger of taking over the story, but never affects it adversely — nothing he does is in any danger of compromising Oswald's bridal quest or progression to sanctity, because he is too different from Oswald to be in direct competition.[87] Being a raven — or rather, not being human — adds to his freedom 'outside' the plot, a freedom to move about without affecting the humans he encounters, precisely because he is not one of them.

Conclusion

It is impossible to come to any clear estimation of the date and origins of the *Münchner Oswald*, but this should not affect an interpretation of the text too adversely. The most fruitful line seems to be to collate the information we do have about the text and attempt to interpret it as a coherent object.

Neither Oswald's bridal quest nor his chaste marriage need be considered problematic when the development of the cult of St Oswald is considered in sufficient detail; St Oswald has always been both saint and king, and the conversion of his father-in-law is well attested. The preservation of chastity in marriage seems a suitable compromise of the two roles he fulfils and highlights the turn to a more ascetic model of sanctity, and the quest itself enables a display of Oswald's sainthood and the spread of Christianity. Potentially more problematic is the intrusion of comic elements into the narrative of a saint, but the comedy is contained in episodes that are largely digressive and do not affect the 'basic' plot of Oswald's path to sanctity.

The *Münchner Oswald* seems to be a text that is given greater freedom by the security of the knowledge of God's miraculous powers and the tradition (both of this saint and of sanctity in general) in which it stands. It is, therefore, the religious nature of the text that allows the oddity and comedy, which — rather paradoxically — might seem curious and self-undermining. Yet this need not necessarily be the case, for there is no reason why the *Münchner Oswald* may not be both serious and comedic, instructive and entertaining.

I have so far studiously avoided attempting to attribute the *Münchner Oswald* to a specific genre, but see no reason, particularly given its transmission, that it could not be considered to be an extended version of the life of the saint.[88] Yet how would its function be different from the shorter lives of the *Heiligen Leben* strand, which are much more formulaic and have posthumous miracles to attest to the sanctity of their subject? Can we suggest — tentatively — that the *Münchner Oswald* is a more entertaining life for a more secular public?

It must be stressed once again that this argument is not to suggest that the created world of the *Münchner Oswald* is not intelligible. That there are elements of the secular and indeed of the comedic need not be problematic; this is only so if we as readers insist upon strict generic boundaries. The *Münchner Oswald* is not an unhappy combination of religious and secular, but rather an accepted life of St Oswald that is funny without compromising its essential seriousness.

Notes to Chapter 3

1. Clare Stancliffe, 'Oswald, "Most Holy and Most Victorious King of the Northumbrians"', in *Oswald: Northumbrian King to European Saint*, ed. by Clare Stancliffe and Eric Cambridge (Stamford: Paul Watkins, 1995), pp. 33–83 (p. 34).
2. Bede, *Ecclesiastical History of the English People*, trans. by Leo Shirley-Price, 4th edn (London: Penguin, 1990), esp. book III.
3. On the spread of the cult of St Oswald, see Peter Clemoes, *The Cult of St Oswald on the Continent* (Jarrow Lecture 1983) and Dagmar Ó Riain-Raedel, 'Edith, Judith, Matilda: The Role of Royal Ladies in the Propagation of the Continental Cult', in *Oswald*, ed. by Stancliffe and Cambridge, pp. 210–29.
4. 'Von sant Oswald', in *Der Heiligen Leben*, I: *der Sommerteil*, ed. by Margit Brand and others (Tübingen: Niemeyer, 1996), pp. 358–68; 'Von sand Oswalden dem chunig', in

Das Märterbuch, ed. by Erich Gierach (Berlin: Weidmann, 1928), pp. 292–96; 'Van sunte Oswaldo deme konninghe', in *Dat Passionael* and 'Ósvalds saga', in *Reykjahólabók*, ed. and trans. by Marianne Kalinke, in her *St. Oswald of Northumbria: Continental Metamorphoses. With an Edition and Translation of 'Ósvalds saga' and 'Van sunte Oswaldo deme konninghe'* (Tempe: Arizona Center for Medieval and Renaissance Studies, 2005), pp. 173–91; pp. 105–71.

5. *Der Wiener Oswald*, ed. by Georg Baesecke (Heidelberg: Winter, 1912); *Der Münchner Oswald*, ed. by Michael Curschmann (Tübingen: Niemeyer, 1974). All quotations from these texts will come from these editions. For details of the manuscripts, see *Marburger Repertorium*, <www.mr1314.de> [accessed 20 September 2010].

6. A. P. Edzardi, 'Die Stuttgarter Oswaldprosa', *Germania*, 20 (1875), 190–206 and *Germania*, 21 (1876), 466–91; András Vizkelety, 'Der Budapester Oswald', *PBB* (Halle), 86 (1964), 107–88; M. Haupt, 'Oswalt', *ZfdA*, 13 (1867), 466–91 (the *Berliner Oswald*). The East Swabian prose redaction is included in Curschmann's edition of the *Münchner Oswald*, pp. 189–213.

7. Michael Curschmann, '"Sant Oswald von Norwegen": Ein Fragment eines Legendenepos', *ZfdA*, 102 (1973), 101–14.

8. For the former argument, see Curschmann, *Der Münchener Oswald und die deutsche spielmännische Epik*, the latter Rolf Bräuer, *Das Problem des 'Spielmännischen' aus der Sicht der St.-Oswald Überlieferung* (Berlin: Akademie, 1969).

9. *Der Münchener Oswald: Text und Abhandlung*, ed. by Georg Baesecke (Breslau: Marcus, 1907), especially pp. 214–15.

10. Ibid., pp. 237–80. The Rhenish origins of all bridal-quest epics is one of the primary arguments for Bornholdt, *Engaging Moments*.

11. Most recently by Kalinke, who argues for the primacy of the 'Ósvalds saga'.

12. Walter Haug, 'Struktur und Geschichte: Ein literaturtheoretisches Experiment an mittelalterlichen Texten', in Haug, *Strukturen als Schlüssel zur Welt* (Tübingen: Niemeyer, 1989), pp. 236–56 (p. 241).

13. Ibid., p. 237: 'Es wäre also der Versuch zu machen, literarhistorisch dort anzusetzen, wo Strukturen insbesondere dadurch, daß ihre Möglichkeiten bis zum Ende durchgespielt sind, ihre Geschichtlichkeit ins Bewußtsein drängen und damit einen Prozeß auslösen, der zum kritischen Umschlag weiterführt'.

14. Ibid., p. 246: 'man überwindet eine traditionelle Position, indem man die Mittel dazu so gut wie vollständig aus dieser Tradition bezieht. Man arbeitet mit der Gesetzlichkeit vorgegebener Strukturen, man verwendet vorgegebenes Motivmaterial, es bleibt die literarische Tradition damit scheinbar ungebrochen präsent, man scheint sie zu akzeptieren, doch nur, um sie dann in einem überraschenden Gegenzug zu überspielen. [...] das Neue [wird] nicht dadurch erreicht, daß man eine gegebene Welt darstellt und sie dann diskreditiert, wie eine gängige Etikettierung gerade der besprochenen Werke als klerikal weltfeindlich dies verkennt; das Wesentliche dieses Innovationsprozesses besteht vielmehr darin, daß man die gegebene Welt aus ihrer eigenen strukturalen Gesetzlichkeit heraus kritisch übersteigt.'

15. Curschmann, *Der Münchener Oswald und die deutsche spielmännische Epik*, pp. 84–85; pp. 188–97.

16. Ibid., pp. 180–81: 'Im *Münchener Oswald* ist das Wissen um die historische Person Oswald noch unmittelbar lebendig, genauso wie das Wissen um die Eigenschaften, die ihn zum heiligen Herrscher erhoben: Oswald ist als im Heidenkampf Gefallener Märtyrer und Missionsförderer, also *quasi sacerdos*, zugleich *rex iustus* und Fürsorger der Armen; vor allem: bereits zu seinen Lebzeiten mit übernatürlichen Kräften begabt.' (p. 180). I see no reason why these latter characteristics cannot also apply to the *Wiener*

Oswald and *Der Heiligen Leben* strand of lives. See also Bräuer, *Das Problem des 'Spielmännischen'*, p. 2, who argues that the fact that Oswald is German king in the *Wiener Oswald* does not necessarily imply a later dating of this text.

17. Ibid., p. 83. See also Vollmann-Profe, p. 219, who agrees with this standpoint and the early dating of the *Münchner Oswald*, but also argues that the text is concerned with the more general problem of worldly life.
18. Curschmann, *Der Münchener Oswald und die deutsche spielmännische Epik*, pp. 76–77. Vollmann-Profe, p. 218, attributes what she considers to be the slightly odd narrative course of the text to the disparate models of protagonist of Saint's Life and bridal-quest epic: 'Die Legende stellt ein ganz vom göttlichen Willen gelenktes und beherrschtes Leben dar, dessen Träger als vollkommenes Werkzeug der göttlichen Planung erscheint; die Brauwerbungserzählung aber lebt von einem Helden, der gegen alle Widerstände schließlich den eigenen Willen durchsetzt'. Miller, pp. 227–30, offers an insightful criticism of Curschmann's analysis, arguing that its fundamental problem is a division of theme (*minne*) and structure (Brautwerbungsschema) and therefore, despite claiming to examine the text as a coherent structure, ends up speaking of a 'Konstruktionsfehler'.
19. Ibid., pp. 188–90. See also Stephan Müller, 'Oswalds Rabe: Zur institutionellen Geschichte eines Heiligenattributs und Herrschaftszeichens', in *Institutionalität und Symbolisierung: Verstetigungen kultureller Ordnungsmuster in Vergangenheit und Gegenwart*, ed. by Gert Melville (Cologne, Weimar, and Vienna: Böhlau, 2001), pp. 451–75 (pp. 461–62). Vizkelety, pp. 140–41, argues that the raven on the Dollinger Oswald was a later addition. According to his argument on p. 134, the first iconographical example of the raven occurred in Regensburg c.1370.
20. de Boor, pp. 254–56.
21. Bräuer, *Das Problem des 'Spielmännischen'*.
22. Kalinke, p. 35: 'The ultimate source of *Ósvalds saga* represents [...] the oldest version of the legend in the German language area, while the metrical version, that is, the *Münchner Oswald* and *Wiener Oswald*, is a derivative work that transmuted a martyr's vita and passio into a hagiographical romance inspired by and emulating the legends of virginal royal saints.' See also p. 37 for her 'tree' of sources and influences. For the opposite opinion, see Curschmann, *Der Münchener Oswald und die deutsche spielmännische Epik*, pp. 206–09, who argues that version zn (*Der Heiligen Leben*) comes directly from the *Münchner Oswald*.
23. Der grosse Gottesfreund, *Fünfmannenbuch*, ed. by Philipp Strauch (Halle: Niemeyer, 1927), pp. 34–50. Unhappy with the suggestion of chastity, the wife says: *so wil ich dir heissen eine bvtte mit kalteme wasser in die kammer seczen, also das dv dich sant Ossewalde nach vebende sist, vnd lo sehhen, wie lange dv das triban wilt* (pp. 37–38). The cold-water bath becomes one of several forms of suffering the lay brother must undergo before successfully relinquishing the worldly life and becoming a priest. This example demonstrates at least that lives of Oswald had common currency in Strassburg at this time.
24. The *Münchner Oswald* is transmitted with the following texts: MS I with *Goldenes Ave Maria*, a prose German *Salve regina*, a rhyming prayer on the death of Christ, a prayer to Mary, *Jüngeres Marienlob* and *Unser vrouwen klage*. MS Mk (a fragment) also contains a German *Cantica canticorum*. MS S contains Heinrich Beck's *Passionshistorie* and *Christus und die sieben Laden*. MSs M and W contain no other texts. For further details, see the *Marburger Repertorium*, <www.mr1314.de> [accessed 20 September 2010].
25. On the *miles christianus* and the influence of the heroic model on Christian saints' lives, see Wolfgang Haubrichs, 'Labor sanctorum und labor heroum: Zur konsolatorischen

Funktion von Legende und Heldenlied', in *Die Funktion außer- und innerliterarischen Faktoren für die Entstehung deutscher Literatur des Mittelalters und der frühen Neuzeit*, ed. by Christa Baufeld (Göppingen: Kümmerle, 1994), pp. 27–49.
26. Bede, III.7, 153.
27. Kalinke, p. 74. For Drogo's vita, see *Oswaldus rex et M. in Anglia. Vita. Auctore D. Drogone monacho*, Acta Sanctorum Aug. II, Dies 5.
28. Reginald of Durham, *Vita S. Oswaldi regis et martyris*, in *Symeonis Monachi Opera Omnia. Historia Ecclesiae Dunhelmensis*, I, ed. by Thomas Arnold (London: Longman & co, 1882), pp. 326–85. On Reginald, see Victoria Tudor, 'Reginald's *Life of St Oswald*', in *Oswald*, ed. by Stancliffe and Cambridge, pp. 178–94. Reginald of Durham is posited as an influence for the *Münchner Oswald* by Curschmann, *Der Münchener Oswald*, p. 79, Kalinke, pp. 63–64 and, more tentatively, by Annemiek Jansen, 'The Development of the St Oswald Legends on the Continent', in *Oswald*, ed. by Stancliffe and Cambridge, pp. 230–41 (pp. 233–35).
29. Reginald of Durham, cap. XI (p. 349): 'And because the holy King, after he had been chastized with the whips of God, endeavoured diligently to emend completely anything that had thus far been excessive in anyone, it came to pass after this vision of glory that he removed his wife, the daughter of King Cynegils, from the community of a shared bed, and thereafter preserved the purity of unimpaired chastity. Previously, however, he had obtained a child from her, the only son he possessed in the world.'
30. Ibid., cap. III (p. 342): *Non enim volebat gloriosus rex Oswaldus infidelis divitis, licet et regis nobilis, filiam accipere, nisi prius Dei dispositione et ipsius sedula admonitione patrem illius, quam ducturus erat, posset Domino adquirendo de diaboli jugo eripere* ('For the glorious King Oswald did not want to take the daughter of the rich heathen, although he was also a noble king, unless, by God's prior disposition and his own [Oswald's] diligent admonition, he were able to snatch the father of her whom he was about to marry from the yoke of the devil for God to receive'); cap. XI (p. 349): *Tandem, agente et suadente Ostrilda regina Merciorum, Oswin regis filia, cujus vir erat rex Ethelredus, monachata est et sancto fine consummata* ('At last, through the deeds and persuasion of Ostrilda, queen of Mercia, daughter of King Oswin and husband of King Ethelred, she took the veil and reached perfection in complete sanctity').
31. See James Brundage, *Law, Sex and Christian Society in Medieval Europe* (Chicago: University of Chicago Press, 1987), pp. 176–416 and Christopher Brooke, *The Medieval Idea of Marriage* (Oxford: Oxford University Press, 1989), esp. pp. 61–92.
32. Henry's wife Kunegunde was also canonized for her chastity: see Jürgen Petersohn, 'Die Litterae Papst Innocenz' III: Zur Heiligsprechung der Kaiserin Kunigunde (1200)', *Jahrbuch für fränkische Landesforschung*, 37 (1977), 1–25.
33. Dyan Elliott, *Spiritual Marriage: Sexual Abstinence in Medieval Wedlock* (Princeton: Princeton University Press, 1993), p. 123. She also points out that Henry's cult was promoted by the bishopric of Bamberg, which he has founded and funded during his lifetime (p. 119). For more information on Henry, see Georges Duby, *The Knight, the Lady and the Priest: The Making of Modern Marriage in Medieval France*, trans. by Barbara Bray (London: Allen Lane, 1984), pp. 57–59. Duby states that, at the time of his assumption of the throne, Henry had already been married for eight years without offspring. He argues that this made him an ideal candidate to succeed Otto III in the eyes of the bishops, who were hoping for a break in succession; moreover, his canonization could be seen as an attempt by the church to aggravate Henry V and Henry VI, both of whom were enemies of the reforming papacy.
34. Elliott, p. 125.
35. Ibid.

36. Kalinke, pp. 44–45, expands on her argument by showing that the *vita* of Henry and Kunegunde immediately precedes that of Oswald in the *Reykjahólabók* and cites the example of the late twelfth-century Hildesheim reliquary, on which Christ is flanked by Henry and Oswald.
37. Ebernand von Erfurt, *Heinrich und Kunegunde*, ed. by Reinhold Bechstein (Quedlinburg: Basse, 1860), chs xii–xiii. Kalinke, p. 61, argues, rather oddly, that the *vita* of Henry and Kunegunde also provides the Oswald stories with the council scene; it is unclear whether she means that this scene, considered by so many to be a central feature of the bridal-quest schema, had its origins in the life of Henry, who would therefore then provide the model for all bridal-quest epics. This seems highly unlikely, as *König Rother* was certainly composed before 1220.
38. See in particular Ó Riain-Raedel, pp. 223–29.
39. The metaphor of 'dying to the world' is commonly used of medieval saints and holy men and was given widespread currency in Western ascetic Christendom by Gregory the Great. The metaphor is originally Pauline (Colossians 2:20), but is explicated in S. Gregorii Magni, *Moralia in Iob*, ed. by Marcus Adriaen, II (Turnholt: Brepols, 1979), 18.54.89.
40. Curschmann, *Der Münchener Oswald und die deutsche spielmännische Epik*, pp. 35–39, discusses the widespread tradition of a water-bath as an ascetic practice.
41. Miller, p. 240. He also mentions the legend of St Alexius in this context (p. 239), for, unlike Oswald, Alexius' (chaste) marriage is the impetus for his ascetic life: 'Die Ehe erscheint nicht als Ziel der Handlung, vielmehr als eine dem Heiligen aufgenötigte Ausgangssituation, die durch dessen Handeln gerade suspendiert wird. Der Weg des Hauptakteurs ist daher als Negation dieses Ausgangspunktes bestimmt'. The presence of the Alexius *vita* in two manuscripts of prose versions (u and b, see Curschmann's edition of *Der Münchner Oswald*, pp. xxx–xxxii) of the Oswald story, both of which are very closely related to the *Münchner Oswald*, suggests that the common theme of male chastity may have been of some importance to readers. On Alexius, see Elliott, pp. 104–08, who relates his popularity to the rise of lay piety in the context of the reform movements: 'for the religious fervor of the masculine laity [...] as well as for clerical opponents to nicolaitism, the legend was peculiarly expressive of the age: an age in which purity was found outside rather than inside of marriage and in which this purity was portrayed as primarily the province of the male.' (p. 106) On the agency of God in the *Münchner Oswald*, see also Florian Kragl, 'Wer hat den Hirsch zum Köder gemacht? Der "Münchner Oswald" *spiritualiter* gelesen', *Amsterdamer Beiträge zur älteren Germanistik*, 63 (2007), 157–78, and Stefan Seeber, 'Sanctity and Comedy in the "Munich Saint Oswald"', in *Intertextuality, Reception, and Performance: Interpretations and Texts of Medieval German Literature (Kalamazoo Papers 2007–2009)*, ed. by Sibylle Jefferis (Göppingen: Kümmerle, 2010), pp. 95–109.
42. See, in particular, Bräuer, *Das Problem des 'Spielmännischen'*.
43. We can hope that Kiening's recent essay on the *Wiener Oswald* will spark more interest. Christan Kiening, 'Heilige Brautwerbung: Überlegungen zum *Wiener Oswald*', in *Impulse und Resonanzen: Tübinger mediävistische Beiträge zum 80. Geburtstag von Walter Haug*, ed. by Gisela Vollmann-Profe and others (Tübingen: Niemeyer, 2007), pp. 89–100.
44. The protagonists in Ebernand von Erfurt's *Heinrich und Kunegunde* also want to preserve their chastity from the outset (chs xii–xv).
45. Kragl, pp. 172–75, argues that Oswald's dream is one instance of the transcendent (rather than immanent) presence of God in the text.
46. When Warmunt tells Oswald about Paug, his first reaction is *ich hilf in zuo der tauf*

(l. 256) and his proposal is always qualified by an agreement to believe in Christ (l. 265; 599; 1104). Marriage is also inseparable from conversion when Oswald decides to go to Aron himself; he sets out his intentions first as *cristenleichen glauben meren* (l. 1534), then obtaining the princess (l. 1539). Those men who die in the process will be granted eternal life (ll. 1546-52). Just as marrying Oswald would be unthinkable without baptism (or even symbolic of baptism and a total assumption of the Christian church in the figure of the saint), so wooing the princess is unthinkable without converting heathens; the bridal quest is completely fused with the crusading mission. For the opposite opinion, see Kalinke, p. 73, who argues that the bride is the 'real reason' for the bridal quest in the *Münchner Oswald*, whereas *Ósvalds saga* is more motivated by conversion. I see no reason why conversion and the bride cannot be mutually representative.

47. This fact could be used to counter Schulz's argument that Oswald's *erbe* is made up of the heathens he converts. Monika Schulz, 'Die falsche Braut: Imperative feudaler Herrschaft in Texten um 1200', *ZfdPh*, 121 (2002) 1-20 (p. 14): 'Der Held einer Legende kümmert sich nicht um leibliche Nachkommen, andererseits wird eine aufwendige Werbungsfahrt in dem Moment sinnlos, wo nun plötzlich ein göttliches Gebot zur Keuschheit verpflichtet. [...] Freilich gibt es keinen leiblichen Zeugungsakt, und es ist auch weniger der Fortbestand und die Expansion eines irdischen Reiches von Interesse, das Ganze ist sozusagen nach oben transponiert: Im 'Oswald' und im 'Orendel' geht es um das Reich Gottes, um eine Allianz mit dem Heiligen also, für das die gottesfürchtigen Minnepaare in Heidenkampf und Zwangstaufe zigtausende von 'Gotteskindern' gewinnen.' Ebernand von Erfurt, however, can be read according to Schulz's argument, because Henry, urged to marry by his men, has a different view of what his *erbe* should be: *ze erben hate er* [Henry] *ime erkorn, | der von der meide wart geborn, | der durch uns starb unt wart begraben, | nechein andern wolde er haben | wan unsen hêren Jêsum Kristen* (ch. XII, 757-61). Such explicit reasoning is not found in the *Münchner Oswald*.

48. Curschmann, *Der Münchener Oswald und die deutsche spielmännische Epik*, pp. 50-51, argues that this parallel marks out the status of the wife as a material good.

49. It should be noted that the title *Die Hochzeit* is not found in the rubric of the text, but was given to it by its earliest editor, Th. G. von Karajan, in 1846. See Peter Ganz, art. 'Die Hochzeit', *VL*, vol. IV, cols 77-79.

50. *Die Hochzeit* is often interpreted as making use of worldly, oral-based themes familiar to a lay public and synthesizing them with the spiritual, thus making the spiritual more accessible. See Peter Ganz, '*Die Hochzeit*: Fabula et Significatio', in *Studien zur frühmittelhochdeutschen Literatur: Cambridge Colloquium 1971*, ed. by L. P. Johnson, H.-H. Steinhoff, and R. A. Wisbey (Berlin: E. Schmidt, 1974), pp. 58-73, who suggests the possibility of 'propaganda fidei' and a religious counterpart to heroic epic, and Klaus Gantert, 'Erzählschema und literarische Hermeneutik: Zum Verhältnis von Brautwerbungsschema und geistlicher Tradition im *Wiener Oswald* und in der Hochzeit', *Poetica*, 31 (1999), 381-414, who concentrates on the use of worldly themes to explain the hermeneutic functions of religious texts, as well as to maintain the supposed 'Geltungsanspruch' of the oral schema. A more complex discussion of the use of allegory in *Die Hochzeit* is found in Kuhn, 'Allegorie und Erzählstruktur'.

51. *Die Hochzeit*, in *Kleinere deutsche Gedichte des 11. und 12. Jahrhunderts*, II, ed. by Albert Waag and Werner Schröder (Tübingen: Niemeyer, 1972), pp. 132-70.

52. Ganz, 'Die Hochzeit', p. 68, suggests that not everything within the *spel* is subject to exegesis, perhaps because its interpretation is well-known or obvious.

53. Bräuer, *Das Problem des 'Spielmännischen'*, especially pp. 149-56. See also Baesecke, p. 218, who was not convinced of the originality of the involvement of the goldsmiths,

and counted their presence among his list of later interpolations. Curschmann, *Der Münchener Oswald und die deutsche spielmännische Epik*, pp. 22–23, finds significance not in the goldsmiths themselves, but the fact that there are twelve of them; twelve is a common number of helpers, or companions to a hero in a variety of epics (for example in Pfaffe Konrad's *Rolandslied*).

54. Bräuer, *Das Problem des 'Spielmännischen'*, pp. 155–56: 'diese ungewöhnlich große Rolle, die den Goldschmieden in einem Legendenroman eingeräumt wird [...], die Erfindung und Einschaltung dieser Episode, die die Handlung nicht vorantreibt und sogar den kompositorischen Zusammenhang empfindlich stört und Widersprüche auf Widersprüche häuft, macht im Zusammenhang mit den bereits besprochenen Goldschmiedepisoden die Annahme eines Goldschmiedes als Bearbeiter der Münchener Fassung wahrscheinlich.'

55. Ibid, pp. 49–50. Bräuer, p. 63, also supports his argument for the primacy of the *Wiener Oswald* through the fact that it contains no goldsmiths. There are, however, goldsmiths in the *Ósvalds saga*, the version of the story discussed at length by Kalinke; if her argument for the primacy of the *Ósvalds saga* is to be taken seriously, it could provide a considerable stumbling block to Bräuer.

56. The provenance of the stag has been much discussed. Kalinke, pp. 91–95, argues that it has its origins in the typical hagiographical topos, where the stag is a symbol of Christ, or shows the way to Christian belief: for example Ps 42:1/2, where the image of the stag comments on the soul's yearning for God; the hind sent by God showing Clovis how to ford the river Vienne (the links between the Clovis and Oswald stories are central to Kalinke); Christ in the form of a stag exhorting St Eustace to accept Christianity. The stag in the *Münchner Oswald* also 'shows the way', but has no explicit connection with Christ (although, indirectly, Oswald does eventually convert Aron and his men); this leads Kalinke to suggest it has lost its hagiographical function. Curschmann, *Der Münchner Oswald und die deutsche spielmännische Epik*, pp. 25–27, emphasizes the magic and fascination of the stag, which he links to his argument that Pamige remains, to a certain degree, a heathen 'Zauberin'. Bräuer, *Das Problem des 'Spielmännischen'*, pp. 156–60, suggests the influence of the stag in the life of St Eustace. See also Elliott, p. 76, on the life of St Osyth, who, desperate to keep her chastity intact, manages to consecrate herself as a virgin when her husband is distracted hunting a miraculous white stag.

57. On the problematic motivation of the stag episode, see Kragl, who interprets it according the scholastic conception of God (in particular the arguments of Anselm of Canterbury and Thomas Aquinas), which focused simultaneously on his transcendence and immanence. He finds it odd that the princess suggests the plan involving the stag, but does not know what the result of this plan will be; she is not aware that the castle will empty because of a desire to catch the stag, which will in turn enable her escape. In contrast to the immanent presence of God in much of the text, this episode displays his transcendent 'Präsenz': '[D]ie List des Hirsch-Köders könnte dann [...] quasi tiefenstrukturell auf ein kaum erkennbares und doch irgendwie manifestes Interagieren einer ephemeren göttlichen Instanz verweisen; ein Verweis, der freilich auf einer Eben stattfindet, die von jener der gewissermaßen oberflächenstrukturellen, personalisierten Gottesreferenzen — Gott als Auftraggeber, Gott als Helfer, der sich mit Gebeten bezahlen lässt und mit dem man handeln kann — radikal verschieden ist' (p. 172).

58. The stag is also heaven-sent in the Oswald stories of the *Heiligen Leben* strand.

59. This raises another possible explanation for the goldsmiths, that they are present in order to gild the deer (perhaps in other versions it was miraculously golden, but here must be made gold in some artisanal way).

60. Kiening, 'Heilige Brautwerbung', p. 98, argues that the stag and raven in the *Wiener Oswald* are connotative beings — they are not directly allegorical, but carry a variety of religious connotations — and help the progression of the story but do not directly enable its outcome. Final agency must remain in the hands of God. The animals and the magic rings Oswald and the princess give one another form 'Metonymien des Heils' which give the text coherence (p. 100): 'Er [the *Wiener Oswald*] liefert den exemplarischen Fall eines Textes, der stärker mit Kontiguitäten (Berührungen und Angrenzungen) als mit Kausalitäten (Folgerungen und Ableitungen) operiert, stärker mit präsentischen als mit mimetischen Strategien und stärker mit Zirkulationen als mit Motivationen'.
61. Miller, p. 235, also explores the temporal complexity of Oswald's promise, relating it to the instant (short-term) yet also constant (long-term) presence and effect of God: 'Im Gelübde wird die situationsbezogene Hilfe Gottes mit dem Gelöbnis späteren Gottesgehorsams verknüpft und so die immerwährende Anwesenheit des höchsten Willens im augenblicklichen Sprechakt realisiert'.
62. Haug, 'Das Komische und das Heilige', p. 30. See also Miller, p. 235: 'Gott also läßt die Brautwerbungshandlung durch *Wunder* glücken: ohne seine Hilfe vermögen die Akteure des Schemas die ihnen beggegnenden Gefahren gar nicht zu bestehen. So verdeutlichen die Wunder einerseits die extreme Gefährlichkeit der Brautwerbung und fungieren somit im Sinne des Schemas.'
63. Haug, 'Das Komische und das Heilige', p. 30. See also Kalinke, p. 77, who finds the conversion miracles overblown and comic in comparison to other versions of the Oswald story.
64. Haug, 'Das Komische und das Heilige', p. 22.
65. Benedicta Ward, *Miracles and the Medieval Mind: Theory, Record and Event 1000–1215* (Aldershot: Wildwood House, 1987), p. 211.
66. Haug, 'Das Komische und das Heilige', pp. 30–31.
67. Ernst Robert Curtius, *European Literature and the Latin Middle Ages*, trans. by Willard R. Trask (Princeton: Princeton University Press, 1990), pp. 425–28; Max Wehrli, *Literatur im deutschen Mittelalter: Eine poetologische Einführung* (Stuttgart: Reclam, 1984), pp. 166–71.
68. Seeber, 'Sanctity and Comedy', p. 98. For a more detailed discussion of classical rhetoric and comedy, see Seeber, *Poetik des Lachens: Untersuchungen zum mittelhochdeutschen Roman um 1200* (Berlin: de Gruyter, 2010), pp. 35–62.
69. Seeber, 'Sanctity and Comedy', p. 102.
70. The concept of *miraculum* in the Middle Ages was complex, but Augustine's argument that miracles were not *contra naturam* but rather *praeter* or *supra naturam* was highly influential (*City of God* XXI, 8). In this sense it was believed that only God, who created the rules of nature, could change the conventions of nature; nothing could happen outside the rules, just happen differently from usual. Thus the miracles performed by a saint are in fact performed by God and proof of his presence and the favoured nature of the saint. See W. Schröder, art. 'Wunder (Patristik und Mittelalter)', in *Historisches Wörterbuch der Philosophie*, ed. by Joachim Ritter, Karlfried Gründer, and Gottfried Gabriel, XII (Darmstadt: Wissenschaftliche Buchgesellschaft, 2004), cols 1055–58 and F. Wagner, art. 'Miracula, Mirakel', in *Lexikon des Mittelalters*, VI (Munich: Artemis and Winkler, 1999), cols 656–59.
71. Seeber, 'Sanctity and Comedy', p. 102: '[sanctity] occasionally comes into contact with the comic, but is never occupied by the latter'.
72. Anja Grebe, 'Heilige Narren: Einleitende Überlegungen zur Ästhetik von Sakralität und Komik im Mittelalter', in *Komik und Sakralität: Aspekte einer ästhetischen Paradoxie in Mittelalter und früher Neuzeit*, ed. by Anja Grebe and Nikolaus Staubach (Frankfurt

a. M.: Lang, 2005), pp. 9–15 (p. 11): 'Die Komik besitzt ihren eigenen Existenz- und Wahrnehmungsbereich, in dem selbst extreme possen und parodien für die 'ernste' Welt nicht existenzgefährdend sind. Diese Feststellung gilt es im Hinblick auf die Frage nach der Ästhetik der Komik im Mittelalter im Auge zu behalten.'

73. Ex. 17:6: *en ego stabo coram te ibi super petram Horeb percutiesque petram et exibit ex ea aqua ut bibat populus fecit Moses ita coram senibus Israhel* ('Behold, I will stand before thee there upon the rock in Horeb; and thou shalt smite the rock, and there shall come water out of it, that the people may drink. And Moses did so in the sight of the elders of Israel').

74. Ward, pp. 167–71.

75. Ibid., pp. 170–71. This is made explicit in Gregory's life of St Benedict; after hearing a series of Benedict's miraculous deeds, Peter, Gregory's dialogue partner and deacon, states that they remind him of other saints and biblical events. Saint Gregory the Great, *Dialogues*, trans. by Odo John Zimmermann (New York: Fathers of the Church, Inc., 1959), II.8: 'The water streaming from the rock reminds me of Moses, and the iron blade that rose from the bottom of the lake, of Eliseus. The walking on the water recalls St Peter, the obedience of the raven, Elias, and the grief at the death of an enemy, David.' Gregory, however, is insistent that, despite this, Benedict was only inspired by Christ; it seems that saints may resemble one another in their deeds, but without direct influence, which can only come from God. It could be suggested that the similarity of their miracles acts as a code and reminder of their inspiration.

76. See also Noah (Genesis 8:7); Job 38:41. See Kiening, 'Heilige Brautwerbung', pp. 97–98.

77. The provenance of the raven has been much discussed and the nineteenth-century theories of a link to Wodan are now largely dismissed. Müller, 'Oswalds Rabe', pp. 458–60, offers a succinct overview of the symbolic possibilities of a raven, both positive (feeding Elias and becoming a preacher in Job) and negative (unreliability at the Flood; depicted as a thief, talkative, and greedy in various legends). The talkative nature of the raven also marks him out as a good messenger, a role often assumed by this type of bird. Kalinke, p. 51, stresses the link between *vitae* of St Oswald and Clovis; according to the legend of St Remigius, the lost chrism for Clovis's baptism was delivered to the saint from heaven by a dove. In the *Der Heiligen Leben* strand of Oswald *vitae*, it is a raven who brings the missing chrism to his baptism; Kalinke suggests that it is only a natural step from here for the raven to become the proxy wooer.

78. See *König Rother*, ll. 281–87, where the appearance of the messengers reflects explicitly and positively on their master.

79. In the *Budapester Oswald*, ll. 166–70, Oswald himself suggests the raven's ornamentation.

80. Conversely, the raven waits until Aron has drunk and eaten before making his entrance, as he believes that food and drink will have dulled his wits (ll. 821–24).

81. Haug 'Das Komische und das Heilige', p. 25. Bräuer, *Das Problem des 'Spielmännischen'*, p. 84, argues that the raven's obsession with food supports his theory of a later medieval reworking of the text: '[E]s sind die typischen Bearbeitungsmerkmale einer Zeit und eines Standes, die dem Sujet und dem Wesen des Urgedichtes bereits völlig gegenüberstanden'.

82. Miller, p. 236, argues that the mermaid episode is an exposition of fairy-tale rather than hagiographical miracles, an instance of the different structure-types in which the text consists; yet his theory is that the *Münchner Oswald* is a coherent, religiously motivated work, so the peculiar motivation behind the inclusion of this scene is not sufficiently addressed. Bräuer, *Das Problem des 'Spielmännischen'*, p. 63, also believes this episode to be a sloppy mixture of religious and profane, which he sees as characteristic of the late Middle Ages. For Curschmann, *Der Münchener Oswald und*

die deutsche spielmännische Epik, p. 17, mermaids embody 'die drohenden und zugleich faszinierenden Kräfte der Tiefe' and their ambivalence reflects 'in zauberischer Brechung die Doppelnatur der *minne*'; the problem of *minne* and its acceptance into a religious narrative is for him the major theme of the text.

83. On the function of the raven as 'a provider of *kurtzweil*', see Seeber, 'Sanctity and Comedy', p. 100.
84. Miller, p. 232, argues that the forgotten raven emphasizes his functionality. This is reflected in his rivalry with the deer, which stresses the very fact he is a raven and, like the deer, not a human member of Oswald's court.
85. Haug, 'Das Komische und das Heilige', p. 28.
86. Contrary to this, see Seeber, 'Sanctity and Comedy', p. 101, on the anthropomorphism of the raven.
87. Miller, pp. 231–32. See also Müller, 'Oswalds Rabe', pp. 456–57.
88. There is no shortage of extended saints' lives among the corpus of medieval German texts, and they vary greatly in style and content, resonating with a variety of different texts and genres, from Heinrich von Veldeke's *Servatius* to Hartmann von Aue's *Gregorius* and Reinbot von Durne's *Georg*.

CHAPTER 4

~

Grauer Rock: Orendel and the Grey Robe

Grauer Rock and the *tunica inconsutilis*

The seamless robe — or *tunica inconsutilis* — is the robe or coat that Christ is said to have worn to his crucifixion.[1] Most commonly considered by the church fathers to be a symbol of the unity of the Christian church,[2] it is traditionally thought to have been brought to Trier by St Helena, mother of Constantine and supposed founder of Trier cathedral, or by St Agritius, the first attested Bishop of Trier, on her behalf. Connections to Trier and to Helena began rather late, however; early historians made claims for a completely different resting place for the robe. According to Gregory of Tours (d. 594), relics of Christ were to be found in Galatia, and the seventh-century chronicle of Fredegar claims that the robe was found in Zafad, near Jerusalem, and brought to Jerusalem in AD 590, where it was buried in marble at the site of the crucifixion.[3] These explanations were widely taken up in the early medieval period.[4] The first mention of St Helena in the context of relics of Christ is found in the *Vita St Helenae* of Altman of Hautvillers, a Benedictine monk from Reims, which can be dated to the mid-ninth century and states that Helena brought several relics to Trier, apparently the city of her birth (this is highly unlikely), including the knife from the Last Supper.[5] The seamless robe is not mentioned explicitly. In the double *vita* of Sts Helena and Agritius, written by an unknown Trier religious in the mid-eleventh century, it is unclear whether the relics brought to Trier included the seamless robe.[6] In this period, Trier archbishops were officially campaigning for the city to have the title of *Roma secunda*, and the primacy of the city is claimed in the double *vita* because it was supposedly the birthplace of Helena.[7]

The robe is first mentioned explicitly in the final, fifth version of the so-called *Silvesterdiplom*, a faked legal document of St Silvester asserting the primacy of the Archbishopric of Trier, dated to the start of the twelfth century.[8] This found its way into the *Gesta Treverorum* and the presence of the seamless robe in Trier seemed to gain currency relatively quickly, as evidenced by two works of the mid-twelfth century: the *Kaiserchronik* and the so-called *Hillinbrief,* a letter supposedly written by the Emperor Friedrich I to Hillin, Archbishop of Trier, in 1158.[9] This latter example is almost certainly a forgery, written for the benefit of Trier's claim for primacy over all churches of Gaul, a claim that would be strengthened by the supposed possession of a relic of great importance, in this case the seamless robe of Christ.[10]

The robe — or whatever the Trier archbishopric was claiming to be the robe — was moved from the Nicholas altar of the cathedral to the main altar in 1196 in the time of the archbishop Johannes I (d. 1212), reported not long after his death in the *Gesta Treverorum continuata*.[11] It then remained hidden in the altar until its rediscovery in 1512. Yet before 1512 the presence of the seamless robe in Trier was not an officially recognized certainty. Unsurprisingly, given the small number of relics of Christ and their utmost importance, a number of other religious institutions claimed possession of the robe, in particular Argenteuil.[12] Despite the clear benefits that the robe would bring to Trier, both financial (thanks to the 'tourist' income of pilgrims) and political (it could finally ensure the supremacy of Trier over surrounding religious centres, particularly Aachen and Cologne, in possession of the robe of the Virgin and the remains of the Magi respectively), it seemed to be too much of a risk to assert its presence officially. At the start of the fifteenth century, Friedrich Schavard, the Provost of St Paulin in Trier, suggested displaying the robe to the public, but the reaction was not favourable, possibly because of the other claims and a lack of concrete evidence.[13] Emperor Maximilian's 'rediscovery' of the robe in 1512 was supposedly divinely inspired, but the subsequent exhibition of the robe occurred against the wishes of the Archbishop elect, Richard von Greiffenklau, and a large part of the cathedral chapter.[14]

The relationship of *Grauer Rock*, or *Orendel*, to the events surrounding the seamless robe at Trier is unclear.[15] The text has not had a particularly glorious history in literary scholarship, largely being condemned as poorly written or thematically confused.[16] Older studies and literary histories concentrated for the most part on the epic origins of the narrative and Orendel himself; they now focus increasingly, however, on its relationship with the history of the relic of the seamless robe at Trier and the rediscovery of the robe by Maximilian I in 1512, which caused the work to be printed in two forms, verse (D) and prose (P).[17] In *Grauer Rock*, this robe is discovered by Orendel, a prince of Trier seeking to woo Bride, the princess of Jerusalem, and he wears it and is identified by it while defending the Holy Grave against heathens. He eventually returns to Trier to defend the city against invading heathens and leaves the robe there, enclosed in a stone chest, but returns to Jerusalem, becomes king and marries Bride in a chaste union. Thanks to the large amount of documentation concerning the events of 1512, we know a fair amount about the reception and potential function of the prints of *Grauer Rock*; as will be discussed below, it seems clear that the aim of the prints was to spread the word about the discovery of the robe and the importance of Trier as a pilgrimage destination, even if the success of the text was rather short-lived. Yet we also know that *Grauer Rock* was not written specifically for the rediscovery of the seamless robe of Christ in 1512: there was a manuscript (H) dated to 1477 (Strassburg Stadtbibliothek Cod. B 92), burnt in Strassburg in 1870, but transcribed beforehand by Ch. M. Engelhardt (Berlin, mgq 817a).[18] The two prints — particularly the verse redaction — are related closely to the manuscript, although some episodes are expanded or clarified in the prose version.[19]

The composition of *Grauer Rock* is traditionally dated to the late twelfth century and often precisely to 1196 on the occasion of the *depositio* of the robe in the main altar of Trier cathedral.[20] As we have already seen, the notion of *Spielmannsepik* as a genre is dependent on dating all the constituent texts to the twelfth century, partly because of the early dating of *König Rother* and *Herzog Ernst*, and partly because one of the founding principles of *Spielmannsepik* is that it forms a precursor to the courtly romances of the *Blütezeit*. Yet for *Grauer Rock*, as is also the case for the *Münchner Oswald* and *Salman und Morolf*, if the generic demands of *Spielmannsepik* and the associated demand for dating the text to the twelfth century are removed, the possibilities of a considerably later dating are opened up. There is no concrete evidence for dating the text to 1196 and the main critical work on its language, Ernst Teuber's 1954 Göttingen dissertation, *Zur Datierungsfrage des mittelhochdeutschen Orendelepos* (not generally available), dates it to the twelfth century but, as pointed out by Biesterfeldt, only had access to Steinger's edition of the text, the language of which is heavily altered in the attempt to recreate an archetype.[21]

The first scholar to question the early dating of *Grauer Rock* (as well as the *Münchner Oswald*) was de Boor, who argued that its style was reminiscent of the late medieval ballad, that the themes of the text picked up on stories popular in the later Middle Ages (particularly the Apollonius-story), and that the 'mechanical' depiction of wonders suggested a late medieval mass-audience.[22] Other than the burnt MS H, the only evidence of knowledge of the text prior to 1512 comes from the fifteenth century. *ain hübsch buoch genant der graw rok und künk alexander* is mentioned in a mid-fifteenth-century register from the workshop of Diebold Lauber; this is presumably a scribal error and accidental conflation of an Orendel-story with an Alexander-story, as there is no other evidence of Alexander being mentioned in connection with the robe of Christ, which would in any case be highly improbable, given the popularity of Alexander stories in their own right.[23] Orendel is also mentioned in the introduction to the mid fifteenth-century *Straßburger Heldenbuch*:

> Kunig Erendelle von Triere, der was der erste heilt, der ie geborn wartt; der fuor uber mer, vnd do er vff das mer kam, do hette er gar vil kiele, wanne er was gar ein richer kinig. do gingen ym die kiele alsaman vnder; doch kan er mitt sim lib vsz, vnd kam ein vischer faren vnd halff dem heren vs. vnd also wz er lang by dem vischer vnd halff ym vischen; vnd hinden nach kam er gon Jherusalem vnd kam zuo dem heiligen grab. do was sin frowe einz kingez dohtter, die was geheissen frowe Bride, vnd wz ouch die schoenstte ob aln wiben. Vnd do nach wartt ym geholffen von andern grossen heren, vnd kam wider gen Triere, vnd starp ouch zuo Triere vnd litt ouch zu Triere. vnd also ertrunken ym al sin diener, vnd verlor grosz guott vff dem mere.[24]

This description of Orendel does not mention the robe at all, concentrating solely on the hero himself, which could suggest the existence of a different version of the story, completely disconnected from the Trier relic. It is also distinctly possible that the story could have been received flexibly depending on context; for the purpose of the introduction to the *Heldenbuch*, the necessary focus would be on the heroic achievements of Orendel, not the translation of the robe.[25]

Regardless of the dating of *Grauer Rock*, all scholars are faced with the same problem: why was it composed? From the twelfth century, as we have seen, St Helena was widely believed to have brought about the *translatio* of the seamless robe of Christ to Trier. Her role in moving the robe would have been highly plausible: she was known to have spent a long time in Palestine and to have found the true cross.[26] It seems very odd, therefore, that *Grauer Rock* should offer a different version of the *translatio* of the robe, replacing a well-attested saint with an otherwise unknown king, a problem that has been addressed frequently in scholarship on the text. The most obvious answer to this problem would be that *Grauer Rock* is directed at a different audience from narratives about Helena, a lay audience, with the aim of popularizing Trier's claim to the relic with an entertaining story in the vernacular.[27]

Yet if the aim of *Grauer Rock* is to popularize Trier and the relic, then why choose Orendel? Various scholars have argued that Orendel himself must be a well-attested local heroic figure; this would enable him to be meaningful and historically believable.[28] Ebenbauer returns to the etymological exploration of the name 'Orendel', forging a connection to Apollo Grannos, who may have entered Germanic mythology as *Auzavandilaz (OHG *Orwandil; MHG Orendel); there is also a link to Horvendil in Saxo Grammaticus and Aurvandill in the Younger Edda.[29] This hero would be some kind of personification of the morning sun, potentially even identified with Christ, who is referred to as *earendel* (light coming from the East) by Cynewulf. Jungandreas argues that there are a few traces of the original myth remaining in *Grauer Rock*: the hero (the sun) is under the control of Winter (Ise), but manages to escape and comes back from the East, bringing great blessing with him.[30] As attractive as the notion of Orendel as a local hero may seem, there appears to be no concrete evidence for his being so; it is also a theory that does not help illuminate the complexities of the text.

Meves also suggests that Orendel may be a particular hero of Trier, albeit less specifically, and argues that he replaces Helena because of disputes between the religious institutions of Trier; because of this, he dates the text to the late twelfth century. The support of the Archbishop Johannes I (d. 1212) meant that the seamless robe in the Trier cathedral gained considerably more importance than the various other relics in the city and that the cathedral itself diverted attention from other churches and monasteries and their relics: the monastery of St Matthew, for instance, possessed bones of St Matthew and the monastery of St Maximian the knife from the Last Supper. The competing institutions, so Meves argues, no longer wanted to share claims to relics and saints. The monastery of St Maximian, as well as the cathedral, had previously claimed Helena as its founder, but owing to her connection with the seamless robe, began to place more emphasis on the efforts of her son, Constantine. St Agritius was thought to be connected with the founding of both St Maximilian and the cathedral church; St Maximilian and the monastery of St Matthew both claimed to have his grave. Since Helena and Agritius were not only connected to the cathedral, but also to competing institutions, Meves argues that an alternative translator would be needed for the seamless robe.[31] This theory seems extremely tenuous and does not solve the problem of the seeming secularization in replacing St Helena with Orendel and a traditional *translatio*-report with a more heroic, adventurous narrative. Moreover — as will be discussed in more detail below — *Grauer Rock* appears to be something of a one-off and never actually replaced accounts of Helena or Agritius bringing the robe to Trier; Meves's argument implies a major rejection of Helena, which was never the case.

Another possibility is that *Grauer Rock* was not intended to replace Helena's translation of the seamless robe, but to fulfil an entirely different purpose, demonstrating what the robe — which was not publicly visible or officially acknowledged by the church authorities in Trier before 1512 — might symbolize and giving it agency. Kiening suggests that 'sie [*Grauer Rock*-stories] beziehen sich explizit oder implizit auf etwas, was im klerikalen oder erbaulichen Schrifttum der Zeit (noch) keinen Ort hat und auch als Objekt (noch) unsichtbar bleibt. Sie arbeiten an jenem Imaginären der Reliquie. . .'.[32] The robe's uncertain status as a relic means that there may have been more freedom to write about it and its relationship to Trier before its presence became official and the Helena translation was established as doctrine, hence the connection to Orendel and the relatively entertaining narrative. Such an interest in making an inaccessible relic in some way accessible could suggest that the text in its extant form was composed in the fifteenth century, given the marked increase in the later Middle Ages in demand for physical, visible proof for devotion and a desire to see God and to see relics, more and more of which were being displayed openly.[33]

It is, however, impossible to make such an argument with any certainty, particularly given that *Grauer Rock*, despite its interest in the appearance of the robe, is not explicitly concerned with devotional practice. All we do know for certain is that the text was written before the rediscovery of the seamless robe by Maximilian in 1512, so was concerned with an inaccessible relic. In this sense, it is unsurprising that it cannot be thought to function as a conventional *translatio*-report; it does not concentrate solely on the translation of the robe and does not describe it in detail, as we shall see.[34] Instead, there seems to be a looser concern in 'exhibiting' the robe and making its properties and presence in Trier public. Yet *Grauer Rock* is not just about the relic, and it would be to ignore a portion of the text to say this; perhaps the main focus is the grey robe, as the *tunica inconsutilis* is known, but the story of the man who wears it, which interlinks and sporadically breaks away from that of the robe, must not be forgotten. In this chapter, the text will be discussed in two respects: first, I shall consider how the properties of the robe are made apparent and clarify the indexical function of Orendel; second, I shall discuss the continuation of Orendel's narrative after the deposition of the robe and the effect of his maintaining the name *grower roc*.

Robe and Man: A Relationship of Indexicality?

Grauer Rock begins with a short prologue (ll. 1–20), encouraging the audience to think of Christ and his salvation of mankind, in particular his fasting of forty days and nights. The grey robe is then introduced: *Nun wil ich mier selber begynen | Von dem grauwen rock sprechen und singen* (ll. 21–22) and linked explicitly with the acts of salvation of Christ, because he wore it while fasting (l. 37). The robe was spun by Mary and woven by St Helena (ll. 25–28), which may suggest that there was some knowledge of her involvement with the seamless robe, but nothing certain or doctrinal.[35] Kiening discusses the 'overdetermination' of the narrative with respect to the description of the robe in the prologue, suggesting that the syntagmatic description of the robe is paradigmatically loaded with meaning, to the extent that the robe becomes an 'überdeterminiertes Dingsymbol'. It is woven not sewn, so is a symbol of unity; it is made on the Mount of Olives, so inextricably linked to the passion of Christ; it was worn during Christ's period of fasting; it was made by Mary and Helena, the latter of whom provides a connection to stories of its discovery and translation. The mention of Helena acts as a participation in the

Helena-tradition, but opens up space for a new *translatio*, 'eine eigensinnige Neubesetzung des Übergangs'.[36] The notion of paradigmatic overdetermination is perhaps rather ambitious for this text; moreover, Helena and the Mount of Olives are never mentioned again and a symbolic connection to the unity of the church is never made explicit. Instead — at least at the start of the story — the grey robe is a visual symbol of the crucifixion of Christ, bearing traces of his blood that cannot be washed out. After the crucifixion, a group of Jews request the robe from King Herod (unlike in the Bible, no lots are drawn for it), wash it, and dry it in the sun. But:

> Unser herre Jhesus Kristus das gebot,
> Das sin rosen varbes blut so rot
> An dem grawen rock stunt,
> Also es noch wol ist kunt,
> In allen den geberden,
> Als er erst gemartelt were. (ll. 73–78)

Herod demands never to see the robe again and has it locked in a chest and thrown to the bottom of the sea. A water-sprite (*siren*) breaks the chest open and drags it to a beach, where it buries it nine fathoms under the ground. The robe remains there for eight years and in the ninth year returns to the surface and is found by a pilgrim, Tragemunt, who also tries to wash out the bloodstains without success. The miraculous persistence of the blood causes him to recognize the true identity of the robe and think of the death of Christ and the salvation of mankind it brought about:

> Ach, du hymelscher Trechtin,
> Dis mag wol din rock sin:
> Herre, du empfinge den sper stich,
> Den litte du, herre, durch mich
> Vnd durch alles menschen konne,
> Wie du uns von der bittern hel gewonne. (ll. 145–50)

Aware that it would not be fitting for him to wear the robe (ll. 151–52), he throws it back into the sea, where it is swallowed by a whale and remains in its stomach for eight years, before finally being discovered by Orendel.

This prehistory of the seamless robe before the involvement of Orendel establishes that the value of the robe does not only consist in the fact that it belonged to and was worn by Christ, but that it still bears the visible sign of his death and pain: his blood. A relic is, in the words of Geary, often simply a 'bone or a bit of dust', so needs some kind of signifying framework through which it may be understood, such as a reliquary or a narrative describing its provenance, translation, or miraculous properties.[37] The grey robe is not just a simple piece of material, but is seamless and inscribed with the text of Christ's blood, which is read by those who look at it. The pilgrim reads the robe correctly, recognizing its provenance, but the blood has some kind of effect on all those described looking at it: Herod demands never to see the robe again and the Fisher-King Ise misinterprets the stains, assuming that the robe belonged to a nobleman who was attacked by robbers (ll. 637–40), which could be an allegory of Christ's betrayal and sacrifice. We, the audience, know the true provenance of the robe from the prologue, and how the bloodstains should be read — as a reminder of the suffering of Christ — and can therefore correct the incorrect readings in our minds.

The reactions to the robe stress the importance of visual response. It is looking at the robe, not touching it, that has an effect, and in later sections of the text, as shall be discussed below, when Orendel is wearing the robe, the visual reaction of other characters is also emphasized. The robe is not made visible through ekphrasis, which we might expect for making a hidden object visible; the author does not provide a really detailed description, or even a more literal illustration, of an inaccessible object for veneration. Illustrated books or single-page prints ('Flugblätter') of relics were not unusual in the fifteenth and early sixteenth centuries, a result not only of the increasing development of printing and the increase of indulgence propaganda before the onset of the Reformation, but also of the phenomenon of increasingly less distant pilgrimages ('Nahwallfahrten'), which brought about a kind of competition between religious institutions, fought out with 'pilgrimage propaganda'.[38] The specifics of pilgrimage propaganda with respect to the seamless robe after its rediscovery in Trier in 1512 will be discussed in more detail further on, as will the role of the prints of *Grauer Rock* in this context. Suffice to say that it was quite common for information about relics to be disseminated after they had been established as locations for pilgrimage, or as a means of establishing them as such locations; the descriptions were often illustrated and could act as advertisements, objects for veneration, or as a means of gaining indulgence. Cordez discusses the various extant examples of these illustrated leaflets, books, and single-leaf prints, which he calls 'Heiltumsverzeichnisse mit Reliquienbildern' or 'illustrierte Reliquienverzeichnisse'; from between 1460 and 1520 there are twenty-two extant printed examples and seven non-printed examples of these, all varying in presentation and function.[39] It is important that illustrations of relics could act as a kind of *ostentio* themselves, a replacement for a 'real' pilgrimage, particularly when an indulgence could be gained by saying a specific prayer while looking at the depiction of the relic.[40] We can think in this context of 'Pilgrims' signs' as well, small models of the relic that could be bought by pilgrims as a reminder of their journey and a devotional reminder of the relic itself; there is an extant Pilgrim's sign from Trier of the seamless robe, dated to the early sixteenth century after the rediscovery of 1512.[41]

Regardless of the reasons behind printing *Grauer Rock* in 1512, the visual interest in the text cannot be thought of as analogous to these various drawings or models of relics, as it was written before the relic was displayed to the public and before the seamless robe became a popular pilgrimage destination, with the associated paraphernalia. Even if *Grauer Rock* was adapted to this framework of publicizing and popularizing the robe as a relic worthy of visitation, it cannot have been written with this function in mind. The 'invisibility' of the robe also — paradoxically — means that the text has to make it publicly known in a less conventional, less ekphrastic sense; it is not yet an object with a recognized, official appearance that can be closely described or reproduced for some kind of veneration, but still something of an 'idea'. Therefore, despite the interest in the spots of blood, the focus in *Grauer Rock* is more on narrative, on making the properties — symbolic or otherwise — of the robe 'public'. Indeed, this is also the primary significance of the spots of blood: a memory device for the passion of Christ, and an unwashable mark to make people aware of the miraculous nature of the robe, not a diagrammatic description of what the robe looks like that can be reproduced accurately.[42]

The grey robe is an item of clothing, so it can — and should — be worn, and its emptiness not only emphasizes the absence (and therefore, paradoxically, the 'presence') of its original wearer (Christ), but also its wearability.[43] It needs to be worn, so that it may have agency and manifest its powers, and it is here that Orendel himself comes into play. Orendel, the third son of King Ougel of Trier, decides after his investiture that he should marry, and Ougel mentions Bride, the Queen of Jerusalem, as a suitable match. The journey to Jerusalem is fraught with difficulties and all Orendel's ships are eventually sunk; he is the only man to survive. He is washed up on a beach, naked, and says that he looks like a robber:

> Wer mich nun hie siecht nackent stan,
> Der sprich zu den stunden,
> Ich sy von einer roupp gallen entrunen
> Vnd sig ein roüber und ein diep (ll. 498–501)

For three days he lies in a hole dug in the beach (ll. 511–12), reminiscent of Christ in his grave before the resurrection, but his expectations of being taken for a robber are fulfilled when he is found by Ise, a rich fisherman, who says: *Ich sich an dissen stunden, | Du bist ab einer roup gallen entrunen, | Du bist ein rouber und ein diepp* (ll. 527–29). The audience knows, however, that Orendel is not a thief, and he says himself: *Wie wol mier stellen nie wart liep | Vnd mir uff disser erden, | Ob Got wil, niemer wil werden.* (ll. 502–04) Orendel is taken in as a servant by Ise, after proving — with divine help — that he is able to catch fish, but he remains in an utmost state of destitution, naked except for a *walt ruche* to protect him from shame (ll. 554–55). Ise catches the whale that has swallowed the grey robe — we are reminded here of Jonah, whose 'rebirth' connected him typologically with Christ — and Orendel asks to have the robe, but Ise says that he first must earn it:

> Er sprach: 'er wirt niemer dier,
> Du vergeltest in dan mier
> Also türe, also er wert müg sin,
> Vnd must daran min diener sin (ll. 651-54)

Orendel is instead bought cheap clothing and shoes (ll. 669-74) but looks naked without the grey robe (l. 675-76). He prays that he may have the robe and is sent thirty golden pennies from heaven with which he may buy it (ll. 709-12), a price linked to the thirty pieces of silver for which Judas betrayed Christ.

It is clear that Orendel must undergo a process of utmost degradation in order to prepare himself for wearing the robe and follow the 'narrow path' trodden by many saints (Matthew 7:13). The topos of being washed up naked on a beach, unknown and unrecognizable, and being taken on as a servant by a local lord is also the major link in *Grauer Rock* to the story of Apollonius, the late classical romance that became very popular in both Latin and vernacular throughout the Middle Ages. It is undeniable that this section of the text is influenced by the Apollonius romance — the themes of shipwreck, nakedness, servitude, and being given clothes by the lord are pronouncedly close — but it is impossible to speak of an 'Apolloniusvorlage'.[44] Tomasek argues that the Apollonius story was widely transmitted in Europe in the twelfth century in both Latin and the vernacular, and that it was highly influential in this period; he notes its influence not only on *Grauer Rock*, but also on the Faustinian episode of the *Kaiserchronik*, on *Tristan* romances, Manekine stories, and the Old French *Jourdain de Blaye*.[45] The first problem here is one of dating; Tomasek argues that the Apollonius material was really only influential for other stories in the twelfth century, when it was one of the most established and widespread narratives in Europe. Yet there was no written vernacular Apollonius in Germany until the fourteenth-century version by Heinrich von Neustadt and the text was perhaps at its most popular in fifteenth-century Germany, with three prose versions, including the *Volksbuch* of Heinrich Steinhöwel, first printed in 1471 and going through at least ten more editions before 1556.[46] Tomasek takes the twelfth-century dating of *Grauer Rock* for granted and his argument does not prove his assumption, particularly given that some of the other texts he draws upon seem unlikely to have been influenced by Apollonius, especially the *Tristan* romances. The other problem is exactly what is meant by 'influence', since single motifs shared by medieval stories are no proof of intertextuality. In the case of *Grauer Rock*, it seems highly likely that the shipwreck scene is influenced directly or indirectly by the Apollonius material, but Tomasek argues that use of an Apollonius-motif causes the recipients of a text to expect certain developments. If — as I have argued with respect to the bridal quest — medieval texts use a variety of motifs that occur in other works but can be developed in completely different ways, with different results and different 'meanings', then this standpoint must be reconsidered. The Apollonius material seems forgotten by the time Orendel meets Bride, so it is hard to accept (or explain away) Bride's kidnap and the chastity of the pair as Apollonius-driven expectations of separation, testing, and reconciliation.

In *Grauer Rock*, the Apollonius shipwreck motifs are given a meaning specific to Orendel and the grey robe, in that Orendel's nakedness prepares him for his role as bearer of the robe. The scenes after his shipwreck are full of implicit theological references, including the parallels with Christ and Jonah mentioned above, which do not form any kind of coherent schema but centre on notions of rebirth, baptism, and the chosen nature of Orendel. Orendel comes naked from the sea as if baptized and, like Adam, he rips a leaf from a bush to cover his shame (ll. 554–55), a postlapsarian act that is nonetheless reminiscent of prelapsarian nakedness. Prelapsarian nakedness was understood by Augustine as a robe of mercy ('Gnadenkleid'), which was connected to the robe of baptism.[47] According to Paul, in baptism the Christian man puts on Christ as a robe, which (like the seamless robe) represents the unity of the Christian church, and in this way becomes part of the body of Christ.[48] The fact that Orendel loses his clothing and his name, both symbols of his worldly life, is reminiscent of investiture as a monk, a process also connected to baptism, where worldly connections are laid aside for new clothing and a new life — even, like Orendel, a new name, as from this point on he is called *grower* (or *groger*) *roc* by the narrator and all those he meets.[49] Notably, Orendel (wearing the grey robe) is mocked by the Knights Templar, who say that he looks like a monk:

> Sy sprachent: 'was kuniges ist das gewesen?
> Wir getruwent wol vor jm zu genesen;
> Er enfürt nit ander wat,
> Dan einen growen rock, der jm wol an stat,
> Und wie er an disen stunden
> Uss[er] einem closter sig entrunnen (ll. 1671–76)

The similarity of the grey robe to a monk's habit indicates its simplicity and the humility of its owner, further emphasized by the description of the armour of one of Orendel's adversaries, a heathen giant (ll. 1218–74). The giant's armour is highly elaborate: his shield is covered with precious stones and his nineteen-cornered helmet is decorated with four golden spikes, masterfully decorated with letters, on top of which is a golden crown, with a golden linden tree and a golden bird flying above. A sack of air with six golden pipes is attached to this bird and can be pressed by the giant to make it sing *recht als ob si lebten* (l. 1255). In the linden tree are a dozen shells which make a sound when the air from the sack passes through them; the combination of this sound and the birdsong is astounding: *Wer do gewesen aller seiten spiel, | So kund es dem nit glichen ziel* (ll. 1265–66). The giant's opponent, Orendel, *fürt nit anders zwor | Dann einen rock, der ist gro* (ll. 1291–92). It is clear that the reader should draw a contrast between the two figures, not only between elaborateness and humility, but also between the mechanical and the miraculous. The 'magical' sound-making devices of the giant's armour are described in great detail, with particular interest on how they work mechanically. The power of Orendel's robe is not man-made but God-given: it is impenetrable (we are first told this at ll. 729–30), but miraculously so, not because of any technical prowess.

The impenetrability of the robe is only one instance of its miraculous immutability. The persisting bloodstains have been discussed above, and it is notable that the introductory section of the text sees the robe undergo a number of processes that should incur change or destruction: it is thrown in the sea, buried under the ground, and eaten by a whale. Oddly, the miraculous immutability is inverted into miraculous mutability when it comes to Orendel's acquisition of it. When other people try it on it falls apart:

> Wer den rock angreiff,
> Wie vast er von einander reisz!
> In allen den geberden,
> Als ob er ful were. (ll. 753–56)

Yet when Orendel wears it, it becomes as good as new:

> Do wart er, an den trüwen,
> Den rock, als wer er nüwen,
> In allen den geberden,
> Als ob er erst gemacht were. (ll. 767–70)

It is unclear whether the blood of Christ has disappeared with this miraculous renewing; it is never mentioned again. Now that the robe has been recognized as the robe of Christ, it seems more important that Orendel is miraculously chosen as its wearer, and that he wear it to defend the Holy Grave and continue the Christian project of salvation.

When Orendel is given the thirty golden pennies from heaven with which to buy the robe, he is told by an angel what he is to do while wearing it: *Du solt darin fechten mit lobe | Mit XV heidischen hertzouwen* (ll. 731–32). The majority of the text then consists in often seemingly endless battles against heathens, who are killed in their thousands by Orendel, now known as *grower roc*. The Grey Robe, which has been a reminder of the passion of Christ, is a symbol of the salvation of mankind, and when worn by Orendel, the project of salvation is continued in the defence of the Holy Grave and battles against heathens. The memory of a past act of salvation is transposed to a new action, and the robe seems to subsume Orendel's identity completely. As soon as he takes possession of the robe, it is the only way by which he can be identified. When he approaches Jerusalem, he is addressed by a man who calls him *groger roc* because he does not know what else he might call him:

> Do er in vere an sach,
> Gern mügent jr hören, wie er sprach:
> 'Got grüsse vch, Groger Rock,
> Ich kan uch nit nenen, das wisz Got,
> Ob ich uch, her, erkante,
> Wie gern ich uch nantte!' (ll. 855-60)

This formula is repeated several times throughout the text and from this point on the former Orendel is called *grower rock* by the narrator and everyone he meets; he even denies his previous identity (ll. 1471-74).

There is not, however, complete identity between Orendel and the Grey Robe. The text is not constructed as an allegory of the salvation of mankind; although Orendel loses his name and is known and recognized by the robe he wears, he does not *become* it. Equally, he does not have identity with Christ, whom he might be considered to imitate by wearing the coat. Instead, the relationship between Orendel and the Grey Robe (and ultimately Christ) is one founded on *indexicality*: the quality of a sign that is linked to its object by an actual connection or real relation in such a way as to compel attention (thus smoke is an index of fire).[50] In this sense, we could talk about Orendel as a kind of 'inverse' reliquary. Reliquaries are similar to stories about relics, making sense of what might otherwise be without significance. They present and interpret their contents; they 'create sacral presence'.[51] Orendel is a kind of inverse reliquary, in that the relic covers him, but he does still give the relic the necessary 'writing', bestowing it with some form of sense by continuing the salvation project of Christ and giving the relic agency. In this sense, Orendel can be thought of as an index of the robe, which is in turn an index of Christ.

The indexical function of Orendel is further clarified by the fact that he is always (and only) called 'Orendel' by the heavenly figures of Mary and the angels, who talk to him to give help or instructions. In this way it is made clear that the action is being directed from heaven; Orendel is told from the very beginning exactly what he should do while wearing the robe and is actively helped in battle by angels when the number of heathen opponents becomes too much. Yet even if the guiding function of the text is Orendel's indexicality, it cannot account for everything that happens, and there is no doubt that he also has his own story, which continues after the deposition of the robe in Trier.

Orendel and the Holy Grave

We have seen that there are two protagonists in *Grauer Rock*: the robe, whose story is made clear by the reactions of others and whose symbolic project is continued by the man who wears it, with whom it has a relationship of indexicality, and the man himself, whose story continues after the deposition of the robe in Trier. And because of the continuation of Orendel's own narrative, it cannot be said that he is simply a reliquary for the Grey Robe, and that his only function is to ensure its translation to Trier and act as an index for the robe and, ultimately, Christ. This leads to probably the greatest difficulty in interpreting *Grauer Rock*, namely the often unclear way in which the stories of Orendel and the Robe are merged. For *Grauer Rock* is a text that continually defies attempts to make it tidy, which is certainly not a bad thing; in this case, however, it is because of the kind of literary complexity of a work such as Gottfried's *Tristan*. The impression is instead — in line with much of the criticism on the text — that *Grauer Rock* is something of a ramshackle mess. This does not mean that it is impossible to say anything fruitful about it, but that straightforward, one-sided interpretations simply do not work. The discussion above of the introductory part of the text showed that the narratives of man and robe start separately and join together symbolically when Orendel buys the Robe with the heaven-sent pennies. It then seems as if Orendel's role is largely indexical. Yet there are other elements to the narrative — most notably Orendel's relationship with Bride — and Orendel's story continues after the Robe has been deposited in Trier. There is the sense (if perhaps not a very clear one) that the narratives of man and robe converge and split apart sporadically — and not always very cleanly — until the deposition, which provides the conclusion to the narrative of the Robe. This will be clarified by the following discussion.

Divine interference continues after the deposition of the robe, and Mary interacts not only with Orendel but also at one point with his men, when Orendel is in trouble. She does this not in the form of a vision but by having a turtledove deliver a letter, objects which in medieval texts often have the character of absolute truth.[52] The remarkable and unusual nature of this intervention is stressed by the fact that the letter is delivered during mass, which is then broken off; the narrator insists that this is not normal and should, in all other circumstances, never happen:

> Das geschach sit, noch ee,
> Vnd geschiet ouch niemer me;
> Vnd sehe ein priester ein minster brinnen,
> So sol er sin messe vol bringen (ll. 3689–92)

Heavenly concern goes beyond Orendel's usefulness as a vessel for the robe, for ensuring the deposition of the robe in Trier is not his only task; his other purpose is to defend the Holy Grave at Jerusalem. In order to do this, he becomes King of Jerusalem, achieved by the not uncommon motif of marrying the besieged female ruler (such as Gahmuret's marriage to Belacane in *Parzival*), but his kingship is not clearly defined; unlike in *König Rother*, for example, his manner of ruling is not expanded on in detail or described as a model for imitation. In contrast to the region around Trier and the Mosel, Jerusalem is not well-defined in the text and the Holy Grave itself is a rather vague object; we are not even given a rough idea of its appearance. Being King is equated with being chief protector of the Holy Grave, which is more of an idea than a real object and thus, rather than a real political role, it is more akin to being God's greatest warrior and defending Christianity itself. It is therefore unsurprising that Orendel is never seen to rule in an active sense; his role does not seem to involve the protection of his people or the maintenance of social stability, as in *König Rother*. His duty is, it seems, exclusively to the Holy Grave, of which he is the chief protector. In this sense, we could speak of his kingship as not of the worldly sort, but entirely directed towards God. Hence also the lack of interest in providing an heir and the utmost necessity of his chastity.[53]

The nature of Orendel's kingship over Jerusalem and the Holy Grave is clarified by a rather odd episode in which Ise comes to Jerusalem. After Orendel has been recognized for who he is and crowned king (it is predestined he shall be king, as Bride has been told so in her sleep by the voice of God, ll. 1457–68), Ise arrives in Jerusalem searching for his former servant. Orendel welcomes him warmly and apologizes for being out of his service for so long, sending Ise to Bride to ask her permission for him to leave and rejoin his master. Bride — who, as a queen, is socially superior to Ise — says that Orendel can no longer be his servant: *Sin dienst kumet dir nit recht* (l. 2220). Ise tells Orendel that *Ir sollent wesen künig und herre | Uber die burg zu Iherusalem* (ll. 2237–38) and Orendel is happy, buying a beautiful new robe for Ise's wife as recompense for the *aldes nider gewete* (l. 2265) she gave him; this is surely the means by which he may absolve himself completely of Ise's service and of any debt he may owe. Ise returns home, but Orendel still — and rather unexpectedly — asks permission of Bride to follow him and serve him. Perhaps this is meant to be a sign of his humility; in any case Bride will not allow him to go and summons Ise again, and on his arrival, Orendel states that he should become a duke of the Holy Grave. This whole episode is rather peculiar, and it could even be argued that it is a conflation of two versions of the story, in one of which Ise returns home with the new robe, in the other of which he remains to serve the Holy Grave. Yet the narrative as we have it has a twofold effect, however, because it frees Orendel from any duties he might have as servant to Ise and also, through Orendel's rather awkward volte-face, recruits another servant for the Holy Grave. In this sense, both Orendel and Ise serve not one another, but a higher master: the Grave, or God. This rather odd scene clarifies that God, not Orendel, is master, and that Orendel does not view himself (and should not be viewed) as king in any worldly sense.

The clearest parallel to Orendel is King David, whom the text claims was Bride's father; Orendel is given his sword (with which he kills giants) and his crown. By carrying David's attributes, Orendel (almost literally) puts himself in his shoes, but the symbolic function of the sword and crown is much less developed than that of the grey robe itself. Orendel, like David, is both *rex et sacerdos*, God's chosen King; David was also thought to be an ancestor of Mary and Christ, providing a link between Bride and Christ as well and, presumably, justifying her rightful place as Queen of Jerusalem. Notably, unlike David, Orendel remains untempted by women. Like Oswald, he is ordered by heaven to retain his chastity with his wife, but unlike Oswald, there is no known historical model of marriage and kingship to make this compromise necessary. Orendel's monkishness and suffering have been discussed above, and much of his story follows the path of the *vita* of a saint, which is not incompatible with his status as warrior;[54] the obvious question to ask, therefore, is why Orendel should marry at all, and quite what the function of Bride might be. The bridal-quest motif is introduced in the typical fashion — noble seeks a bride, receives advice, she lives overseas — but is quickly abandoned as soon as Orendel comes into contact with the grey robe. This is again evidence that the bridal-quest motif does not have to be a symbolic structure for a text and that it can be combined flexibly with a variety of other story-motifs for a variety of different purposes. In *Grauer Rock*, the bridal-quest motif is an excellent way of starting the story and gives the hero an impulse to travel to Jerusalem; the description of Orendel in the *Heldenbuch*-prologue, quoted above, also suggests that there may have been other stories concerned with an Orendel-hero wooing an Eastern princess. Yet when Orendel arrives in Jerusalem, wooing Bride seems completely forgotten and more importance is instead placed on defending the Holy Grave. We have already seen that there is a relationship of indexicality between Orendel and the robe, and there is also a sense of partial identity between Bride and the Holy Grave, in that wooing her can be equated with defending it. It is striking that the text is roughly constructed around two people (Orendel and Bride), two places (Trier and Jerusalem), and two symbolically determined objects (the Robe and the Grave), which can be split into two triads: Orendel — Trier — Grey Robe; Bride — Jersualem — Holy Grave.

Functionally, marrying Bride enables Orendel to become King of Jerusalem legitimately, as well as to ally himself with the house of David. She is also a means of temptation through which his chastity may be tested. Bride asks Orendel to marry her (ll. 1796–98), but Orendel refuses, saying that she should wait for a King. She has already told him, as mentioned above, that the voice of God has told her about Orendel's story and that she should marry him, making him King of Jerusalem, and Orendel has denied that he is this man, so it seems slightly odd that she should still want to marry him, perhaps a sign that she can see through his denial. In any case, she gives him a robe worn by King David and, after feasting, they go to bed together (ll. 1811–24); it is striking that the seamless robe is (implicitly — it is certainly explicitly put back on later) removed before this worldly temptation. An angel then appears to Orendel and states that he must not sleep with Bride for nine years (ll. 1827–32), and he lays a sword between him and Bride to prevent this (ll. 1834–40), although Bride tells him to remove this, saying that she could last for ten years without a man (l. 1856). At the end of the text, an angel appears again to warn the pair against sexual relations, this time without any time limit, although they are both to die within the year (ll. 3903–10). Such a limited lifespan is reminiscent of the *Münchner Oswald*; again, there is the sense that the protagonist has achieved as much as possible and attained such a state of perfection that it would be pointless to live longer. The chaste marriage in *Grauer Rock* is also a kind of compromise, combining the story-motifs of marriage to the unprotected queen (who enables legitimate kingship) and a saintly, ascetic way of life.[55] Yet the relationship between Orendel and Bride is one of equals and is not based on traditional gender roles; there are no comments about their love or even attraction towards each other, and Bride acts in a male way, joining battle herself.[56] Earlier in the text she also attacks a servant whom she has ordered to fetch her father's (David's) sword, but brings her a fake, thus proving the 'special' nature of the real sword (the fake sword shatters against the stone wall) and her own strength (ll. 1622–42).

Bride's 'masculine' strength — and indeed the asexual way in which she is treated by Orendel — is not incompatible with the 'type' of the female saint, who often has to show such strength in order to protect her chastity. The threat to Bride's chastity by the heathen King Minold, who wants to marry her, is also reminiscent of many female saints' lives, as is her torture after refusing him, which emphasizes her naked body and physical pain:

> Er leit die maget here
> (Nacket) in einen [tieffen] kerckere,
> Do schlugent sy die gute,
> Das jr das rote blute
> (Vber den leib zu tal flosz
> Vnd von ir auff die erden gosz
> Vnd) uber jren lip zu tal ran. (ll. 3281–87)

Bride's character may be constructed from a number of types (courtly lady, warrior queen, female saint), but these types are not incompatible with one another. Equally, Orendel's own story and actions away from the grey robe are not incompatible with the story of the robe itself, despite the often unclear way in which these stories are merged.

This is partly because Orendel retains the name *grower rock* even after he has admitted his true identity and even after the robe has been translated to Trier, the result of which is that the robe is never entirely forgotten.[57] Yet it is notable that the formula with which other characters address him admits that the name *grower rock* is insufficient and even not actually a name: *Ob ich uch, her, erkante, | Wie gern ich uch nantte!*. Nonetheless, *grower rock* is the name by which Orendel becomes known when he arrives in Jerusalem, so is the name with which he establishes himself not only as bearer of the robe, but also as the defender of Jerusalem and Trier in his own right. In this sense, the name *grower rock*, which has an indexical function as described above, is also established as an independent name for the hero. That this occurs is naturally not a completely separate phenomenon from that of making the robe as relic active and publicly known; Orendel could not become the hero Grey Robe without the indexical function of the robe, but the name Grey Robe becomes — particularly later in the text and after the deposition of the robe in Trier — a name for the hero, separate from that of the robe. It is under this name that the former Orendel establishes his heroic prowess, becomes King of Jerusalem, and dies.

It is unclear whether Orendel achieves what he does solely because of the robe, for although it is impenetrable, there is nothing to suggest that it endows its wearer with extraordinary strength or other miraculous powers. The relationship between robe and wearer does not follow the Proppian sequence of protagonist and adjutant, according to which the adjutant is a necessary piece of equipment for the success of the protagonist (we could perhaps think of the relationship between Oswald and his raven in this manner).[58] Orendel is never dependent on the robe for his success. Yet the fact that the robe chooses him as its wearer with a miraculous sign (and that it rejects other wearers) demonstrates that he is already in some way special and chosen by God. Equally, it is only under the name *grower rock* that Orendel can become King of Jerusalem and defender of the Holy Grave, because this name inevitably points to the relic and all it signifies, even if the relic itself is by this point not visible.

Conclusion: The Reception of *Grauer Rock*

After the 'rediscovery' of the *tunica inconsutilis* by Maximilian I in Trier cathedral in 1512, *Grauer Rock* was, as mentioned above, printed in verse by Hans Froschauer and in a prose version by Hans Othmar, both Augsburg printers. Both, particularly the verse print, are little changed from the manuscript text, but each mentions the discovery of the robe by Maximilian in its title and the prose redaction contains an epilogue with further details, pointing to the fact that the text was printed for a specific reason: to celebrate or popularize the discovery and presence of the robe.[59] The prints were made in Augsburg partly because there was no printing-house in Trier at the time, but also because of the imperative to spread the news of the relic and the newfound potential of Trier as a pilgrimage destination as widely as possible.[60] Augsburg was also an important cultural and political centre for Maximilian; *Weiß Kunig* and *Ehrenpforte*, two of Maximilian's autobiographies, both of which mention the discovery of the seamless robe, would be printed in Augsburg by Hans Schönsperger the elder.[61]

The sheer number of writings about the relic and its discovery printed between 1512 and 1517 — no fewer than forty — demonstrates the attempt made to publicize both Trier and Maximilian's divinely inspired achievement.[62] It was important for Trier to establish itself as a rival pilgrimage site to nearby Aachen and Cologne; furthermore, the relic gave Maximilian the opportunity to style himself in the tradition of a saintly ruler, as seen particularly in the 'Lied' about its discovery, printed in 1512.[63] Therefore it is unsurprising that *Grauer Rock* was printed, even if it did not correspond to the conventional *translatio* of the robe through St Helena. The demand for publicizing the relic was probably greater than any need for consistency.[64]

It is perhaps also unsurprising that *Grauer Rock* was not successful. There are very few extant copies of either print and the text was never printed again, despite regular exhibitions of the relic; moreover, it was considered by some contemporaries to be neither accurate nor of any value. The doctor Johannes Adelphus Muling wrote negatively about the text in a report of the discovery of the robe printed in 1513:

> Noch ist ein ander gedicht mit Rymen harfür kommen von künig Orendel, wie er den Rock hab funden zuo Jherusalem: mit vyl fabeln und dantmeren, ynziehend etliche personen der künig und künigin, so nie uff erde gewesen seind, noch zuo Jherusalem regieret, als er sagt, und in keiner hystorien funden werden.[65]

In the German version of his *Medulla Gestorum Treverensium*, written in 1514, the future Trier suffragan bishop Johann Enen also complains about the unserious style of the text:

> Es sind auch diss vergangen iare vyle und mancherley brieff unnd clein tractatel getrückt, welcher eins teyls neben der warheit hin geschlichen sind [...] in besonderheit ein tractatel oder büchelin von einem könig genannt Orendel welches doch gar falsch erdicht und (alls ich glaub) umb eigents nutz wille angefangen sey So es gar in keinen berümbten angenommenden historiographen schrifften fonden wiirt.[66]

Furthermore, a comment, written in a humanist hand, at the end the Munich copy of the prose print of *Grauer Rock* reads: 'fictitium est non verum'.[67]

It seems, therefore, that despite its dissemination soon after the rediscovery of the seamless robe, *Grauer Rock* was not suitable to describe a relic that was publicly accessible and officially authenticated, for after the presence of the robe had been established and its *translatio* therefore made factually true, the story could be nothing but a 'fictitium'.

The reception of *Grauer Rock* tells us little about why — or indeed when — it was written, a problem that is impossible to solve. It is clear, though, that the text is interested in making the robe meaningful, which it achieves through a man, who makes the nature and properties of the robe obvious in a relationship of indexicality, and enables the continuation of project of salvation it symbolizes. The man, Orendel, has his own narrative, however, wooing Bride, Queen of Jerusalem and defending the Holy Grave — a narrative that is never entirely unconnected to the robe itself. Orendel maintains the name of the robe, even when it is not visibly present, and in this sense, a reminder of the robe and what it symbolizes permeates the whole text and creates the hero *grower roc*, King of Jerusalem and defender of the Holy Grave.

Notes to Chapter 4

1. The robe is described in John 19:23-24:

    milites ergo cum crucifixissent eum acceperunt vestimenta eius et fecerunt quattuor partes unicuique militi partem et tunicam erat autem tunica inconsutilis desuper contexta per totum / dixerunt ergo ad invicem non scindamus eam sed sortiamur de illa cuius sit ut scriptura impleatur dicens partiti sunt vestimenta mea sibi et in vestem meam miserunt sortem et milites quidem haec fecerunt.

    [Then the soldiers, when they had crucified Jesus, took his garments, and made four parts, to every soldier a part; and also his coat: now the coat was without seam, woven from the top throughout. / They said therefore among themselves, Let us not rend it, but cast lots for it, whose it shall be: that the scripture might be fulfilled, which saith, They parted my raiment among them, and for my vesture they did cast lots. These things therefore the soldiers did.]

    The scripture referred to here is Ps. 22:19.
2. Ekkart Sauser, 'Die Tunika Christi in der Vätertheologie', in *Der Heilige Rock zu Trier: Studien zur Geschichte und Verehrung der Tunika Christi*, ed. by Erich Aretz and others (Trier: Paulinus, 1996). pp. 39–66. Of central importance are Cyprian, *de unitate ecclesiae*, and Augustine, *Tractatus in evangelium Johannis*, 118, who stressed the inseparability of the robe as a warning against schism and heresy. Sauser, pp. 52–56, also stresses the variety of interpretations of the seamless robe; christological theology considered it to be representative of Christ's humanity (the robe was made of linen, which came from the earth (Origen)) or of his godliness (the robe was woven from top down (John Chrysostom)), or indeed of the unity of Christ's humanity and divinity. Others viewed the robe as a simple item of clothing, perhaps symbolic of Christ's simplicity, or stressed the importance of fulfilling the prophecy of Ps 22:19.
3. *Gregorii Tvronensis opera*, I (MGH Scriptores rerum Merovingicarum, I) (Hannover: Hahn, 1951), pp 492–93; *Chronicarum quae dicuntur Fredegarii scholastici*, Liber IV.11, ed. by Bruno Krusch (MGH Scriptores rerum Merovingicarum, II, 126–27) (Hannover: Hahn, 1888). On these two sources, see Bernhard Schmitt, '"Heilige Röcke" anderswo: Die außerhalb der Trierer Domkirche vorkommenden sogenannten "Tuniken" Christi', in *Der Heilige Rock zu Trier*, pp. 549–605 (pp. 551–56).
4. Michael Embach, 'Im Spannungsfeld von profaner "Spielmannsepik" und christlicher Legendarik: der Heilige Rock im mittelalterlichen Orendel-Gedicht', in *Der Heilige Rock zu Trier*, pp. 763–97 (p. 768, esp. fn. 5).

5. *Acta Sanctorum* 15 Aug III, Dies 18, ch. 43.
6. H. V. Sauerland, *Trierer Geschichtsquellen des XI. Jahrhunderts* (Trier: Paulinus, 1889), esp. pp. 63–66.
7. Bernward Plate, 'Orendel — König von Jerusalem: Kreuzfahrerbewußtsein (Epos d. 12. Jhs.) und Leidenstheologie (Prosa von 1512)', *Euphorion*, 82 (1988), 168–210 (p. 170).
8. Embach, 'Im Spannungsfeld', p. 770.
9. *Die Kaiserchronik eines Regenburger Geistlichen*, ll. 10385–10400:

> si [Helena] vuor ze Jerusalêm in daz lant,
> daz hailige crûce si dâ vant.
> si sant ouch zu êren
> Trieren der urmâren:
> den rok den got selbe ze der marter truoch,
> und den nagel den man durch sîne baide vuoze sluoch,
> und daz houbet sancti Andrei,
> sancti Petri zant
> und ain cheten dâ mit er dolte diu bant,
> und sancti Mathie gebaine,
> und dar zuo golt und gestaine
> und ander vil manige hêrscaft
> frumte si ze Trieren in die stat.
> daz tet diu chunigîn umbe daz,
> wande si von Triere geborn was.

For the Hillinbrief, see *Kaiser Friedrich I. an Erzbischof Hillin von Trier*, in Norbert Höing, 'Die *Trierer Stilübungen*: Ein Denkmal der Frühzeit Kaiser Friedrich Barbarossas', *Archiv für Diplomatik*, 1 (1955), 257–329 (p. 321).

10. Embach, 'Im Spannungsfeld', p. 770.
11. *Gesta Treverorum continuata*, Continuata quarta, Additamentum alius auctoris (MGH Scriptores, XXIV, 396).
12. These other claims are documented thoroughly by Schmitt, '"Heilige Röcke" anderswo'.
13. Christian Kiening, 'Hybriden des Heils: Reliquie und Text des *Grauen Rocks* um 1512', in *Literarische und religiöse Kommunikation in Mittelalter und Früher Neuzeit*, ed. by Peter Strohschneider (Berlin: de Gruyter, 2009), pp. 371–410 (p. 385).
14. Michael Embach, 'Die Trierer Heiltumsschriften des 16. Jahrhunderts zwischen Wallfahrtspropaganda und Maximiliansapotheose', in *Wallfahrt und Kommunikation: Kommunikation über Wallfahrt*, ed. by Bernhard Schneider (Mainz: Gesellschaft für mittelrheinische Kirchengeschichte, 2004), pp. 229–44 (p. 232). The veracity of the seamless robe has also been doubted more recently; a widespread discussion was initiated at its exhibition in 1844 thanks in particular to Gildermeister and von Sybel, the major doubters. See Johann Gildermeister and Heinrich von Sybel, *Der Heilige Rock zu Trier und die zwanzig andern Heiligen ungenähten Röcke* (Düsseldorf: Buddeus, 1844) and Hartmut Kühne, *Ostensio reliquiarum: Untersuchungen über Entstehung, Ausbreitung, Gestalt und Funktion der Heiltumsweisungen im römisch-deutschen Regnum* (Berlin: de Gruyter, 2000), pp. 12–13.
15. The title of the text is disputed, though it is becoming increasingly common to refer to it as *Grauer Rock*. Uwe Meves, *Studien zu König Rother, Herzog Ernst und Grauer Rock (Orendel)*, pp. 227–43, has argued very strongly for this title, given the primary importance of the seamless robe. I have chosen to follow the trend and refer to it as *Grauer Rock*, not in order to imply that the robe is the text's main protagonist, but — as I shall discuss below — because this is also the name adopted by Orendel for much of the work.

16. Steinger, an editor of the text, states for example that it is 'eine Dichtung ohne Grundsatz'. *Orendel*, ed. by Hans Steinger (Halle: Niemeyer, 1935), p. xxvii.
17. The first scholar to direct attention away from the heroic, 'literary' nature of the text and towards its more cultural-historical role, stressing the primary importance of the seamless robe of Christ, was Ernest Tonnelat, 'Le roi Orendel et la tunique sans conture du Christ', in *Mélanges offerts à M. Charles Andler par ses amis et ses élèves* (1924), pp. 351–70, repr. as 'König Orendel und Christi nahtloses Gewand' (1924), trans. by Dorothea Kleinmann, in *Spielmannsepik*, ed. by Schröder, pp. 145–67. See also Uwe Meves, 'Das Gedicht vom "Grauen Rock" (Orendel) und die Trierer Reliquientradition', *Kurtrierisches Jahrbuch*, 15 (1975), 5–19; Embach, 'Im Spannungsfeld'; Embach, 'Die Trierer Heiltumsschriften'; and most recently Kiening, 'Hybriden des Heils'.
18. It is also reproduced very closely in the edition by von der Hagen: *Der ungenähte Rock Christi: Wie König Orendel von Trier ihn erwirbt, darin Frau Breiden und das heilige Grab gewinnt, und ihn nach Trier bringt. Altdeutsches Gedicht, aus der einzigen Handschrift, mit Vergleichung des alten Drucks*, ed. by Friedrich von der Hagen (Berlin: Schultze, 1844). All quotations will come from von der Hagen's text; there is no reliable modern edition.
19. There is one extant copy of the verse print redaction of *Grauer Rock* (Munich, BSB, 4° P.o.germ. 161n) and three copies of the prose print redaction (Munich, BSB, 4° P.o.germ. 161m; Berlin, Staatsbibliothek, Yu 1731; London, British Library, C.175.d.29). Both Munich prints are reproduced in a facsimile edition: *Orendel (Der Graue Rock): Faksimileausgabe der Vers- und der Prosafassung nach den Drucken von 1512*, ed. by Ludwig Denecke (Stuttgart: Metzler, 1972). See also Hans-Joachim Koppitz, *Studien zur Tradierung der weltlichen mittelhochdeutschen Epik im 15. und beginnenden 16. Jahrhundert* (Munich: Fink, 1980), pp. 202–08.
20. Arguments for dating *Grauer Rock* to the last decade of the twelfth century are found in almost all literary histories and critical works on the text: for these see the introduction of this study.
21. Corinna Biesterfeldt, *Moniage — Der Rückzug aus der Welt als Erzählschluß: Untersuchungen zu 'Kaiserchronik', 'König Rother', 'Orendel', 'Barlaam und Josephat', 'Prosa-Lancelot'* (Stuttgart: Hirzel, 2004), p. 64.
22. de Boor, pp. 256–57. See also Kiening, 'Hybriden des Heils', p. 389, who argues that the notion of a twelfth-century *Orendel* is nothing more than a 'germanistische[s] Fantasma'. Peter K. Stein, 'Orendel 1512: Probleme und Möglichkeiten der Anwendung der *theory of oral-formulaic poetry* bei der literaturhistorischen Interpretation eines mittelhochdeutschen Textes', in *Hohenemser Studien zum Nibelungenlied*, ed. by Achim Masser (Dornbirn: Voralberger Verlagsanstalt, 1981), pp. 322/148–348/174, argues that the 'Motivkomplexe' used in the text — the bridal quest, crusading, adventurous journey, Arthurian crisis of the self — are always 'frustrated' and never completed as might be expected, which he suggests is characteristic of the age of written heroic epic, the thirteenth century. He asserts that *Grauer Rock* was therefore written in this period, although he thinks that the origins of the story probably date to 1196.
23. Heidelberg Universitätsbibliothek cpg 314 f. 4r. On Lauber's register, see Denecke, p. 3.
24. *Heldenbuch: Altdeutsche Heldenlieder aus dem Sagenkreise Dietrichs von Bern und der Nibelungen*, I, ed. by Friedrich von der Hagen (Leipzig: Schultze 1855), p. cxi.
25. It is curious that all pre-1512 evidence comes from south-west Germany; the manuscript of the text was owned by a Strassburg library, the *Heldenbuch* is also from Strassburg, and Lauber worked in Hagenau in the Alsace. This certainly indicates that the pre-1512 reception of *Grauer Rock* was not restricted to Trier, although it is unclear whether the presence of the work in south-west Germany would have been an attempt to publicize the robe or simply the chance dissemination of an entertaining story. Scholarship is

unanimous about the fact that the text originated in or near Trier, however, thanks to its good geographical knowledge of the Mosel region and traces of the Mosel Franconian dialect, as well as the emphasis on Trier itself, which is even described as the location for the Last Judgement (ll. 3187-90).
26. Tonnelat, p. 164.
27. See in particular Klaus Gantert, 'Durch got und des heiligen grabes eren und ouch durch die schonen juncfrowen: Reliquientranslation und Brautwerbungshandlung im *Orendel*', *Kurtrierisches Jahrbuch*, 39 (1999), 123-44 (p. 135): 'Der Epiker bemüht sich darum, den inhaltlich sakral bestimmten Stoff — die Überführung der Reliquie vom Heiligen Land nach Trier — einem laikalen Publikum unter Zuhilfenahme weltlicher Erzählstrukturen nahezubringen. Das traditionelle Erzählschema fungiert hierbei als Vehikel, mit dessen Hilfe versucht wird, geistliche Erzählinhalte rezipientengerecht zu realisieren.' Denecke, pp. 12-13 views *Grauer Rock* as both entertaining and didactic, an example of 'Männerliteratur' perhaps composed for an order of knights, possibly in conjunction with the Litauerreisen of the fourteenth century, given the emphasis on chastity and the animosity towards the Knights Templar. See also Tonnelat, p. 167.
28. See Alfred Ebenbauer, 'Orendel — Anspruch und Verwirklichung', in *Strukturen und Interpretationen: Studien zur deutschen Philologie gewidmet Blanka Horacek zum 60. Geburtstag*, ed. by Alfred Ebenbauer and others (Vienna: Braumüller, 1974), pp. 25-63 (p. 44): '[I]ch glaube nicht, daß es inhaltliche Gründe waren, die dem Dichter die Orendel-Figur für seine Absichten geeignet erscheinen ließen, sondern vermute vielmehr, daß Orendel in einer engen Beziehung zu Trier gestanden ist, und daß es eine Tradition gegeben hat, in der Orendel als besonderer Held dieser Stadt galt. Der Dichter hätte dann nicht eine beliebig erfundene Person oder irgendeinen alten Helden der aus dem gepriesenen Trier stammenden Helena vorgezogen, sondern einen in seiner Stadt bekannten, — und geglaubten — Helden ihrer Frühzeit. Mit einer solchen Darlegung konnte er dann freilich auf Zustimmung beim Publikum rechnen und zwar sowohl im Hinblick auf dessen literarische Erwartungen als auch angesichts seines eigenen Anspruchs, historisch glaubwürdig zu sein und mit den reliquiengeschichtlichen Interessen der Trierer Kirche im Einklang zu stehen.'
29. See also de Boor, p. 257.
30. Wolfgang Jungandreas, 'Orendel und der Heilige Rock', *Kurtrierisches Jahrbuch*, 8 (1968), 84-95 (p. 84).
31. Meves, 'Das Gedicht vom "Grauen Rock"' and *Studien*, pp. 227-43.
32. Kiening, 'Hybriden des Heils', p. 390.
33. Ibid., p. 380. On the complexities of the so-called 'Schaufrömmigkeit' of the fifteenth century, see Caroline Walker Bynum, 'Seeing and Seeing Beyond: The Mass of St. Gregory in the Fifteenth Century', in *The Mind's Eye: Art and Theology in the Middle Ages*, ed. by Jeffrey Hamburger and Anne-Marie Bouché (Princeton: Princeton University Press, 2005), pp. 208-40, who argues that there was a concurrent tradition of intense scepticism regarding images and visible signs of devotion. The interest in the immutability and unseeability of God meant that there was interest in seeing 'beyond' the image or relic to a presence that was more than just visual.
34. On the *translatio* as literary genre, see Patrick Geary, *Furta Sacra: Thefts of Relics in the Central Middle Ages*, 2nd edn (Princeton: Princeton University Press, 1990), pp. 9-15.
35. Tonnelat, pp. 164-65. Gantert, 'Durch got und des heiligen grabes eren', p. 144, who argues that *Grauer Rock* offered a story of the seamless robe and Trier that differed deliberately from church versions — a story more suited for a lay public — suggests that Helena's involvement in the production of the robe is a failed attempt at integration: '[D]as vergebliche Bemühen des Epikers, auch die traditionelle Fassung

des Translationsberichtes in seine Neukonzeption zu integrieren, dokumentiert der Versuch, die Kaisermutter Helena in vollkommen anachronistischer Weise als die Weberin des Grauen Rockes in das mittelhochdeutsche Epos einzufügen'.
36. Kiening, 'Hybriden des Heils', p. 398.
37. Geary, p. 5. See also Kiening, 'Hybriden des Heils', pp. 376-77.
38. Philippe Cordez, 'Wallfahrt und Medienwettbewerb: Serialität und Formenwandel der Heiltumsverzeichnisse mit Reliquienbildern im Heiligen Römischen Reich (1460-1529)', in *'Ich armer sundiger mensch': Heiligen- und Reliquienkult am Übergang zum konfessionellen Zeitalter*, ed. by Andreas Tacke (Göttingen: Wallstein, 2006), pp. 37-73 (p. 37).
39. Cordez, pp. 37-39.
40. Kühne, p. 6, defines the *ostensio* as follows: 'Heiltumsweisungen waren Veranstaltungen, zu denen sich ein zahlreiches, nach Stand und Herkunft unterschiedliches Publikum, Geistliche und Weltliche, städtische Gruppen, die Landbevölkerung der Umgegend, aber auch von weiter her kommende 'Wallfahrer' und unter diesen auch weltliche und geistliche 'Herren', vom Kaiser bis zum Grafen, vom Erzbischof bis zum Prälaten, versammelte, um die Heiltümer einer Kirche zu sehen, die in einem liturgisch geregelten Prozedere und einer von der öffentlichen Gewalt überwachten Weise auf einem öffentlichen Platz gezeigt und ausgerufen wurden.' Cordez, pp. 64-65, discusses a book containing depictions of relics from Maastricht, Aachen, Kornelimünster, Düren, Cologne, and Trier in this context, which ends with a picture of the Immaculate Conception with a prayer written down below it; by saying the prayer, the reader could gain an indulgence. See also Jeffrey Hamburger, 'Vision and the Veronica', in Hamburger, *The Visual and the Visionary: Art and Female Spirituality in Late Medieval Germany* (New York: Zone Books, 1998), pp. 317-82, who discusses the phenomenon of images of the Veronica in the later Middle Ages, especially those inserted into the margins of manuscripts as 'Kußbilder', objects for kissing and veneration, which could satisfy to some degree the desire to come face to face with Christ and act as a kind of spiritual pilgrimage.
41. This 'Pilgerzeichen' is reproduced in H. J. E. van Beuningen, A. M. Koldeweij, and D. Kicken, *Heilig en Profaan 2. 1200 laatmiddeleeuwse insignes uit openbare en particuliere collecties* (Cothen: Stichting Middeleeuwse Religieuze en Profane Insignes, 2001), p. 365.
42. On the phenomenon of blood veneration in the later Middle Ages, see Caroline Walker Bynum, *Wonderful Blood: Theology and Practice in Late Medieval Northern Germany and Beyond* (Philadelphia: University of Pennsylvania Press, 2007). Blood — in particular the blood of Christ — usually refers to the Eucharist (although it does not have to) and the problem of the presence of Christ in the host, much discussed by theologians of the time, had repercussions on blood relics (Bynum focuses in particular on the Wilsnack blood cult). In *Grauer Rock* it is not the blood itself that is important, but rather the fact that it allows the robe to be identified and proves that it belonged to Christ. The problem of the blood of Christ — whether it could be left behind at all, whether it is entative or signative (i.e. Christ's real blood or just a red colour to trigger memory) — is not addressed.
43. The play between presence and absence is a general phenomenon of relics: they are a part of the saint (or Christ) and therefore point unavoidably to sacral presence, but also point to the absence of the saint and the difference of the relic to him. See Geary, p. 22: 'They [relics] were part of the sacred, the numinous; but incarnated in this world, as had been Christ, without losing their place in the other'.
44. Tomas Tomasek, 'Über den Einfluß des Apolloniusromans auf die volkssprachliche Erzählliteratur des 12. und 13. Jahrhunderts', in *Mediävistische Komparatistik: Fest-*

schrift für Franz Josef Worstbrock zum 60. Geburtstag, ed. by Wolfgang Harms and Jan-Dirk Müller (Stuttgart and Leipzig: Hirzel, 1997), pp. 221-39 (p. 227).

45. The influence of the Apollonius romance on *Grauer Rock* has been noted for some time: see Elard Hugo Meyer, 'Quellenstudien zur mittelhochdeutschen Spielmannsdichtung', *ZfdA*, 37 (1893), 321-56 and Samuel Singer, *Apollonius von Tyrus: Untersuchungen über das Fortleben des Antiken Romans in spätern Zeiten* (Halle: Niemeyer, 1895), pp. 3-15. Both Meyer and Singer also note the similarities between *Grauer Rock* and the Old French *Jourdain de Blaye (Blavies)*. More recently, see Ebenbauer, 'Orendel — Anspruch und Verwirklichung', p. 57.
46. Elizabeth Archibald, *Apollonius of Tyre: Medieval and Renaissance Themes and Variations. Including the Text of the Historia Apollonii Regis Tyri with an English translation* (Cambridge: Brewer, 1991), pp. 45-51; 194-95; 201-02. It is unfortunate that Archibald, p. 55, makes a fundamental error in her description of the plot of *Grauer Rock* in relation to the Apollonius material; contrary to what she suggests, Bride is not taken for dead and thrown into the sea in a chest.
47. Kraß, pp. 39-45.
48. Galatians 3:26-29:

    pomnes enim filii Dei estis per fidem in Christo Iesu / quicumque enim in Christo baptizati estis Christum induistis / non est Iudaeus neque Graecus non est servus neque liber non est masculus neque femina omnes enim vos unum estis in Christo Iesu / si autem vos Christi ergo Abrahae semen estis secundum promissionem heredes.

    [For ye are the children of God by faith in Christ Jesus. / For as many of you as have been baptized into Christ have put on Christ. / There is neither Jew nor Greek, there is neither bond nor free, there is neither male nor female: for ye are all one in Christ Jesus. / And if ye be Christ's, then are ye Abraham's seed, and heirs according to the promise.]

49. Kraß, pp. 193-202. He discusses becoming a monk as a kind of 'devestiture as investiture'; the change of clothing in *Orendel* is also mentioned (pp. 210-15), but mainly with respect to the notion of religious justification of kingship. Gabriele Raudszus, *Die Zeichensprache der Kleidung: Untersuchungen zur Symbolik des Gewandes in der deutschen Epik des Mittelalters* (Hildesheim: Olms, 1985), p. 48, also draws a connection between the Grey Robe and the monk's habit. She argues that the habit was often thought of as a kind of miraculous, protective object and was cared for and even venerated as a kind of contact reliquary. It was also of great importance for monks to die and be buried in their habits (p. 50) — note that Orendel always expresses the wish before battle to die in the Grey Robe (for example ll. 1603-04; ll. 1987-88).
50. This understanding of indexicality is from the classic definition by Charles Sanders Peirce, in Winfried Nöth, *Handbook of Semiotics* (Bloomington and Indianapolis: University of Indiana Press, 1990), pp. 39-47.
51. Jeffrey Hamburger, 'Seeing and Believing: The Suspicion of Sight and the Authentication of Vision in Late Medieval Art', in *Imagination und Wirklichkeit: Zum Verhältnis von mentalen und realen Bildern in der Kunst der frühen Neuzeit*, ed. by Klaus Krüger and Alessandro Nova (Mainz: von Zabern, 2000), pp. 47-69 (p. 55).
52. For example the tablet in *Gregorius*, which tells of his true provenance and the letter in *Wolfdietrich* A, which asserts that he is not illegitimate.
53. I therefore find it difficult to agree with those who argue that Orendel's kingship (in the 'real' worldly sense) is the guiding principle of the text. Plate, for instance, argues that the manuscript text of *Grauer Rock*, originally composed in 1196, was directed primarily towards the laity, stressing the importance of kingship in general and

Orendel's David-style kingship in a time in which there were tensions between the archbishopric and the laity in Trier. See also Dobozy, *Full Circle*, pp. 32–51.

54. The similarity between the travails of the saint and the hero is discussed by Haubrichs, 'Labor sanctorum', who suggests that Lives of early Christian saints and martyrs may have been influenced by archaic heroic ideals and that Saints' Lives then influenced later heroic epics.

55. Ebenbauer, 'Orendel — Anspruch und Verwirklichung', p. 61, suggests that the poet of *Grauer Rock* did not view chastity as a particular problem: 'Das *magedum* wird nicht als Problem diskutiert, sondern ist als Voraussetzung für ein heiligenmäßiges Leben ein Faktum und in dem Maße als der Dichter seine Helden in ihrer Vorbildhaftigkeit gestaltete, mußte er diesem Faktum Rechnung tragen'.

56. Vollmann-Profe, p. 223, describes the relationship between Orendel and Bride as follows: 'Minne weder als Erfahrung einer zauberisch-bannenden Macht noch als Rechtsakt, sondern als Freundschaft auf der Basis gemeinsamer Überzeugung'. See also Maria Müller, *Jungfräulichkeit in Versepen des 12. und 13. Jahrhunderts* (Munich: Fink, 1995), pp. 153–55.

57. Stein, 'Orendel 1512', p. 326, ignores the question of naming in his discussion of Orendel's 'identity'. According to his argument, in the first part of the text Orendel attains success in the robe, then must start again without this heavenly guarantee after the deposition: 'Orendel hat im Grauen Rock eine neue Existenz, eine völlig von Gott beherrschte, seine Person zudeckende Identität gefunden. Diese muß er nun ablegen und Helden- wie Kreuzfahrt wieder als 'Orendel' durchführen, als ein Orendel aber, der nun um ein Gewichtiges angereichert ist.'

58. Vladimir Propp, *Morphology of the Folktale*, trans. by Laurence Scott, (Austin: University of Texas Press, 1968), pp. 43–50.

59. The title pages and epilogue are reprinted in Denecke's facsimile; see Denecke, pp. D1; P1; P73–75.

60. Embach, 'Die Trierer Heiltumsschriften', pp. 234–35, suggests that the only publications about the relic destined for reception in Trier itself were those printed in Metz.

61. Embach, 'Im Spannungsfeld', pp. 779–80.

62. Embach, 'Die Trierer Heiltumsschriften', pp. 232–33. Twenty-seven of these publications were in German, and the majority of these anonymous and in prose.

63. 'Ein Lied von der Auffindung des h. Rockes', in Gerhard Hennen, 'Eine bibliographische Zusammenstellung der Trierer Heiligtumsbücher, deren Drucklegung durch die Ausstellung des h. Rockes im Jahre 1512 veranlasst wurde', *Centralblatt für Bibliothekswesen*, 4 (1887), 481–550 (pp. 510–14). See also Embach, 'Die Trierer Heiltumsschriften', pp. 236–37.

64. In this case I disagree with Embach, 'Im Spannungsfeld', pp. 779–80, who suggests that Maximilian may have caused *Grauer Rock* to be printed himself. In 'Die Trierer Heiltumsschriften', pp. 243–44, he qualifies this by arguing that *Grauer Rock* points thematically to kingship as understood by Maximilian and the Habsburgs: a mixture of heroic and religious ideals.

65. 'Des Arztes Johannes Adelphus Bericht über die Auffindung des hl. Rockes', welchen Martin Flach zu Strassburg 1513 druckte', in Hennen, 'Eine bibliographische Zusammenstellung', p. 509.

66. 'Die deutsche Ausgabe der Medulla Gestorum vom Jahre 1514, gedruckt zu Metz von Caspar Hochfeder im Auftrage des Trierischen Verlagsbuchhändlers Mathias Hahn', in Hennen, 'Eine bibliographische Zusammenstellung', p. 542. Koppitz, p. 208, discusses how Enen criticized the exploitation of the discovery of the robe by printers desirous of profit.

67. 'It is a fiction and not true.' See Denecke, p. 5.

CONCLUSION

In the introduction to this study, an examination of some permissive theories of genre demonstrated that they commonly have at their core the idea of some kind of constant that is historically recognizable and definable. Both Jauss and Grubmüller argue that a medieval text can participate in more than one genre, and that genres change through time. Jauss suggests, however, that medieval genres have a synchronically recognizable 'dominant', whereas Grubmüller argues that genres can only be recognized or described historically in the context of a process of change, thus preferring to refer to generically related groups of texts as 'Werkreihen'. It is possible for a text to belong to more than one 'Werkreihe', but a genre is only present and describable when the 'Werkreihe' is clear and can be discerned in a process of historical change. The aim of this study was to investigate the group of texts known variously as *Spielmannsepik* or *Brautwerbungsepik* and to attempt to understand whether they can be thought of as a genre — or, more specifically, whether the so-called bridal-quest schema can be thought of as a dominant or formative of a 'Werkreihe'.

The common understanding of the bridal-quest schema is of a set of conventions, known and expected by the audience, whose understanding of the text in question is shaped exclusively by the way it 'distorts', inverts, or negates these conventions. The conventions of the bridal-quest schema are usually that a king (or other high-born person) wants a bride, and, after a council scene, must travel across the sea to find her. There must be some sort of obstacle to the marriage, and after this is resolved, the hero and the bride return home. The process may then be repeated. This schema is sometimes described as the 'dangerous' bridal quest to distinguish it from the 'simple' or unproblematic bridal quest, in which the marriage is achieved swiftly without overcoming any obstacles.

The bridal-quest schema is usually considered to have originally been a narrative structure for oral storytelling, which became more complex when written down; the move from oral to written story-model has been discussed at length by Haug with respect to *König Rother*, *Salman und Morolf*, and the *Münchner Oswald*, and the move from orality to literacy has become particularly important in much criticism on the former text. It seems likely that some kind of bridal-quest structure did exist as an oral narrative structure, but problems occur in the attempt to interpret a written text through the way it has changed the structure in the move away from orality; assumptions are inevitably made about the nature of the oral form and the written text is consequently read backwards with respect to its relationship with a hypothetical before. It is also difficult to treat the so-called *Brautwerbungsepen* as a group of texts positioned on the cusp of orality and literacy, as early examples of written literature, as was often the case in descriptions of *Spielmannsepik*, given that the early dating of *Salman und Morolf*, the *Münchner Oswald* and *Grauer Rock* is increasingly in doubt. The earliest manuscripts of these three texts are from the fifteenth century and, although this in itself is insufficient to prove a late dating, there is little evidence to suggest the texts were composed or written down in the twelfth century. Even if they were, it is impossible to know how they may have changed over time.

The problem of dating does not dismiss the possibility of a generic relationship, however, given that genres exist and develop through time; the question is rather whether the bridal quest is constitutive of genre. The notion of the bridal-quest schema has been shown to be problematic on several counts. If meaning is created in individual texts through the way in which they distort or deviate from the schema, then it is necessary that the audience has a clear knowledge of the schema, through either other written texts or the oral tradition. Yet there is no evidence that the so-called bridal-quest epics were ever transmitted together and there is no idealized, prototypical realization of the bridal-quest schema. Equally, it is doubtful whether the structure of the bridal quest ever constitutes the entire system of meaning of a specific text.

There is no doubt that there is such a thing as a bridal-quest motif that appears in many medieval texts, the basic idea being that a king (or other high-born person) wants a wife, calls a council and sets out (or sends someone out) to woo her. Yet as it appears in so many different forms in different texts, it is impossible to pin down more specifically. The question to ask, therefore, is whether this more loosely defined bridal-quest motif is a genre-forming constant. Questing for a bride can constitute the whole of a narrative — as in *König Rother* — but it can equally lead to the exploration and investigation of a number of other matters (perhaps *König Rother* is more about being a king than about wooing a bride). In *Salman und Morolf*, the narrative is also driven by the act of wooing (and retrieving) a woman, but by various different men; the bride is ambiguous and much of the narrative taken up by the unusual actions and behaviour of Morolf. The *Münchner Oswald* manages to combine the bridal-quest motif with the Life of a saint, and *Grauer Rock* uses the motif as its starting point, but soon loses sight of it in a narrative that seems to be as much about relic as man.

The implicit assumption of much previous criticism is that the bridal-quest motif is a set of recognizable conventions that determine the understanding of the text in question through variation or negation. I hope to have shown that this assumption is both historically unfounded and theoretically questionable, and that, more importantly, it promotes an unnecessarily restrictive mode of reading the texts in question, obscuring many other interesting features and themes. A more productive starting point for the reading of these texts would be to take the bridal-quest motif as nothing more than a generator of narrative and possibility that can be used variously and flexibly.

In this sense, the bridal-quest motif need not be the dominant principle of the texts that contain it; these texts could equally (or perhaps even more so) belong to other 'Werkreihen' or narrative groupings of some kind, hence the emphasis in this study *away* from the bridal-quest motif. *Grauer Rock* and the *Münchner Oswald* have been interpreted here largely according to their specific contexts — the relic of the *tunica inconsutilis* at Trier and the development of the cult of St Oswald respectively. Although these texts inevitably resonate with other literary works, they can fruitfully be read as part of a wider cultural context and need not necessarily be thought of as part of an exclusively literary genre. *König Rother* and *Salman und Morolf* are rather harder to place, but *König Rother* shares similarities with other twelfth-century texts, not with respect to a closeness to orality or another such 'developmental' theory, but with respect to shared themes and interests. *Salman und Morolf* is something of an anomaly, but importantly an anomaly that makes sense in itself.

The four texts discussed here — in particular *Salman und Morolf*, the *Münchner Oswald*, and *Grauer Rock* — have suffered in literary history and scholarship in general from being, in a sense, 'lost texts' that do not fit into canonical genres or have a clear place in the progression of literary history, either chronologically and thematically. This is, to a large extent, because of the genre label of *Spielmannsepik*, which, as has been shown, arose from the distinction between 'Volkspoesie' and 'Kunstpoesie' and became itself canonical, if never clearly defined or uncontroversial. Even if *Spielmannsepik* as a term is increasingly neglected, its ghost remains and with it the notion that the texts it was created to describe belong together. The present investigation of the bridal-quest motif could have treated other texts (such as *Ortnit*, *Kudrun*, and *Dukus Horant*, or even the *Nibelungenlied* or *Tristan*), but it seemed particularly important to attempt to dispel the idea that the four texts dealt with here are somehow generically linked, as either *Brautwerbungsepik* or *Spielmannsepik*. In attempting to rid the critical standpoint on these texts from such classificatory dogmatism I hope to have opened the field to new possibilities: the potential the texts have for further investigation, in directions that are neither schematic nor determined by the presumptions of *Spielmannsepik*, is great and will, I hope, be pursued further.

BIBLIOGRAPHY

Editions and translations

Chronicarum quae dicuntur Fredegarii scholastici, Liber IV.11, ed. by Bruno Krusch (MGH Scriptores rerum Merovingicarum, II, 126–27) (Hannover: Hahn, 1888)
Dukus Horant, ed. by P. F. Ganz, F. Norman, and W. Schwarz (Tübingen: Niemeyer, 1964)
Gesta Treverorum continuata, Continuata quarta, Additamentum alius auctoris (MGH Scriptores, XXIV, 396) (Hannover: Hahn, 1879)
Gregorii Tvronensis opera, I (MGH Scriptores rerum Merovingicarum, I) (Hannover: Hahn, 1951)
Heldenbuch: Altdeutsche Heldenlieder aus dem Sagenkreise Dietrichs von Bern und der Nibelungen, I, ed. by Friedrich von der Hagen (Leipzig: Schultze 1855)
Herzog Ernst, ed. and trans. by Bernhard Sowinski, 2nd edn (Stuttgart: Reclam, 1970)
Die Hochzeit, in *Kleinere deutsche Gedichte des 11. und 12. Jahrhunderts*, II, ed. by Albert Waag and Werner Schröder (Tübingen: Niemeyer, 1972), pp. 132–70
Die Kaiserchronik eines Regenburger Geistlichen, ed. by Edward Schröder (MGH, Scriptorum qui vernacula lingua usi sunt, I) (Hannover: Hahn, 1892)
König Rother: Mittelhochdeutsche Text und neuhochdeutsche Übersetzung, ed. by Ingrid Bennewitz and trans. by Peter K. Stein (Stuttgart: Reclam, 2000)
Kudrun, ed. by Karl Stackmann (Tübingen: Niemeyer, 2000)
Das Nibelungenlied, ed. by Helmut Brackert, 27th edn (Frankfurt a. M.: Fischer, 2001)
Orendel, ed. by Hans Steinger (Halle: Niemeyer, 1935)
Orendel (Der Graue Rock): Faksimileausgabe der Vers- und der Prosafassung nach den Drucken von 1512, ed. by Ludwig Denecke (Stuttgart: Metzler, 1972)
Ortnit und die Wolfdietriche, ed. by Arthur Amelung and Oskar Jänicke, 2 vols (Berlin: Weidmann, 1871–73)
'Ösvalds saga', in *Reykjahólabók*, ed. and trans. by Marianne Kalinke, in Kalinke, *St. Oswald of Northumbria: Continental Metamorphoses. With an Edition and Translation of* Ösvalds saga *and* Van sunte Oswaldo deme konninghe (Tempe: Arizona Center for Medieval and Renaissance Studies, 2005), pp. 105–71
VIZKELETY, ANDRÁS, 'Der Budapester Oswald', *PBB* (Halle), 86 (1964), 107–88
Der Münchener Oswald: Text und Abhandlung, ed. by Georg Baesecke (Breslau: Marcus, 1907)
Der Münchner Oswald, ed. by Michael Curschmann (Tübingen: Niemeyer, 1974)
Der Wiener Oswald, ed. by Georg Baesecke (Heidelberg: Winter, 1912)
'Von sant Oswald', in *Der Heiligen Leben*, I: *der Sommerteil*, ed by Margit Brand and others (Tübingen: Niemeyer, 1996), pp. 358–68
CURSCHMANN, MICHAEL, '"Sant Oswald von Norwegen": ein Fragment eines Legendenepos', *ZfdA*, 102 (1973), 101–14

'Von sand Oswalden dem chunig', in *Das Märterbuch*, ed. by Erich Gierach (Berlin: Weidmann, 1928), pp. 292–96

'Van sunte Oswaldo deme konninghe', in *Dat Passionael*, ed. and trans. by Marianne Kalinke, in Kalinke, *St. Oswald of Northumbria: Continental Metamorphoses. With an Edition and Translation of* Ösvalds saga *and* Van sunte Oswaldo deme konninghe (Tempe: Arizona Center for Medieval and Renaissance Studies, 2005), pp. 173–91

EDZARDI, A. P., 'Die Stuttgarter Oswaldprosa', *Germania*, 20 (1875), 190–206; *Germania*, 21 (1876), 466–91

Oswaldus rex et M. in Anglia. Vita. Auctore D. Drogone monacho, Acta Sanctorum Aug. II, Dies 5

HAUPT, M., 'Oswalt', *ZfdA*, 13 (1867), 466–91

Der ungenähte Rock Christi: Wie König Orendel von Trier ihn erwirbt, darin Frau Breiden und das heilige Grab gewinnt, und ihn nach Trier bringt. Altdeutsches Gedicht, aus der einzigen Handschrift, mit Vergleichung des alten Drucks, ed. by Friedrich von der Hagen (Berlin: Schultze, 1844)

The Saga of Thidrek of Bern, trans. by Edward R. Haymes (New York and London: Garland, 1988)

Salman und Morolf, ed. by Alfred Karnein (Tübingen: Niemeyer, 1979)

Salomon et Marcolfus, ed. by Walter Benary (Heidelberg: Carl Winter, 1914)

Salomon und Markolf: Das Spruchgedicht, ed. by Walter Hartmann (Halle: Niemeyer, 1934)

Primary Sources

BEDE, *Ecclesiastical History of the English People*, trans. by Leo Shirley-Price, 4th edn (London: Penguin, 1990)

CHRÉTIEN DE TROYES, *Cligés*, ed. by Stewart Gregory and Claude Luttrell (Cambridge: Brewer, 1993)

EBERNAND VON ERFURT, *Heinrich und Kunegunde*, ed. by Reinhold Bechstein (Quedlinburg: Basse, 1860)

DER GROSSE GOTTESFREUND, *Fünfmannenbuch*, ed. by Philipp Strauch (Halle: Niemeyer, 1927)

GOTTFRIED VON STRASSBURG, *Tristan*, ed. and trans. by Rüdiger Krohn, 9th edn (Stuttgart: Reclam, 2001)

SAINT GREGORY THE GREAT, *Dialogues*, trans. by Odo John Zimmermann (New York: Fathers of the Church, Inc., 1959)

S. GREGORII MAGNI, *Moralia in Iob*, ed. by Marcus Adriaen, II (Turnholt: Brepols 1979)

HARTMANN VON AUE, *Erec*, ed. and trans. by Thomas Cramer, 24th edn (Frankfurt a. M.: Fischer, 2002)

HARTMANN VON AUE, *Gregorius*, ed. by Friedrich Neumann and trans. by Burkhard Kippenburg (Stuttgart: Reclam, 1963)

HARTMANN VON AUE, *Iwein: Text der siebente Ausgabe von G. F. Benecke, K. Lachmann und L. Wolff*, trans. by Thomas Cramer, 4th edn (Berlin: de Gruyter, 2001)

KAUFRINGER, HEINRICH, *Drei listige Frauen*, in *Novellistik des Mittelalters: Märendichtung*, ed. and trans. by Klaus Grubmüller (Frankfurt a. M.: Deutscher Klassiker Verlag), pp. 840–71

DER ARME KONRAD, *Frau Metze die Käuflerin*, in *Neues Gesamtabenteuer*, I, 2nd edn, ed. by Werner Simon (Dublin and Zürich: Weidmann, 1967), pp. 70–83
PFAFFE LAMBRECHT, *Alexanderroman*, ed. and trans. by Elisabeth Lienert (Stuttgart: Reclam, 2007)
NOTKER DER DEUTSCHE, *Der Psalter*, III, ed. by Petrus W. Tax (Tübingen: Niemeyer, 1983)
REGINALD OF DURHAM, *Vita S. Oswaldi regis et martyris*, in *Symeonis Monachi Opera Omnia: Historia Ecclesiae Dunhelmensis*, I, ed. by Thomas Arnold (London: Longman & co, 1882), pp. 326–85
WOLFRAM VON ESCHENBACH, *Parzival*, ed. by Eberhard Nellmann (Frankfurt a. M.: Deutscher Klassiker Verlag, 2006)

Secondary Sources

ARCHIBALD, ELIZABETH, *Apollonius of Tyre: Medieval and Renaissance Themes and Variations. Including the text of the Historia Apollonii Regis Tyri with an English translation* (Cambridge: Brewer, 1991)
BACHORSKI, HANS-JÜRGEN, 'Serialität, Variation und Spiel: Narrative Experimente in *Salman und Morolf*', in *Heldensage, Heldenlied, Heldenepos: Ergebnisse der II. Jahrestagung der Reinecke-Gesellschaft, Gotha, 16.-20. Mai 1991* (Amiens: Université de Picardie, Centre d'études médiévales, 1992), pp. 7–29
BAHR, JOACHIM, 'Der "Spielmann" in der Literaturwissenschaft des 19. Jahrhunderts', *ZfdPh*, 73 (1954), 174–96, repr. in *Spielmannsepik*, ed. by Walter Johannes Schröder (Darmstadt: Wissenschaftliche Buchgesellschaft, 1977), pp. 289–322
BAKHTIN, MIKHAIL, *Rabelais and his World*, trans. by Hélène Iswolsky (Bloomington: Indiana University Press, 1984)
BATTS, MICHAEL S., *A History of Histories of German Literature: Prolegomena* (New York: Lang, 1987)
BEUNINGEN, H. J. E. VAN, A. M. KOLDEWEIJ, and D. KICKEN, *Heilig en Profaan 2. 1200 laatmiddeleeuwse insignes uit openbare en particuliere collecties* (Cothen: Stichting Middeleeuwse Religieuze en Profane Insignes, 2001)
BIESTERFELDT, CORINNA, *Moniage — Der Rückzug aus der Welt als Erzählschluß: Untersuchungen zu 'Kaiserchronik', 'König Rother', 'Orendel', 'Barlaam und Josephat', 'Prosa-Lancelot'* (Stuttgart: Hirzel, 2004)
BOOR, HELMUT DE, *Die deutsche Literatur von Karl dem Großen bis zum Beginn der höfischen Dichtung 770-1170: Geschichte der deutschen Literatur von den Anfängen bis zur Gegenwart* ed. by Helmut de Boor and Richard Newald, I (Munich: Beck 1949)
BORNHOLDT, CLAUDIA, *Engaging Moments: The Origins of Medieval Bridal-Quest Narrative* (Berlin: de Gruyter, 2005)
——'*in was zu schouwen also not*: Salman und Morolf bildlich erzählt', in *Visualisierungsstrategien in mittelalterlichen Bildern und Texten*, ed. by Horst Wenzel and C. Stephen Jaeger (Berlin: Erich Schmidt, 2006), pp. 226–47
BRANDT, RÜDIGER, 'Spielmannsepik: Literaturwissenschaft zwischen Edition, Überlieferung und Literaturgeschichte. Ein nicht immer unproblematisches Verhältnis', *Jahrbuch für internationale Germanistik*, 37 (2005), 9–49

BRÄUER, ROLF, *Das Problem des 'Spielmännischen' aus der Sicht der St.-Oswald Überlieferung* (Berlin: Akademie, 1969)
—— *Literatursoziologie und epische Struktur der deutschen Spielmanns- und Heldendichtung* (Berlin: Akademie, 1970)
——, ed., *Dichtung des europäischen Mittelalters: Ein Führer durch die erzählende Literatur* (Munich: Beck, 1990)
BROOKE, CHRISTOPHER, *The Medieval Idea of Marriage* (Oxford: Oxford University Press, 1989)
BRUNDAGE, JAMES *Law, Sex and Christian Society in Medieval Europe* (Chicago: University of Chicago Press, 1987)
BUMKE, JOACHIM, *Mäzene im Mittelalter: Die Gönner und Auftraggeber der höfischen Literatur in Deutschland 1150-1300* (Munich: Beck, 1979)
—— *Geschichte der deutschen Literatur im hohen Mittelalter*, 5th edn (Munich: dtv, 2004)
BYNUM, CAROLINE WALKER, 'Did the Twelfth Century discover the individual?', *Journal of Ecclesiastical History*, 31 (1980), 1–17
—— 'Seeing and Seeing Beyond: The Mass of St. Gregory in the Fifteenth Century', in *The Mind's Eye: Art and Theology in the Middle Ages*, ed. by Jeffrey Hamburger and Anne-Marie Bouché (Princeton: Princeton University Press, 2005), pp. 208–40
—— *Wonderful Blood: Theology and Practice in Late Medieval Northern Germany and Beyond* (Philadelphia: University of Pennsylvania Press, 2007)
CLEMOES, PETER, *The Cult of St Oswald on the Continent* (Jarrow Lecture 1983)
COLDITZ, CARL, 'Über die Anwendung der Morolfstrophe im Mittelalter und im deutschen Lied', *Modern Philology*, 31 (1933/34), 243–52
CORDEZ, PHILIPPE, 'Wallfahrt und Medienwettbewerb: Serialität und Formenwandel der Heiltumsverzeichnisse mit Reliquienbildern im Heiligen Römischen Reich (1460-1529)', in *'Ich armer sundiger mensch': Heiligen- und Reliquienkult am Übergang zum konfessionellen Zeitalter*, ed. by Andreas Tacke (Göttingen: Wallstein, 2006), pp. 37–73
CURSCHMANN, MICHAEL, *Der Münchener Oswald und die deutsche spielmännische Epik* (Munich: Beck, 1964)
—— '*Spielmannsepik*: Wege und Ergebnisse der Forschung von 1907-1965', *DVjS*, 40 (1966), 434–78; 597–647
CURTIUS, ERNST ROBERT, *European Literature and the Latin Middle Ages*, trans. by Willard R. Trask (Princeton: Princeton University Press, 1990)
DEUTSCH, LORENZ, 'Die Einführung der Schrift als Literarisierungsschwelle: Kritik eines mediävistischen Forschungsfaszinosums am Beispiel des *König Rother*', *Poetica*, 35 (2003), 69–90
DINKELACKER, WOLFGANG, *Ortnit-Studien* (Berlin: E. Schmidt, 1972)
DINSER, GUDULA, *Kohärenz und Struktur: Textlinguistische und erzähltechnische Untersuchungen von König Rother* (Cologne and Vienna: Böhlau, 1975)
DOBOZY, MARIA *Full Circle: Kingship in the German Epic; Alexanderlied, Rolandslied, Spielmannsepen* (Göppingen: Kümmerle, 1985)
—— 'The Function of Knowledge and Magic in *Salman und Morolf*', in *The Dark Figure in Medieval German and Germanic Literature*, ed. by Edward R. Haymes and Stephanie Cain Van D'Elden (Göppingen: Kümmerle, 1986), pp. 27–41

DUBY, GEORGES, *The Knight, the Lady and the Priest: The Making of Modern Marriage in Medieval France*, trans. by Barbara Bray (London: Allen Lane, 1984)

EBENBAUER, ALFRED, 'Orendel — Anspruch und Verwirklichung', in *Strukturen und Interpretationen: Studien zur deutschen Philologie gewidmet Blanka Horacek zum 60. Geburtstag*, ed. by Alfred Ebenbauer and others (Vienna: Braumüller, 1974), pp. 25–63

—— 'Andere Großepen', in *Deutsche Literatur: Eine Sozialgeschichte*, ed. by Horst Albert Glaser, I: *Aus der Mündlichkeit in die Schriftlichkeit 750–1320*, ed. by Ursula Liebertz-Grün (Hamburg: Rowohlt 1988), pp. 279–89

EHRISMANN, GUSTAV, *Geschichte der deutschen Literatur bis zum Ausgang des Mittelalters*, II: *Die Mittelhochdeutsche Literatur. I. Frühmittelhochdeutsche Zeit* (Munich: Beck, 1922)

ELLIOTT, DYAN, *Spiritual Marriage: Sexual Abstinence in Medieval Wedlock* (Princeton: Princeton University Press, 1993)

EMBACH, MICHAEL, 'Im Spannungsfeld von profaner "Spielmannsepik" und christlicher Legendarik: Der Heilige Rock im mittelalterlichen Orendel-Gedicht', in *Der Heilige Rock zu Trier: Studien zur Geschichte und Verehrung der Tunika Christi*, ed. by Erich Aretz and others (Trier: Paulinus, 1996), pp. 763–97

—— 'Die Trierer Heiltumsschriften des 16. Jahrhunderts zwischen Wallfahrtspropaganda und Maximiliansapotheose', in *Wallfahrt und Kommunikation: Kommunikation über Wallfahrt*, ed. by Bernhard Schneider (Mainz: Gesellschaft für mittelrheinische Kirchengeschichte, 2004), pp. 229–44

ENGELEN, ULRICH, *Die Edelsteine in der deutschen Dichtung des 12. und 13. Jahrhunderts* (Munich: Fink, 1978)

ERB, EWALD, *Geschichte der deutschen Literatur von den Anfängen bis 1160*, 2 vols: *Geschichte der deutschen Literatur von den Anfängen bis zur Gegenwart*, I, I–II, ed. by Klaus Gysi and others, (Berlin: Volk und Wissen Volkseigener Verlag, 1965)

FISCHER, HUBERTUS, 'Gewalt und ihre Alternativen: Erzähltes politisches Handeln im *König Rother*', in *Gewalt und ihre Legitimation im Mittelalter: Symposium des Philosophischen Seminars der Universität Hannover vom 26. bis 28. Februar 2002*, ed. by Günther Mensching (Würzburg: Königshausen & Neumann, 2003), pp. 204–34

FLEISCHMANN, SUZANNE, 'The Non-lyric Texts', in *A Handbook of the Troubadours*, ed. by. F. R. P. Akehurst and Judith M. Davis (Berkeley: University of California Press, 1995), pp. 167–84

FOWLER, ALASTAIR, *Kinds of Literature: An Introduction to the Theory of Genres and Modes* (Oxford: Clarendon Press, 1982)

FRIEDMAN, JOHN BLOCK, *The Monstrous Races in Medieval Art and Thought* (Cambridge, MA: Harvard University Press, 1981)

FRINGS, THEODOR, 'Die Enstehung der deutschen Spielmannsepen', *Zeitschrift für deutsche Geisteswissenschaft*, 2 (1939/40), 306–31, repr. in *Spielmannsepik*, ed. by Walter Johannes Schröder (Darmstadt: Wissenschaftliche Buchgesellschaft, 1977), pp. 191–212

FRINGS, THEODOR and MAX BRAUN, *Brautwerbung*, I (Leipzig: Hirzel, 1947)

FROMM, HANS, 'Die Erzählkunst des *Rother*-Epikers', *Euphorion*, 54 (1960), 347–79

—— 'Doppelweg', in *Werk-Typ-Situation: Studien zur poetologischen Bedingungen in der älteren deutschen Literatur*, ed. by Ingeborg Glier and others (Stuttgart: Metzler, 1969), pp. 64–79

FUCHS-JOLIE, STEPHAN, 'Gewalt, Text, Ritual: Performativität und Literarizität im *König Rother*', *PBB*, 127 (2005), 183–207

—— 'Rother, Roland und die Rituale: Repräsentation und Narration in der frühhöfischen Epik', in *Deutsche Königspfalzen: Beiträge zu ihrer historischen und archäologischen Erforschung*, VII: *Zentren herrschaftlicher Repräsentation im Hochmittelalter: Geschichte, Architektur und Zeremoniell*, ed. by Caspar Ehlers, Jörg Jarnut, and Matthias Wemhoff (Göttingen: Vandenhoeck & Ruprecht, 2007), pp. 171–96

GANTERT, KLAUS, 'Durch got und des heiligen grabes eren und ouch durch die schonen juncfrowen: Reliquientranslation und Brautwerbungshandlung im *Orendel*', *Kurtrierisches Jahrbuch*, 39 (1999), 123–44

—— 'Erzählschema und literarische Hermeneutik: Zum Verhältnis von Brautwerbungsschema und geistlicher Tradition im *Wiener Oswald* und in der *Hochzeit*', *Poetica*, 31 (1999), 381–414

GANZ, PETER, '*Die Hochzeit*: Fabula et Significatio', in *Studien zur frühmittelhochdeutschen Literatur: Cambridger Colloquium 1971*, ed. by L. P. Johnson, H.-H. Steinhoff, and R. A. Wisbey (Berlin: E. Schmidt, 1974), pp. 58–73

——, art. 'Die Hochzeit', *VL*, IV, cols 77–79

GEARY, PATRICK, *Furta Sacra: Thefts of Relics in the Central Middle Ages*, 2nd edn (Princeton: Princeton University Press, 1990)

GELLINEK, CHRISTIAN, *König Rother: Studie zur literarischen Deutung* (Bern: Francke, 1968)

GERVINUS, GEORG GOTTFRIED, review, 'Geschichte der neuern deutschen Poesie. Vorlesungen von August Wilhelm Bohtz. Göttingen 1832; Geschichte der deutschen National-Literatur mit Proben der deutschen Dichtkunst und Beredsamkeit. Von Dr Karl Herzog. Jena 1831', *Heidelberger Jahrbücher der Literatur*, 26 (1833), 1194–1239

—— *Geschichte der poetischen National-Literatur der Deutschen*, I: *Von den ersten Spuren der deutschen Dichtung bis gegen das Ende des 13ten Jahrhunderts* (Leipzig: Wilhelm Engelmann 1835)

—— *Geschichte der poetischen National-Literatur der Deutschen, Zweite Auflage*, I: *Von den ersten Spuren der deutschen Dichtung bis gegen das Ende des 13. Jahrhunderts* (Leipzig: Wilhelm Engelmann 1840)

GILDERMEISTER, JOHANN and HEINRICH VON SYBEL, *Der Heilige Rock zu Trier und die zwanzig andern Heiligen ungenähten Röcke* (Düsseldorf: Buddeus, 1844)

GORYS, ERHARD, *Lexikon der Heiligen*, 5th edn (Munich: dtv, 2004)

GREBE, ANJA, and NIKOLAUS STAUBACH, eds, *Komik und Sakralität: Aspekte einer ästhetischen Paradoxie in Mittelalter und früher Neuzeit*, (Frankfurt a. M.: Lang, 2005)

GREEN, D. H., *Medieval Listening and Reading: The Primary Reception of German Literature 800–1300* (Cambridge: Cambridge University Press, 1994)

GRIESE, SABINE, *Salomon und Markolf: Ein literarischer Komplex im Mittelalter und in der frühen Neuzeit* (Tübingen: Niemeyer, 1999)

GRIMM, JACOB, 'Vorrede zu: Über den altdeutschen Meistergesang (1811)', repr. in

Spielmannsepik, ed. by Walter Johannes Schröder (Darmstadt: Wissenschaftliche Buchgesellschaft, 1977), pp. 1–7

GRIMM, WILHELM, 'Ueber die Entstehung der altdeutschen Poesie und ihr Verhältniß zu der nordischen', in *Studien*, ed. by Carl Daub and Friedrich Creuzer, 6 vols (Frankfurt and Heidelberg: Mohr, 1805–11), IV (1808), 75–121, repr. in Gerard Kozielek, *Mittelalterrezeption: Texte zur Aufnahme altdeutscher Literatur in der Romantik* (Tübingen: Niemeyer, 1977), pp. 124–50

GRUBMÜLLER, KLAUS, 'Gattungskonstitution im Mittelalter', in *Mittelalterliche Literatur und Kunst im Spannungsfeld von Hof und Kloster: Ergebnisse der Berliner Tagung, 9.–11. Oktober 1997*, ed. by Nigel F. Palmer and Hans-Jochen Schiewer (Tübingen: Niemeyer, 1999), pp. 193–210

GUILLÉN, CLAUDIO, *Literature as System: Essays toward the Theory of Literary History* (Princeton: Princeton University Press, 1971)

HAMBURGER, JEFFREY, 'Vision and the Veronica', in Hamburger, *The Visual and the Visionary: Art and Female Spirituality in Late Medieval Germany* (New York: Zone Books, 1998), pp. 317–82

—— 'Seeing and Believing: The Suspicion of Sight and the Authentication of Vision in Late Medieval Art', in *Imagination und Wirklichkeit: Zum Verhältnis von mentalen und realen Bildern in der Kunst der frühen Neuzeit*, ed. by Klaus Krüger and Alessandro Nova (Mainz: von Zabern, 2000), pp. 47–69

Handwörterbuch des deutschen Aberglaubens, 10 vols, ed. by H. Bächtold-Stäubli (Berlin: de Gruyter, 1927–42)

HAUBRICHS, WOLFGANG, 'Labor sanctorum und labor heroum: Zur konsolatorischen Funktion von Legende und Heldenlied', in *Die Funktion außer- und innerliterarischen Faktoren für die Entstehung deutscher Literatur des Mittelalters und der frühen Neuzeit*, ed. by Christa Baufeld (Göppingen: Kümmerle, 1994), pp. 27–49

HAUG, WALTER, 'Das Komische und das Heilige: Zur Komik in der religiösen Literatur des Mittelalters', *Wolfram-Studien*, 7 (1982), 8–31

—— 'Brautwerbung im Zerrspiegel', in *Sammlung, Deutung, Wertung: Ergebnisse, Probleme, Tendenzen und Perspektiven philologischer Arbeit. Melanges de littérature médiévale et de linguistique allemande offerts à Wolfgang Spiewok à l'occasion de son soixantième anniversaire par ses collègues et amis*, ed. by Danielle Buschinger (Amiens: Université de Picardie, Centre des études médiévales, 1988), pp. 179–88

—— 'Struktur und Geschichte: Ein literaturtheoretisches Experiment an mittelalterlichen Texten', in Haug, *Strukturen als Schlüssel zur Welt* (Tübingen: Niemeyer, 1989), pp. 236–56

—— 'Struktur, Gewalt und Begierde: Zum Verhältnis von Erzählmuster und Sinnkonstitution in mündlicher und schriftlicher Überlieferung', in *Idee — Gestalt — Geschichte: Festschrift für Klaus von See*, ed. by Gerd Wolfgang Weber (Odense: Odense University Press, 1988), pp. 143–57, repr. in Haug, *Brechungen auf dem Weg zur Individualität: Kleine Schriften zur Literatur des Mittelalters* (Tübingen: Niemeyer, 1997), pp. 3–16

—— 'Die geistliche Umformulierung profaner Typen: *Rolandslied*, Brautwerbungsepen, *Alexanderroman*', in Haug, *Literaturtheorie im deutschen Mittelalter: Von den Anfängen bis zum Ende des 13. Jahrhunderts*, 2nd edn (Darmstadt: Wissenschaftliche Buchgesellschaft, 1992), pp. 75–90

HEINZLE, JOACHIM, *Das Nibelungenlied: Eine Einführung*, 2nd edn (Frankfurt a. M.: Fischer, 1996)
HENNEN, GERHARD, 'Eine bibliographische Zusammenstellung der Trierer Heiligtumsbücher, deren Drucklegung durch die Ausstellung des h. Rockes im Jahre 1512 veranlasst wurde', *Centralblatt für Bibliothekswesen*, 4 (1887), 481–550
HERDER, JOHANN GOTTFRIED, *Auszug aus einem Briefwechsel über Ossian und die Lieder alter Völke*, in *Werke*, ed. by Martin Bollacher, II: *Schriften zur Ästhetik und Literatur 1767–1781*, ed. by Gunter E. Grimm (Frankfurt a. M.: Deutscher Klassiker Verlag, 1993), pp. 447–97
HÖING, NORBERT, 'Die *Trierer Stilübungen*: Ein Denkmal der Frühzeit Kaiser Friedrich Barbarossas', *Archiv für Diplomatik*, 1 (1955), 257–329
HUNGER, ULRICH, 'Romantische Germanistik und Textphilologie: Konzepte zur Erforschung mittelalterlicher Literatur zu Beginn des 19. Jahrhunderts', *Sonderheft zur DvjS*, 61 (1987), 42–68
JAKOBSON, ROMAN, 'The Dominant', in *Readings in Russian Poetics: Formalist and Structuralist Views*, ed. by Ladislav Matejka and Krystyna Pomorska (Ann Arbor: University of Michigan, 1978), pp. 82–87
JANSEN, ANNEMIEK, 'The Development of the St Oswald Legends on the Continent', in *Oswald: Northumbrian King to European Saint*, ed. by Clare Stancliffe and Eric Cambridge (Stamford: Paul Watkins, 1995), pp. 230–41
JAUSS, HANS-ROBERT, 'Theorie der Gattungen und Literatur des Mittelalters', *Grundriss der romanischen Literaturen des Mittelalters*, 6 (1972), 93–138
JUNGANDREAS, WOLFGANG, 'Orendel und der Heilige Rock', *Kurtrierisches Jahrbuch*, 8 (1968), 84–95
KALINKE, MARIANNE, *St. Oswald of Northumbria: Continental Metamorphoses. With an Edition and Translation of Ósvalds saga and Van sunte Oswaldo deme konninghe* (Tempe: Arizona Center for Medieval and Renaissance Studies, 2005)
KERTH, THOMAS, *King Rother and his Bride: Quests and Counter-Quests* (Rochester, NY: Camden House, 2010)
KIENING, CHRISTIAN, 'Arbeit am Muster: Literarisierungsstrategien im *König Rother*', in *Neue Wege in der Mittelalter-Philologie: Landshuter Colloquium 1996*, ed. by Joachim Heinzle, L. Peter Johnson, and Gisela Vollmann-Profe (Berlin: Schmidt, 1998), pp. 211–44
—— 'Heilige Brautwerbung: Überlegungen zum *Wiener Oswald*', in *Impulse und Resonanzen: Tübinger mediävistische Beiträge zum 80. Geburtstag von Walter Haug*, ed. by Gisela Vollmann-Profe and others (Tübingen: Niemeyer, 2007), pp. 89–100
—— 'Hybriden des Heils: Reliquie und Text des *Grauen Rocks* um 1512', in *Literarische und religiöse Kommunikation in Mittelalter und Früher Neuzeit*, ed. by Peter Strohschneider (Berlin: de Gruyter, 2009), pp. 371–410
KLEIN, THOMAS, 'Zur Thidreks saga', in *Arbeiten zur Skandinavistik: 6. Arbeitstagung der Skandinavisten des deutschen Sprachgebietes*, ed. by Heinrich Beck (Frankfurt a. M.: Lang, 1985), pp. 487–565
—— 'Ermittlung, Darstellung und Deutung von Verbreitungstypen in der Handschriftenüberleiferung mittelhochdeutscher Epik', in *Deutsche Handschriften 1100–1400*, ed. by Volker Honemann and Nigel F. Palmer (Tübingen: Niemeyer 1988), pp. 110–67
KOBERSTEIN, AUGUST, *Grundriß der Geschichte der deutschen National-Litteratur* (Leipzig: Vogel, 1827)

—— Grundriß der Geschichte der deutschen National-Litteratur, 4th edn, I (Leipzig: Vogel 1847)
KOKOTT, HARTMUT, Literatur und Herrschaftsbewußtsein. Wertstrukturen der vor- und frühhöfischen Literatur: Vorstudien zur Interpretation mittelhochdeutscher Texte (Frankfurt a. M.: Lang, 1978)
KOPPITZ, HANS-JOACHIM, Studien zur Tradierung der weltlichen mittelhochdeutschen Epik im 15. und beginnenden 16. Jahrhundert (Munich: Fink 1980)
KOZIELEK, GERARD, Mittelalterrezeption: Texte zur Aufnahme altdeutscher Literatur in der Romantik (Tübingen: Niemeyer, 1977)
KRAGL, FLORIAN, 'Wer hat den Hirsch zum Köder gemacht? Der "Münchner Oswald" spiritualiter gelesen', Amsterdamer Beiträge zur älteren Germanistik, 63 (2007), 157–78
KRASS, ANDREAS, Geschriebene Kleider: Höfische Identität als literarisches Spiel (Tübingen: Francke, 2006)
KUHN, HUGO, 'Gattungsprobleme der mittelhochdeutschen Literatur', in Kuhn, Dichtung und Welt im Mittelalter (Stuttgart: Metzler, 1959), pp. 41–61
—— 'Erec', in Kuhn, Dichtung und Welt im Mittelalter (Stuttgart: Metzler, 1959), pp. 133–50
—— 'Allegorie und Erzählstruktur', in Formen und Funktionen der Allegorie, ed. by Walter Haug (Stuttgart: Metzler, 1979), pp. 206–18
—— 'Versuch einer Literaturtypologie des 14. Jahrhunderts', in Kleine Schriften, III: Liebe und Gesellschaft, ed. by Hugo Kuhn and Wolfgang Walliczek (Stuttgart: Metzler, 1980), pp. 121–34
KÜHNE, HARTMUT, Ostensio reliquiarum: Untersuchungen über Entstehung, Ausbreitung, Gestalt und Funktion der Heiltumsweisungen im römisch-deutschen Regnum (Berlin: de Gruyter, 2000)
LIENERT, ELISABETH, Die 'historische' Dietrichepik: Untersuchungen zu 'Dietrichs Flucht', 'Rabenschlacht' und 'Alpharts Tod' (Berlin and New York: de Gruyter, 2010)
LUGOWSKI, CLEMENS, Form, Individuality and the Novel: An Analysis of Narrative Structure in Early German Prose, trans. by John Dixon Halliday (Norman: University of Oklahoma Press, 1990)
MAURER, FRIEDRICH, 'Der Topos von den "Minnesklaven": Zur Geschichte einer thematischen Gemeinschaft zwischen bildender Kunst und Dichtung im Mittelalter', DVjs, 27 (1953), 182–206
MEVES, UWE, 'Das Gedicht vom "Grauen Rock" (Orendel) und die Trierer Reliquientradition', Kurtrierisches Jahrbuch, 15 (1975), 5–19
—— Studien zu König Rother, Herzog Ernst und Grauer Rock (Orendel) (Frankfurt a. M.: Lang, 1976)
—— 'Zur historischen Bedingtheit literarischer Wertung: Das Beispiel "Spielmannsepik" in der Literaturgeschichtsschreibung', in Textsorten und literarische Gattungen: Dokumentation des Germanistentages in Hamburg vom 1. bis 4. April 1979, ed. by Vorstand der Vereinigung der deutschen Hochschulgermanisten (Berlin: Schmidt, 1983), pp. 317–34
——, ed., Alt-deutsche epische Gedichte: Großentheils zum erstenmahl aus Handschriften bekannt gemacht und bearbeitet von Ludwig Tieck. 1. König Rother (Göppingen: Kümmerle, 1979)
MEYER, ELARD HUGO, 'Quellenstudien zur mittelhochdeutschen Spielmannsdichtung', ZfdA, 37 (1893), 321–56

MIKLAUTSCH, LYDIA, 'Salman und Morolf — Thema und Variation', in *Ir sult sprechen willekomen: grenzenlose Mediävistik. Festschrift für Helmut Birkhan zum 60. Geburtstag*, ed. by Christa Tuczay, Ulrike Hirhager, and Karin Lichtblau (Bern: Lang, 1998), pp. 284-306

——*Montierte Texte, hybride Helden: Zur Poetik der Wolfdietrich-Dichtungen* (Berlin: de Gruyter, 2005)

MILLER, NIKOLAUS, 'Brautwerbung und Heiligkeit: Die Kohärenz des *Münchner Oswald*', *DVjs*, 78 (1978), 226-40

MILLET, VICTOR, *Germanische Heldendichtung im Mittelalter* (Berlin: de Gruyter, 2008)

MÜLLER, JAN-DIRK, 'Ratgeber und Wissende in heroischer Epik', *Frühmittelalterliche Studien*, 27 (1993), 125-46

——*Spielregeln für den Untergang: Die Welt des Nibelungenliedes* (Tübingen: Niemeyer, 1998)

——*Höfische Kompromisse: acht Kapitel zur höfischen Epik* (Tübingen: Niemeyer, 2007)

MÜLLER, MARIA, *Jungfräulichkeit in Versepen des 12. und 13. Jahrhunderts* (Munich: Fink, 1995)

MÜLLER, STEPHAN, 'Oswalds Rabe: Zur institutionellen Geschichte eines Heiligenattributs und Herrschaftszeichens', in *Institutionalität und Symbolisierung: Verstetigungen kultureller Ordnungsmuster in Vergangenheit und Gegenwart*, ed. by Gert Melville (Köln, Weimar, and Wien: Böhlau, 2001), pp. 451-75

NAUMANN, HANS, 'Versuch einer Einschränkung des romantischen Begriffs Spielmannsdichtung', *DVjs*, 2 (1924), 777-94, repr. in *Spielmannsepik*, ed. by Walter Johannes Schröder (Darmstadt: Wissenschaftliche Buchgesellschaft, 1977), pp. 126-44

NEUDECK, OTTO, 'Grenzüberschreitung als erzählerisches Prinzip: Das Spiel mit der Fiktion in *Salman und Morolf*', in *Erkennen und Erinnern in Kunst und Literatur: Kolloquium Reisenburg 4.-7. Januar 1996*, ed. by Dietmar Peil, Michael Schilling, and Peter Strohschneider (Tübingen: Niemeyer, 1998), pp. 87-114

NEUENDORFF, DAGMAR, 'Kaiser und Könige, Grafen und Herzöge im Epos von König Rother', *Neuphilologische Mitteilungen*, 85 (1984), 45-58

NÖTH, WINFRIED, *Handbook of Semiotics* (Bloomington and Indianapolis: University of Indiana Press, 1990)

Ó RIAIN-RAEDEL, DAGMAR, 'Edith, Judith, Matilda: The Role of Royal Ladies in the Propagation of the Continental Cult', in *Oswald: Northumbrian King to European Saint*, ed. by Clare Stancliffe and Eric Cambridge (Stamford: Paul Watkins, 1995), pp. 210-29

ORTMANN, CHRISTA, and HEDDA RAGOTZKY, 'Brautwerbungsschema, Reichsherrschaft & staufische Politik: Zur politischen Bezeichnungsfähigkeit literarischer Strukturmuster am Beispiel des *König Rother*', *ZfdPh*, 112 (1993), 321-43

PERKINS, DAVID, *Is Literary History Possible?* (Baltimore: Johns Hopkins University Press, 1992)

PETERSOHN, JÜRGEN, 'Die Litterae Papst Innocenz' III: Zur Heiligsprechung der Kaiserin Kunigunde (1200)', *Jahrbuch für fränkische Landesforschung*, 37 (1977), 1-25

PISCHON, FRIEDRICH AUGUST, *Leitfaden zur Geschichte der deutschen Literatur*, 4th edn (Berlin: Duncker und Humblot, 1838; 1st edn 1830)
PLATE, BERNWARD, 'Orendel — König von Jerusalem: Kreuzfahrerbewußtsein (Epos d. 12. Jhs.) und Leidenstheologie (Prosa von 1512)', *Euphorion*, 82 (1988), 168–210
PROPP, VLADIMIR, *Morphology of the Folktale*, trans. by Laurence Scott, (Austin: University of Texas Press, 1968)
RAUDSZUS, GABRIELE, *Die Zeichensprache der Kleidung: Untersuchungen zur Symbolik des Gewandes in der deutschen Epik des Mittelalters* (Hildesheim: Olms, 1985)
REIFFENSTEIN, INGO, 'Die Erzählervorausdeutung in der frühmittelhochdeutschen Dichtung: Zur Geschichte und Funktion einer poetischen Formel', in *Festschrift für Hans Eggers zum 65. Geburtstag*, ed. by Herbert Backes, *Beiträge zur Geschichte der deutschen Sprache und Literatur*, 94 (Sonderheft) (Tübingen: Niemeyer, 1972), pp. 551–76
RÖCKE, WERNER, 'Höfische und unhöfische Minne- und Abenteuerromane', in *Epische Stoffe des Mittelalters*, ed. by Volker Mertens and Ulrich Müller (Stuttgart: Kröner, 1984), pp. 395–423
—— 'Schälke — Schelme — Narren: Literaturgeschiche des "Eigensinns" und populäre Kultur in der frühen Neuzeit', in *Schelme und Narren in der Literatur des Mittelalters: XXVII. Jahrestagung des Arbeitskreises Deutsche Literatur des Mittelalters (Greifswald), Eulenspiegelstadt Mölln, 24.-27. September 1992* (Greifswald: Reinecke, 1994), pp. 131–49
ROSENKRANZ, KARL, *Geschichte der deutschen Poesie im Mittelalter* (Halle: Anton und Gelbcke, 1830)
RUH, KURT, *Höfische Epik des deutschen Mittelalters*, I: *Von den Anfängen bis zu Hartmann von Aue* (Berlin: Schmidt, 1967)
SAUERLAND, H. V., *Trierer Geschichtsquellen des XI. Jahrhunderts* (Trier: Paulinus, 1889)
SAUSER, EKKARD, 'Die Tunika Christi in der Vätertheologie', in *Der Heilige Rock zu Trier: Studien zur Geschichte und Verehrung der Tunika Christi*, ed. by Erich Aretz and others (Trier: Paulinus, 1996), pp. 39–66
SCHIEWER, REGINA, 'Riskante Theologie? Minnegrotte, Engel und Eucharistie: Eine rezeptionsgeschichtliche Untersuchung', in *Exemplar: Festschrift für Kurt Otto Seidel*, ed. by Rüdiger Brandt and Dieter Lau (Frankfurt a. M.: Lang, 2008), pp. 243–61
SCHLEGEL, A. W., *Kritische Ausgabe der Vorlesungen*, ed. by Ernst Behler, II/I: *Vorlesungen über Ästhetik*, ed. by Georg Braungart (Paderborn: Schöningh, 2007)
SCHLEUSNER-EICHHOLZ, GUDRUN, *Das Auge im Mittelalter*, 2 vols (Munich: Fink, 1985)
SCHMID-CADALBERT, CHRISTIAN, *Der Ortnit AW als Brautwerbungsdichtung* (Bern: Francke Verlag 1985)
SCHMITT, BERNHARD, '"Heilige Röcke" anderswo: Die außerhalb der Trierer Domkirche vorkommenden sogenannten "Tuniken' Christi", in *Der Heilige Rock zu Trier: Studien zur Geschichte und Verehrung der Tunika Christi*, ed by Erich Aretz and others (Trier: Paulinus, 1996), pp. 549–605
SCHMITZ, SILVIA, '*War umbe ich die rede han ir hauen*: Erzählen im *König Rother*',

in *Situationen des Erzählens: Aspekte narrativer Praxis im Mittelalter*, ed. by Ludger Lieb and Stephan Müller (Berlin: de Gruyter, 2002), pp. 167–90

SCHNEIDER, KARIN, *Gotische Schriften in deutscher Sprache*, I: *Vom späten 12. Jahrhundert bis um 1300* (Wiesbaden: Reichert, 1987)

SCHNELL, RÜDIGER, 'Zur Karls-Rezeption in *König Rother* und in Ottes *Eraclius*', *PBB*, 104 (1982), 345–58

—— *Causa Amoris: Liebeskonzeption und Liebesdarstellung in der mittelalterlichen Literatur* (Bern: Francke, 1985)

SCHRÖDER, W., art. 'Wunder (Patristik und Mittelalter)', in *Historisches Wörterbuch der Philosophie*, ed. by Joachim Ritter, Karlfried Gründer, and Gottfried Gabriel, XII (Darmstadt: Wissenschaftliche Buchgesellshaft, 2004), cols 1055–58

SCHRÖDER, WALTER JOHANNES, 'König Rother: Gehalt und Struktur', *DVjs*, 29 (1955), 301–22, repr. in *Spielmannsepik*, ed. by Walter Johannes Schröder (Darmstadt: Wissenschaftliche Buchgesellschaft, 1977), pp. 323–50

—— *Spielmannsepik* (Stuttgart: Metzler, 1962)

SCHULZ, ARMIN, 'Morolfs Ende: Zur Dekonstruktion des feudalen Brautwerbungsschemas in der sogenannten Spielmannsepik', *PBB*, 124 (2002), 233–49

—— *Schwieriges Erkennen: Personenidentifizierung in der mittelhochdeutschen Epik* (Tübingen: Niemeyer, 2008)

SCHULZ, MONIKA, '"Iz ne wart nie urouwe bas geschot": Bemerkungen zur Kemenatenszene im *König Rother*', in *Literarische Kommunikation und soziale Interaktion: Studien zur Institutionalität mittelalterlicher Literatur*, ed. by Beate Kellner, Ludger Lieb, and Peter Strohschneider (Frankfurt and Oxford: Lang, 2001), pp. 73–88

—— 'Die falsche Braut: Imperative feudaler Herrschaft in Texten um 1200', *ZfdPh*, 121 (2002), 1–20

SCHWIETERING, JULIUS, *Die deutsche Dichtung des Mittelalters* (Darmstadt: Gentner, 1957)

SEEBER, STEFAN, *Poetik des Lachens: Untersuchungen zum mittelhochdeutschen Roman um 1200* (Berlin: de Gruyter, 2010)

—— 'Sanctity and Comedy in the "Munich Saint Oswald"', in *Intertextuality, Reception, and Performance: Interpretations and Texts of Medieval German Literature (Kalamazoo Papers 2007–2009)*, ed. by Sibylle Jefferis (Göppingen: Kümmerle, 2010), pp. 95–109

SIEFKEN, HINRICH, *Überindividuelle Formen und der Aufbau des Kudrunepos* (Munich: Fink, 1967)

SINGER, SAMUEL, 'Salomosagen in Deutschland', *ZfdA*, 35 (1891), 177–87, repr. in *Spielmannsepik*, ed. by Walter Johannes Schröder (Darmstadt: Wissenschaftliche Buchgesellschaft, 1977), pp. 72–84

—— *Apollonius von Tyrus: Untersuchungen über das Fortleben des antiken Romans in spätern Zeiten* (Halle: Niemeyer, 1895)

SPIEWOK, WOLFGANG, 'Vom Salman zum Salomon, vom Morolf zum Markolf', in *Schelme und Narren in der Literatur des Mittelalters: XXVII. Jahrestagung des Arbeitskreises Deutsche Literatur des Mittelalters (Greifswald), Eulenspiegelstadt Mölln, 24.–27. September 1992* (Greifswald: Reinecke, 1994), pp. 151–60

STANCLIFFE, CLARE, 'Oswald, "Most Holy and Most Victorious King of the Northumbrians"', in *Oswald: Northumbrian King to European Saint*, ed. by Clare Stancliffe and Eric Cambridge (Stamford: Paul Watkins, 1995), pp. 33–83

STEIN, PETER K., 'Orendel 1512: Probleme und Möglichkeiten der Anwendung der *theory of oral-formulaic poetry* bei der literaturhistorischen Interpretation eines mittelhochdeutschen Textes', in *Hohenemser Studien zum Nibelungenlied*, ed. by Achim Masser (Dornbirn: Voralberger Verlagsanstalt, 1981), pp. 322/148–348/174

—— '*Do newistich weiz hette getan. Ich wolde sie alle ir slagen hanc*: Beobachtungen und Überlegungen zum *König Rother*', in *Festschrift für Ingo Reiffenstein zum 60. Geburtstag*, ed. by Peter K. Stein and others (Göppingen: Kümmerle, 1998), pp. 309–38

STOCK, MARKUS, *Kombinationssinn: Narrative Strukturexperimente im Straßburger Alexander, im Herzog Ernst B und im König Rother* (Tübingen: Niemeyer, 2002)

—— 'Sich sehen lassen: Die Visibilität des Helden und der höfische Sichtraum in *König Rother*', in *Sehen und Sichtbarkeit in der deutschen Literatur des Mittelalters*, ed. by Ricarda Bauschke, Sebastian Coxon, and Martin Jones (Berlin: Akademie, 2011), pp 228–39

TIECK, LUDWIG, 'Die altdeutschen Minnelieder', in *Kritische Schriften: Zum erstenmale gesammelt und mit einer Vorrede herausgegeben von Ludwig Tieck*, I (Leipzig: Brockhaus, 1848), pp. 185–214; repr. in Gerard Kozielek, *Mittelalterrezeption: Texte zur Aufnahme altdeutscher Literatur in der Romantik* (Tübingen: Niemeyer, 1977), pp. 44–62

TOMASEK, TOMAS, 'Über den Einfluß des Apolloniusromans auf die volkssprachliche Erzählliteratur des 12. und 13. Jahrhunderts', in *Mediävistische Komparatistik: Festschrift für Franz Josef Worstbrock zum 60. Geburtstag*, ed. by Wolfgang Harms and Jan-Dirk Müller (Stuttgart and Leipzig: Hirzel, 1997), pp. 221–39

TONNELAT, ERNEST, 'Le roi Orendel et la tunique sans conture du Christ', in *Mélanges offerts à M. Charles Andler par ses amis et ses élèves* (1924), pp. 351–70, repr. as 'König Orendel und Christi nahtloses Gewand' (1924), trans. by Dorothea Kleinmann, in *Spielmannsepik*, ed. by Walter Johannes Schröder (Darmstadt: Wissenschaftliche Buchgesellschaft, 1977), pp. 145–67

TUDOR, VICTORIA, 'Reginald's *Life of St Oswald*', in *Oswald: Northumbrian King to European Saint*, ed. by Clare Stancliffe and Eric Cambridge (Stamford: Paul Watkins, 1995), pp. 178–94

UHLAND, LUDWIG, *Werke*, ed. by Helmut Fröschle and Walter Scheffler, III: *Geschichte der deutschen Poesie im Mittelalter*, ed. by Helmut Fröschle (Munich: Winkler, 1981)

URBANEK, FERDINAND, *Kaiser, Grafen und Mäzene im König Rother* (Berlin: Schmidt, 1976)

VOGT, FRIEDRICH, 'Leben und Dichten der deutschen Spielleute im Mittelalter', in *Vortrag gehalten im wissenschaftlichen Verein zu Greifswald am 29. November 1875* (Halle: Niemeyer, 1876), pp. 3–32, repr. in *Spielmannsepik*, ed. by Walter Johannes Schröder (Darmstadt: Wissenschaftliche Buchgesellschaft, 1977), pp. 18–48

VOLLMANN-PROFE, GISELA, *Wiederbeginn volkssprachlicher Schriftlichkeit im hohen Mittelalter (1050/60–1160/70): Geschichte der deutschen Literatur von den Anfängen bis zum Beginn der Neuzeit*, ed. by Joachim Heinzle, I/II (Königstein/Ts: Athenäum, 1986)

VRIES, JAN DE, 'Die Schuhepisode im König Rother', *ZfdPh*, 80 (1961), 129–41
WACKERNAGEL, WILHELM, *Geschichte der deutschen Litteratur* (Basel: Schweighauserische Buchhandlung, 1848)
WAGNER, F., ART. 'Miracula, Mirakel', in *Lexikon des Mittelalters*, VI (Munich: Artemis and Winkler, 1999), cols 656–59
WARD, BENEDICTA, *Miracles and the Medieval Mind: Theory, Record and Event 1000–1215* (Aldershot: Wildwood House, 1987)
WAREMAN, PIET, *Spielmannsdichtung: Versuch einer Begriffsbestimmung* (Amsterdam: van Campen, 1951)
WEHRLI, MAX, *Geschichte der deutschen Literatur vom frühen Mittelalter bis zum Ende des 16. Jahrhunderts* (Stuttgart: Reclam, 1980)
—— *Literatur im deutschen Mittelalter: Eine poetologische Einführung* (Stuttgart: Reclam, 1984)
WENZEL, HORST, 'Fernliebe und Hohe Minne: Zur räumlichen und zur sozialen Distanz in der Minnethematik', in *Liebe als Literatur: Aufsätze zur erotischen Dichtung in Deutschland*, ed. by Rüdiger Krohn (Munich: Beck, 1983), pp. 187–208
WISHARD, ARMIN, *Oral Formulaic Composition in the Spielmannsepik: An Analysis of Salman und Morolf* (Göppingen: Kümmerle, 1984)
WOLFF, LUDWIG, ART. 'Heinrich von Veldeke', *VL*, III, cols 899–902
WUTH, HENNING, 'Morolfs Tauchfahrt: Überlegungen zur narrativen Bedeutung von "Technik" im *Salman und Morolf*', *Archiv für das Studium der neueren Sprachen und Literaturen*, 235 (1998), 328–44
YOUNG, CHRISTOPHER, 'Ulrich von Liechtenstein in German Literary History: The Don Quixote of the Steiermark', in *Ulrich von Liechtenstein: Leben, Zeit, Werk, Forschung*, ed. by Sandra Linden and Christopher Young (Berlin: de Gruyter, 2010), pp. 1–44
ZIMMERMANN, RITA, *Herrschaft und Ehe: Die Logik der Brautwerbung im König Rother* (Frankfurt a. M.: Lang, 1993)

INDEX

St Adomnán, *Life of Columba* 102
St Afra 78–79
Agamemnon 94
St Agritius, bishop of Trier 137, 141
Alexander the Great, stories of 47 85, 139
   see also Pfaffe Lambrecht, *Alexander*
St Alexius 131 n. 41
Altman of Hautvilliers *Vita St Helenae* 137
St Anthony 121
Apollonius, stories of 17, 139, 146–47
St Augustine of Hippo 134 n. 70, 147, 156 n. 2

Bachorski, Hans-Jürgen 71
Baesecke, Georg 104, 132–33 n. 53
Bahr, Joachim 13
Bakhtin, Mikhail 83, 87
baptism 80, 103, 113, 117, 120, 132 n. 46, 135 n. 77, 147
Bede, *Ecclesiastical History of the English People* 103, 107
Biesterfeldt, Corinna 139
Biterolf und Dietleib 11
Bodmer, Johann Jakob 6
de Boor, Helmut 15, 16, 17, 70, 105, 139
Bornholdt, Claudia 33 n. 119, 71, 95 n. 13, 97 n. 37
Brandan 15
Brandt, Rüdiger 18
Bräuer, Rolf 17, 105, 114
Brautwerbungsepik, *see* bridal-quest epic
bridal-quest epic:
   as bridal-quest motif 23–25, 43–44, 48, 94, 152, 164, 165
   and the bridal-quest schema 1–2, 19–24, 35, 38–39, 70–71, 75, 102, 105, 163–64
   definition of 1–2, 19–25
   double structure of 20–21
   and orality 19–21, 35–37, 71, 163–65
Byzantine, Byzantium 11, 65 n. 58, 68 n. 86, 68 n. 90, 72

Caesarius of Heisterbach, *Dialogus miraculorum* 119
carbuncle 77
Charlemagne 7, 40, 41, 42, 58, 59, 60, 68 n. 90

chaste marriage 108–10, 127, 131 n. 41, 151–53
Chrétien de Troyes 50
   Cligés 73–74
Clovis, Frankish king 133 n. 56, 135 n. 77
Constantine, Roman Emperor 137, 141
conversion 107, 109, 112, 117–18, 120, 121, 127, 131–32 n. 46, 132 n. 47
Cordez, Philippe 144
courtly romance 1, 8, 12, 14, 16, 21, 24, 25, 35, 36–37, 41, 43, 50, 60, 139
crusades, crusading 12, 14, 48, 57–58, 112, 131–32 n. 46
Curschmann, Michael 13, 14, 16, 22, 36, 37, 71, 104, 105, 129 n. 18
Curtius, Ernst Robert 119
Cynewulf 140

David, biblical King 81, 151–53
Deutsch, Lorenz 24, 33 n. 125
Dialogus Salomonis et Marcolfi 72–73, 96 n. 24, 96 n. 27, 99 n. 63
Dießen, house of 59, 67 n. 76
Dietrichs Flucht 21
Dukus Horant 1, 21, 165

Ebenbauer, Alfred 17, 140
Ebernand von Erfurt, *Heinrich und Kunegunde* 108, 131 n. 37, 131 n. 44, 132 n. 47
Edward the Confessor 108
Ehrismann, Gustav 14
'Eigensinn' 82–83, 99 n. 61
Eilhart, *Tristrant* 40
Elliott, Dyan 108
Enen, Johann, *Medulla Gestorum Treverensium* 155
Erb, Ewald 16, 31 n. 95
Eucharist 77, 78, 97–98 n. 42, 160 n. 42
eyes 91–92, 100 n. 81

falcons 91–92, 104 n. 84
'Fernliebe' 43, 53, 98 n. 45
Flore und Blanscheflur 17
Fredegar 137
Friedrich von Schwaben 17

Frings, Theodor 19, 20
Fuchs-Jolie, Stephan 50, 64 n. 43

Geary, Patrick 143
genre:
  in literary history 2, 5, 8
  permissive model of 2–5, 163
  prescriptive model of 2
Gervinus, Georg Gottfried 9–12
Gesta Treverorum 137–38
Gottfried von Strassburg, *Tristan* 16, 21, 24, 97–98 n. 42, 98 n. 51, 99 n. 67, 126, 150, 165
Graf Rudolf 11, 16
Grauer Rock (*Orendel*) 1, 9, 11, 14–18, 21, 25–26, 35, 70, 72, 137–62, 164–65
  dating of 139–42, 158 n. 22
  prints of 138–39, 154–55, 158 n. 19
  reception of 138, 155, 156, 158–59 n. 25
  relationship to seamless robe of Christ 138, 140–49
  sources of 140–41
  title of text 26 n. 1, 157 n. 15
  transmission of 139
  see also seamless robe of Christ
St Gregory the Great 120, 131 n. 39, 135 n. 75
Gregory of Tours 137
Greiffenklau, Richard von 138
Griese, Sabine 71, 79, 89, 90
Grimm, Jakob 6, 8, 13
Grimm, Wilhelm 6, 8, 12, 13
Grubmüller, Klaus 3, 4, 5, 18, 24, 26 n. 6, 163
  'Werkreihe' 4–5, 18, 24, 163, 165
Die Gute Frau 17

von der Hagen, Friedrich 6, 7, 158 n. 18
Hartmann von Aue:
  Der Arme Heinrich 9
  Erec 37
  Gregorius 136 n. 88, 161 n. 52
  Iwein 41, 49
Haug, Walter 20–21, 36, 37, 38, 71, 104, 118, 119, 123, 125, 163
Heinrich von Veldeke:
  Eneasroman 40–41
  Servatius 136 n. 88
St Helena 137, 140, 141, 142, 143, 155
Henry II, Holy Roman Emperor 106, 108–09, 130n33
Herder, Johann Gottfried 6, 13
Herod, King 143, 144
heroic epic 7–8, 9, 10, 12, 13–14, 23, 24, 42, 106–07, 132 n. 50, 158 n. 22, 162 n. 54

Herzog Ernst 1, 2, 9, 10, 11, 15, 16, 17, 19, 40–41, 47, 69 n. 93, 70, 103, 139
Hillinbrief 138
Die Hochzeit 113, 132 n. 50
Hohenstaufen, house of 40, 58, 68 n. 86
Holy Grave 138, 148, 150–52, 154, 156
Hunger, Ulrich 6

indexicality 149, 150, 152
investiture 147, 161 n. 49

Jauss, Hans-Robert 3, 4, 17, 18, 24, 163
  'dominant' 4, 5, 17, 18, 23, 24, 163, 165
Johannes I, Archbishop of Trier 141
Jonah 145–46, 147
Jourdain de Blaye 146
Jungandreas, Wolfgang 140

Kaiserchronik 40–41, 66 n. 59, 138, 146
Kalinke, Marianne 106, 107, 108, 119
Kiening, Christian 37, 38, 50, 62 n. 14, 65 n. 53, 68–69 n. 92, 116, 134 n. 60, 141, 142
Koberstein, August 9, 70, 74
König Rother 1, 7–8, 9–17, 19–21, 25, 35–69, 70, 72, 74, 85, 92, 95 n. 3, 100 n. 80, 102, 103, 135 n. 78, 139, 150–51, 163–65
  disguise in 39, 48, 49–50, 55, 56–57
  double-structure of 36–37, 41, 60, 61–62 n. 6, 63 n. 29
  giants in 47–48, 50–52, 65 n. 53
  patronage of 40
  'Schuhprobeszene' in 53–54, 67 n. 69
  sources of 63 n. 26
  as a transitional work 25, 35–38, 60–61
  transmission of 40, 61 n. 1
  'Ur-Rother' 35–36
Konrad von Würzburg 9
  Engelhard 17
  Partonopier und Meliur 17
Der arme Konrad, *Frau Metze die Käuflerin* 74
Pfaffe Konrad, *Rolandslied* 40–41, 133 n. 53
Kudrun 1, 20, 21, 24, 165
Kuhn, Hugo 3, 4, 23, 37
Kunstpoesie 6–8, 10–13, 165
  see also Volkspoesie

Lachmann, Karl 6
Lambert of Ardres, *Historia comitum Ghisnensium* 72, 96 n. 16
Pfaffe Lambrecht, *Alexander* 40–41, 69 n. 93
Lauber, Diebold 139, 158 n. 25
Laurin 7, 114

'Legendenroman' 15, 16–17, 18, 70
Lugowski, Clemens 54, 62 n. 14

Manessische Liederhandschrift 6
Markolfs buch 9, 16, 72–74, 82, 96 n. 24, 96 n. 27, 98–99 n. 59, 99 n. 63
Mary, mother of God 77, 116, 118, 142, 149, 150, 152
Maurer, Friedrich 80–81
Maximilian I, Holy Roman Emperor 138, 141, 142, 154–55, 162 n. 64
  Ehrenpforte 155
  Weiß Kunig 155
Meran, house of 59
mermaids 93, 122, 124–25, 135–36 n. 82
Merswin, Rulman, *Fünfmannenbuch* 106, 129 n. 23
Meves, Uwe 7, 141
Miklautsch, Lydia 23, 71
Miller, Nikolaus 110, 129n18, 135 n. 82
Millet, Victor 23
Millstätter Sammelhandschrift 113
'Minnesklave' 71, 80–81
miracles 116–21, 134 n. 70, 148
Moriz von Craûn 5
Muling, Johannes Adelphus 155
Müller, Jan-Dirk 24, 41–42, 44, 55, 61 n. 3
Müller, Stephan 135 n. 77
Münchner Oswald 1, 9, 11, 14–18, 21, 24, 25–26, 35, 39, 70, 72, 102–36, 139, 153, 163–65
  and comedy 26, 118–20, 122, 125–27
  dating of 104–06, 109, 126
  goldsmiths in 105, 114–15 132–33 n. 53, 133 n. 55, 133 n. 59
  raven in 121, 122–26, 135 n. 77, 154
  relationship to *Wiener Oswald* 103, 110–13, 115–18, 120, 123, 125
  stag in 113–16, 133 nn. 56–57
  transmission of 103, 120, 129 n. 24
  see also St Oswald, Northumbrian king

names, naming 41–42, 49, 55, 147–49, 153–54
Naumann, Hans 13, 14
Neudeck, Otto 71, 87, 100 n. 74
Nibelungenlied 8, 9, 20, 21, 24, 39, 74, 76, 91, 97 nn. 36–37, 101 n. 84, 126, 165
Notker der Deutsche 72

Orendel, *see Grauer Rock*
Ortnit 1, 7, 9, 21–24, 39, 74, 165
Ossian 6
Ósvalds saga, *see Reykjahólabók*
St Oswald, Northumbrian King:
  development of cult of 26, 102–04, 107–09, 127
  iconography of 104–05
  stories of:
    Berliner Oswald 103
    Budapester Oswald 103, 135 n. 79
    Drogo, *vita* of St Oswald 107
    East-Swabian prose Oswald 103
    Der Heiligen Leben 103, 104, 105, 106 109, 110, 115, 127, 128–29 n. 16, 129 n. 22, 133 n. 58, 135 n. 77
    Linzer Oswald 103
    Das Märterbuch 103, 105, 109, 110, 115, 127, 128–29 n. 16, 133 n. 58, 135 n. 77
    Dat Passional 103, 105, 106, 109, 110, 115, 127, 128–29 n. 16, 133 n. 58, 135 n. 77
    Reginald of Durham, *Vita S. Oswaldis* 107, 109, 129 n. 28
    Reykjahólabók 103, 105, 106, 109, 110, 115, 127, 128–29 n. 16, 133 n. 58, 135 n. 77
    Wiener Oswald 103, 104, 105–06, 109, 110–13, 115–18, 120, 123, 125, 134 n. 60
  see also Münchner Oswald

St Paul 121, 147
Pippin 42, 58–60
Pischon, Friedrich August 9
prelapsarian nakedness 147
Propp, Vladimir 154
Prosa-Lanzelot 5

recognition 54–55, 87–93, 100 n. 80, 100–01 n. 81, 101 n. 86
relics 137–38, 141–45, 149, 159 n. 33, 160 n. 40, 160 n. 43
reliquary 143, 149–50, 161 n. 49
Röcke, Werner 17, 82, 83
Rosengarten 7, 74
Rosenkranz, Karl 9
Ruh, Kurt 16

Salman und Morolf 1, 9–18, 21, 25, 35, 61, 70–101, 139, 163–65
  dating of 73–74
  disguise in 85–90
  print epilogue to 80, 96 n. 24, 98 n. 53
  relationship to 'Spruch' tradition 72–73, 82, 96 n. 27
  'Schwank' in 82–83, 93
  strophic form of 73, 96–97 n. 28
  transmission of 72, 74
Saxo Grammaticus 140
Schavard, Friedrich 138

Schlegel, A. W. 6, 8
Schmid-Cadalbert, Christian 21–23, 24
Schmitz, Silvia 37, 64 n. 43
Schnell, Rüdiger 68 n. 90, 80–81
Schröder, Walter Johannes 13, 56, 61–62 n. 6, 68 n. 88
Schulz, Armin 71, 100–01 n. 81, 101 n. 86
Schulz, Monica 53, 67 n. 69, 132 n. 47
Schwietering, Julius 15
seamless robe of Christ 137–38, 139–41, 154–55, 156 nn. 1–2, 157 n. 14
   see also Grauer Rock
Seeber, Stefan 119
Seneca 94
Siefken, Hinrich 24
Silvesterdiplom 137
Solomon, biblical King 70, 72–74, 78, 81, 84
Spielmannsepik 1–2, 6–8, 12–18, 19–20, 70, 102, 139, 163–65
   and the 'Spielmann' 11–13
Spruchgedicht, see also Markolfs buch
Steinger, Hans 139
Stock, Markus 38, 39, 47, 54, 56, 61 n. 2, 67–68 n. 81
Straßburger Heldenbuch 139–40, 152
Der Stricker, *Pfaffe Amis* 9

Tengeling, house of 40, 59, 68 nn. 91–92
Teuber, Ernst 139

Tieck, Ludwig 6, 7, 8
Tomasek, Tomas 146
Tundalus 15
tunica inconsutilis, see seamless robe of Christ

Uhland, Ludwig 6, 9, 12, 30 n. 59
Ulrich von Liechtenstein, *Frauendienst* 9

Vilcinasaga 36, 66 n. 59
Vizkelety, András 129 n. 19
Vogt, Friedrich 12
Volkspoesie 6–8, 10–13, 165
   see also Kunstpoesie
Vollmann-Profe, Gisela 17, 32 n. 111

Wackernagel, Wilhelm 11, 12
Ward, Benedicta 118, 120–21
Wehrli, Max 16, 119
Welf, house of 40, 65 n. 76, 104
Wilhelm von Orlens 17, 74
Wilhelm von Österreich 17
Wilhelm von Wenden 17
Heinrich Wittenwiler, *Der Ring* 83
Wolfdietrich 7, 9, 21, 22–23, 33 n. 135, 161 n. 52
Wolfram von Eschenbach 14, 71, 105
   Parzival 16, 37, 41, 150

Younger Edda 140

www.ingramcontent.com/pod-product-compliance
Lightning Source LLC
Chambersburg PA
CBHW071230170426
43191CB00032B/1283